NOSTRADAMUS

LES VRAYES CENTURIES
et
PROPHETIES
de Maistre
MICHEL NOSTRADAMUS

A Amsterdam Chez Iean Ianßon à Waesberge, et le Clesre du Feu Elizé Weyerstraet. An 1668.

Frontispiece of the edition printed in Amsterdam in 1668.

Nostradamus

THE MAN
WHO SAW THROUGH TIME

by Lee McCann

GREENWICH HOUSE
Distributed by Crown Publishers, Inc.
New York

TO
MUIRIEL FULLER
WHO SUGGESTED THAT THIS
BOOK BE WRITTEN

This 1984 edition is published by Greenwich House,
a division of Arlington House, Inc.
distributed by Crown Publishers, Inc., 225 Park Avenue South,
New York, New York, 10003,
by arrangement with Farrar, Strauss & Giroux, Inc.

Manufactured in the United States of America

ISBN: 0-517-436930
n m l k j i h

Contents

		PAGE
	Foreword	ix

PART ONE

I.	A Prophet Is Born	3
II.	The Education of a Genius	24
III.	Personages and Politics	54
IV.	Garlands of Fame	81
V.	The Plague Returns	109
VI.	A Prophet's Eyry	138
VII.	Purpose	167
VIII.	On to Paris	194
IX.	The Court of the Valois	224
X.	Toward Familiar Country	255

PART TWO

I.	The Cycle of Valois-Navarre	293
II.	Claude De Savoie	329
III.	In the Twentieth Century	337

Illustrations

Frontispiece of the edition printed in   *Frontispiece*
Amsterdam in 1668

FACING PAGE

Etching made by a woman of Salon, from
the portrait bust by César Nostradamus,
son of the prophet   54

Through this old gate traveled Nostradamus
on errands of mercy and friendship   109

King René, the minstrel-monarch of Provence   167

Blois, setting of royal splendors and tragic
destinies   224

Last resting place of the older Capetian kings   255

Ronsard, who celebrated the arrival of Nostradamus at court with verses in his honor   293

Foreword

THE RICH, ACTIVELY FULFILLED LIFE of the French prophet, Michel de Nostradame, is the story of genius not only in its rarest but its most modern form. His ability foreshadowed a hope, now gaining a first hearing in this our day, that science may, in some not too remote tomorrow, discover principles of mental forces which will permit every man to realize within himself a reflection of the powers of Nostradamus.

Many prophets have crossed the brightly lighted stage of history and paused to utter some astounding bit of prescience. But they are seldom remembered for more than a single episode, some ray of strange illumination that for a moment spotlighted the fate of a throne or a battle. Actually there exist but two written documents of prophecy which have pictured a grand-scale continuity of history, and unfolded a tapestry of world futures. One of these is, of course, the mighty word of Scripture. The other is that cryptic romaunt of Europe's fate, the *Centuries*, written by Nostradamus, Provençal troubadour of destiny.

No one knows as yet what forces shape a prophet, nor how it is that to "remembrance of things past," he adds "remembrance of the things that are to come." Perhaps the Red Queen knew more about it than most.

When Alice asked her why she cried out before, instead of after, she had pricked her finger, her majesty sagely observed that it is a poor rule which doesn't work both ways. Nostradamus would have enjoyed that bit of wit, so like his own, and pertinent to prophecy.

What is "before" and "after"? What is up or down when considered outside the limited, inaccurate criteria of the five senses? The fourth-dimensional vision of Nostradamus, like the Red Queen's cry, transcended the meanings which we give these words. The man who saw through time watched, as through a telescope, the distant stars of future events rise and set, beyond the eye of the present, over a period of four hundred years.

"Heaven from all creatures hide the book of Fate,
All but the page prescrib'd, their present state."

Pope was within his sceptical rights when he penned that couplet, because the vaticinating exceptions among heaven's creatures have always been so few that for people as a whole his words were true. Another Englishman, the modernist Dean Inge, had however a better perspective. As a churchman he accepted prophecy. As an intelligent modern he said that the phenomenon of prevision was quite possibly part of an evolutionary process which would one day become a developed faculty general to man. Considered in this light, Nostradamus, astounding as are his prophecies, is himself, the man, of even greater fascination than his work, because he attained in its completeness the faculty to which it is at least a possibility that all may eventually aspire.

It was only a few years ago that several thousand New Yorkers unhinged one of the bronze doors of the American Museum of Natural History in an effort to hear a talk that few could understand when heard. The lecture was on the mathematics of the strange, and to them, new, fourth dimension which they had visualized, confounding it with the psychic world, as opening exciting secret vistas and miraculous powers. Such an incident is indicative of a dawning intensity of popular interest in the world of unseen forces, physical and metaphysical. Vitamins and visions, telescopes and telepathy, all go together as part of the thrilling new universe expanding within the consciousness of the twentieth century.

Science works always first with physical properties and objectives. Our breakfast newspapers tell of atoms cracked and a new element found, and radio serves us up freshly discovered planets with the evening meal. In all this inrush of knowledge nothing has been of such captivating interest as the new discoveries about time which are giving rise to a new point of view as significant for layman as for scientist. Einstein has substituted new time-concepts and time-mechanics for old in the study of the universe. For half a century new inventions in communications have been telescoping time, bringing true Mother Shipton's words:

"Around the world thoughts shall fly
In the twinkling of an eye."

Now, doctors are timing and graphing the electrical
thought impulses of the human brain. And universities are experimenting in psychology departments
with a kind of time-sense to which may be linked the
phenomena of the psyche.

We are so accustomed to thinking of time as the
straight road separated by present experience into its
two parts, yesterday and tomorrow. But the scientist
is beginning to perceive what the mystic has always
known, that time is an unknown country stretching
boundlessly in all directions. Nostradamus, in whom
awareness of this set him apart from his fellows, was
the Marco Polo of time's uncharted land, in which he
traveled the future as we travel a continent. From
these transcendental voyagings, like Polo, he returned
with incredible stories of strange sights. The prophet's
rare okapis were a vision of events to come.

Both of these men, whose discoveries were beyond
the comprehension of their age, have come late into
their own. Archaeology and exploration have verified
the narrative of Polo's travels. History, not only since
the sixteenth century, but daily, is verifying the time-
travels of that other and greater explorer, Nostradamus.
He is of yesterday, today, and still a long tomorrow.
By virtue of what he was, and of our own hopes, he
deserves the distinguished position today which he had
in the Renaissance, and serious study in the light of

what science is teaching us of the power and forces of the mind.

It is an old and tenaciously held popular idea that interest in and concentration on extra-dimensional qualities of the mind tend inevitably to some form of imbalance which may run the gamut from credulity to insanity. Too often in the past superstition has added to this its dark aura of witchcraft and abnormal rites. Nostradamus was, throughout his life, a striking refutation of such beliefs. His intellectual achievements and emotional balance, his social adaptation and vigorous health show him as the pattern of the well-rounded man. Considering his unique gift, he may be said to have had, besides his genius for prophecy, a veritable genius for normality. Had he never written the *Centuries*, his title to fame would still be clear. The brilliant skill and self-sacrificing devotion which made him the greatest physician in France of his day would alone keep his memory green. Physician, linguist, scholar, diplomat, writer, teacher, *religieux* and prophet, his life touched all phases of Renaissance thought and activity from the hovels of France, where he fought the plague, to the court of the Valois, where he was honored beyond any seer in history.

The Book of Joel, which seems to have made a strong impression upon Nostradamus, contains within its grim forecast the lovely, well-known passage:

"and your sons and your daughters shall prophesy, your old men shall dream dreams, your young men shall see visions." Nostradamus was the greatest of

all who since Biblical ages have given to these words
the substance of fulfillment. And perhaps his life was
prelusive to the "clear seeing" which may be the glory
of the coming age.

The major facts of the life of Nostradamus are
known and fully attested. Much confusion, however,
exists concerning a number of biographical details.
Such questions as which one of the prophet's grandfathers it was who educated him, what was the year of
his second marriage, and which of his sons was the
eldest born are matters of conflicting opinion. Some
commentators have assumed that his son, César, was
born in 1555 simply because Nostradamus dedicated
his prophecies to him in that year. It is impossible to
find out the exact truth about these and other discrep-
ancies because of the loss or destruction of old documents which would provide the proof. In such instances, the author has chosen from old accounts the
story which has seemed in her opinion to be best supported by inference and available evidence.

The fictional treatment employed to present certain
incidents is used in an attempt to give more vitality to
the faded colors of time, but each has underlying facts
or substantial inference. There is one exception to this,
the attributed purpose in the writing of the *Centuries*.
Other commentators besides the author believe, however, that this theory is true. It agrees with what is
known of the prophet's character and type of mind,
and is supported by indications from within the prophecies.
                                                    L. M.

PART ONE

and honey to make Christmas nougat. They chatted of New Year's gifts in the making, and gossiped about holiday masques at the Governor's palace at Aix. Troubadours tuned their harps and memorized romaunts. Through church windows drifted the voices of choir-boys practicing Christmas music, chanting their welcome to the Son of Man, singing of peace on earth which then as now seldom prevailed.

The ancient town, gay with the season, little imagined, least of all the expectant parents, that this child, born in their midst that day, would bring to his birthplace a fame enduring for centuries. Who then could foresee that a future Europe would search his words for an answer to the grim riddle of its fate? Over the Midi town the stars had taken stance to endow this infant with stranger wisdom than prophet had held since the faraway years of those who foretold the coming of the Christ.

On this the 14th day of December by the Julian calendar, "near to the twelve hours of noon," so the chronicle runs, the son of Jacques and Renée de Nostradame was born. The voice of the bronze bell speaking the hour from the town belfry was carried on breezes fragrant of meadows. In the hearts of the parents the bell-notes chimed the olden gratitude: "Unto us a child is born, unto us a son is given."

How long the family of baby Michel de Nostradame had been settled in Provence is not known. But long enough for them to be assimilated into the annals of the country, to have made their contribution of sci-

CHAPTER ONE

A Prophet Is Born

It was nearly Christmas, of the year 1503. San Rémy, ancient Provençal town, namesake of the Saint who baptized Clovis on Christmas Day, was astir with preparations for the coming activities. Everywhere in town and countryside people stopped in the sunshine to greet and talk of plans for Calèndo, the Romance word which Provençals still use for Christmas. Great ladies in silken finery, blithe young knights attended by their squires riding down from châteaux in the hills, peasant women in full skirts and bright-colored bodices, jolly monks, dark-eyed girls and sober town fathers, all were preparing for the year's greatest celebration.

In the town square men talked about yule-logs. Some who owned groves were going to cut down an olive or an almond tree that was too old to be worth keeping. But more would go to the forest to cut their logs, and drag them home behind uncoupled oxen as men had done since the days of the Druids. San Rémy housewives crowded the market-stalls, buying almonds

ence and service, and to reap the rewards of prestige.

The statement that Michel was of Jewish birth has been insistently asserted by most commentators. There seems to be no warrant for this outside of unverified rumors after his lifetime. His race is not important except in relation to his prophecies. But it is of essential interest to know whether he was the last inheritor of the grand Hebrew tradition of prophecy. Or, has the Gentile race, lacking such tradition, really produced one prophet of distinction in whom they can take pride, and whose forecasts are concerned with their destiny? One who, if not comparable to the sublime poetry and exaltation of the prophets of Israel, can be compared with them in the accuracy and authority of his vision.

Nostradamus, in his letter of dedication to King Henry II, speaks of the Biblical computation of years. He says: "I hold that the Scripture takes them to be solar." To a scholar this should be proof enough that Nostradamus did not have Jewish background; if he had, he could not have escaped knowing that the Jewish calculations were always according to the lunar calendar.

Jean-Ayme de Chavigny, doctor of theology, magistrate of Beaune, presumably dependable, was the close friend and pupil of Nostradamus. His biographical sketch of the prophet is the only first-hand account, still available, that has been handed down. He makes no mention of Jewish descent. He writes:

"His grandfathers, maternal and paternal, had a

reputation as great savants in mathematics and medicine, one being physician to René, King of Jerusalem and Sicily, and Count of Provence, the other, of Jean, Duke of Calabria, son of King René. This closes the mouth of the envious who, because they are misinformed, have reflected upon his birth."

The sixteenth century was a period of bitter anti-Semitism and general intolerance. Jews, it is true, were not persecuted in Provence, and many of them rose to wealth and secure standing there. Had Nostradamus been a Jew, his reputation might not have suffered from it in the place of his birth. But it would have suffered as his fame spread to larger fields, particularly Paris. During his lifetime his enemies called him charlatan and sorcerer. Had he been vulnerable to the accusation, he would certainly have been branded as a Jew by attackers overlooking no point that could be raised against him.

Doctor Theophilus Garencières, one of the early commentators, who states that all his life he had been in contact with people who either knew all about Nostradamus or thought they did, likewise makes no mention of Jewish descent. His concern was how God could reveal himself to a man of merely average social position. He says that this wonder agitated the minds of many people who admired Nostradamus as a prophet. This was not because the caste-conscious Renaissance had forgotten the birth of the Son of the Carpenter, but because they had reconciled His origin with their own social standards. Ferne's *Blazen of Gentry*, a sixteenth-century work on heraldry, is at pains to inform its readers that the twelve apostles were all gentlemen of blood, reduced to servile work only through misfortune.

It may have been wishful thinking that led some writers who favored Nostradamus to assert that he was of noble birth. But it must be inferred from the events of his life that he was at least gently born of people whose standing was excellent.

When Nostradamus visited the court of Henry II, as the king's guest, he was accorded almost the honor of a ranking personage, and lodged in the palace of a prince-cardinal of the blood. Henry would have known through his Provençal governor, a lifelong friend of the prophet, the history and standing of the de Nostradame family. It is to be feared that he would not have received the prophet with such public acclaim if the family position had not met with his approval.

It has been argued that the learning of Nostradamus' grandfathers was in advance of Gentile culture, and was therefore Jewish. It is true that the Jews in France had a fine record in the scholarly professions, and particularly in medicine. But there is another theory which, while it cannot be proved, would account for much.

A king of Provence went with Saint Louis to the Crusades, and shared his imprisonment in the Orient. The Saracens, marvelously advanced in medicine and mathematics, showed the Crusaders many wonders. Some of their knowledge found its way back to Europe in this manner. Ancestors of Nostradamus may have been of those who benefited by Arab learning in its own great centers; there may even have been a strain of Arab ancestry. Either or both would account for the prestige which the prophet's grandfathers enjoyed at the court of King René of Provence. It might also account for some ancient, inherited medical *recepte* which crusading ancestors brought back from the Orient, and which Nostrad.mus may have used to conquer the plague; something older than the known, standardized Arab remedies of his own times.

King René had a curious Turko-Arab complex. He preferred people of such blood and customs above all others. Consequently his court for half a century attracted every one who had a drop of the blood or any of its associations and culture. Every Levantine and Arab who had something to sell and the price of the trip came there with his wares. If a subject wanted to put anything across, he had to make the king an Eastern present. René dressed himself and the court in Oriental costume, and his Turkish and Arabian masques were famous.

One amusing incident of René's feeling in such matters concerns a grandfather of Nostradamus. René's queen had a laundress, Charlotte the Turk. In some way Charlotte injured her leg. Anywhere else, she would have been too far below the salt to rate attention from the royal physician. But because of Charlotte's Turkish blood, the king thought nothing too good for her. His own doctor, none other than Doctor de Nostradame, was ordered to attend her with all care, which presumably he did. It is logical to suppose that the learned grandfathers of Nostradamus contributed in some way to the king's passion for Turks and Arabs, and held his patronage to some extent through superiority in the kind of lore and training he most respected and valued.

The grandfathers had long been friends and associates at the court of Provence. When Jacques, the son of Pierre de Nostradame, married Renée, the daughter of Jean de Rémy, it had cemented more closely their existing ties of affection and mutual interest.

Jacques de Nostradame, the father of Michel, was a notary public. This occupation, dwarfed in importance today, had then a scholarly and important rating when so many of the population, even among the upper circles, could not so much as write their name. They depended on the notary, who was called on for services that ranged from writing a love-letter to arranging a transfer of property. His field was a wide one, and included nearly everything in business and property matters that did not require the actual practice of law.

Jacques' income would have provided a comfortable home in keeping with good standards of Provençal living. Through his doors passed the active flow of town affairs, personal, business and civic. Many would seek him out because, through his father and father-in-law, his contacts at the capital were somewhat influential. His house was probably near the center of the town, easy of access to his clients.

Young Michel's earliest recollections of his parents' home would center about its cheerful, fragrant kitchen which, typical of all Provençal homes in the sixteenth century, was the room where both the domestic and the social life was carried on. The center and symbol of the room's activity was the great fireplace, majestic, cavernous, holding a banked fire that had never gone out since first his father and mother came there to live. Shining pots and pans of brass hung low from the mantle shelf, convenient for his mother to bake her delicious bread, cook thick nourishing stews or roast a fowl. At either angle of the fireplace was an oak settle where the grandfathers liked to laze and talk when they came to visit. Across the room stood the buffet. Atop this was the long, flaring wooden trough in which his mother mixed and kneaded the bread. In one corner was a cupboard with shelves and drawers holding all manner of household goods. This, like the buffet, was of strong, deep-toned oak. Michel knew every line of the severe carving in geometrical design which caught the firelight on its mellow wood.

On the walls hung light cabinet shelves holding salt and spice boxes, small pieces of gay earthenware, and special treasures. Perhaps there was an enamel cup or a vase of cunning workmanship, a present from grandfather who had got it at a bargain from a Levantine merchant come to sell his wares at court.

Michel could remember the deep, embrasured windows of his home, and the narrow stoop at the door, points of vantage from which he got his earliest pictures of the life of the town as it streamed by in colorful show on fête days and market days. The charm of the procession was unending, rich merchants on ambling mules with silver bells on the harness, carts piled up with the reds and yellows of oranges and pomegranates for the market, peasants bringing in butter and cheeses from the country, shepherds with their droves, knights and ladies with feathers in their hats, riding on prancing horses.

Unforgettable, too, the first time his mother took him to Mass at the ancient church. Through the great doors, older than the Gothic spire, into the lofty vastness of dim light, he had clung affrighted to his mother's hand, staring into the rich mystery of dusk and gold and stained-glass saints. Kneeling, he had looked up to the carved Virgin and the tapers like flowers at her feet. The notes of the organ and the high clear chant of the choir-boys enfolded him, drew him with ecstasy as if to his mother's breast. It was source and beginning of his passionate, unswerving observance and devotion to the Roman ritual from which he never deviated throughout his life. Such observance was to him never a duty, it was the sacred embroidery of his delight in God.

Another ritual that captivated young Michel was that which pertained to his father's business. He could not remember the time when he had not been fascinated by the things on his father's writing-table. The pewter ink-well with the long quills standing at attention in the small side holes, the little bowl of clean sand, and the rolls of white sheepskin neatly disposed, called to his hands to touch and try them.

He early listened to all that he could of his father's talk of the goings-on in San Rémy. With the big ears for which little pitchers are proverbial he placed together scraps which the grown-ups thought he was too young to take in. He was as curious as a cat about the news from Aix, the capital, and the rumors from Paris, that faraway city, no more than a name to him. He wondered what levies were and why his father said the people grumbled about them; he wondered if the King would go to war with Italy, and what war was like. He found out about the new elections to the town council, and who was traveling to Aix to see the Governor.

His mind observed and pigeonholed with childish literalness all that went on about him. It was his initiation, the beginning of his interest in affairs of state that were so to enchant his later years. Here was the acorn that grew into the tree of the *Centuries*.

It was the charm of these early recollections that kept Nostradamus, the man, always a small-town boy by inclination as he was by birth. In his day as in ours most people were the bits of steel pulled upon by the glamour-magnets of the great cities. The complex brilliance of cities and their mirage of opportunity were woven into the dreams of youth and the ambitions of manhood, and in France all roads led to Paris. Michel remained curiously immune to this lure. He

learned early to prize the smaller world of the town,
that can be compassed in its entirety, its figures known
and studied against their background of the generations. Here in Provence were his personal interests;
these were his people.

Michel was a strong boy, quick and active, full of
the eager vitality of youth. His grandfathers set him
early at his tasks of learning, but being physicians
they wisely allowed him plenty of leisure for boyish
adventure in ranging the countryside under the Midi
sunshine. There was a deeply-felt bond between him
and this lovely Provençal country. Boy and man he
never wanted to be away from it for long. The breath
of its perfume and past drew him always back to its
ancient, fertile valleys watered by winding streams below the lift of Alpine hills. As a child he learned the
seasons by the pink bloom of almond trees, the dun
green of the olive, the gold of harvests and the blood-
purple of vineyards. And always there was music ac-
companying the beauty of Nature's drama, harp and
lute, dancing and song. For Provence is a land set to
music by the Troubadours.

The genius of the Troubadours made an early and
lasting impression on Michel and his brother. The famous lays which told of the honor, the chivalry, the
high adventure of the heroes of Provence were captivating to the imagination of the romantic youngsters.
Nor had it been long since these poets had gone their
way, singing, into the past. Their patron, the minstrel-
monarch René, had been the last to go. Their memory

was ever green through the treasure of their songs, intimately known and sung by all of high and low degree. Michel and Jean heard them with their nursery rhymes. *Le Roman de Renart* seems to have made the deepest impression on Michel, perhaps because it is an allegory in which the characters are animals and the plot tells of their struggle for forest leadership. Cunning and hypocrisy are pitted against force, and weakness as usual loses out. Nostradamus, in the *Centuries*, uses the same animals, denoting the same qualities, as symbols of the contending powers of Europe. The Wolf, the Bear, the Lion, the Fox, the Eagle, the Stag, all play their parts again in his minstrelsy of destiny.

Michel's brother was gifted with a great voice. The home rang with Jean's singing of the *Roman de la Rose*, the *Chanson de Roland* and other celebrated *lays et fabliaux*. Jean, in later life, followed the prosaic though profitable career of attorney for the parliament of Arles. But as his real contribution he left behind him a history of the Troubadours, a monumental tome entitled: "Lives of the Most Famous Ancient Provençal Poets Who Flourished in the Times of the Counts of Provence."

Some say that the songs of the Troubadours weakened the spirit and resistance of Provence. If so, it was in the sense in which today the more sensitive standards of civilization are at the mercy of armed force. "If God would only send peace!" cries Nostradamus in the *Centuries*. He learned his ideals of peace and honor and gentle manners from the minstrels of old Provence.

Sir Walter Scott, in *Anne of Geierstein,* gives a delightful glimpse of the influence of the Troubadours on this land.

He sketches a scene which was familiar to Michel's boyhood:

"The shepherd literally marched abroad in the morning piping his flock to pasture with some love sonnet of an amorous Troubadour. His 'fleecy care' seemed actually under the influence of the music. Instead of being driven before the shepherd, they followed him, and did not disperse to feed, until facing them, he executed variations on his air. His huge wolf-dog, guardian of the flock, followed his master with ears pricked like the chief critic of the performance. At noon the shepherd's audience would be increased by comely matron or blooming maiden who joined her voice to his as they rendezvoused beside some antique fountain. In the cool of the evening there was dancing on the village green or concert before the hamlet door. Travellers were invited to share the little repast of fruits, cheese and bread. Everything gave charm to the illusion and pointed to Provence as the Arcadia of France.

"The greatest singularity was the absence of armed men and soldiers in this peaceful country. In England, no one stirred without his long-bow, sword and buckler. In France, the hind wore armor even betwixt the stilts of the plough. In Germany you could not look

along a mile of road without seeing clouds of dust
from which emerged waving feathers and flashing
armor. But in Provence all was quiet and peaceful, as
if the music of the land had lulled to sleep all wrathful
passions. Now and then a mounted cavalier would
pass, harp at saddle-bow or carried by an attendant, at-
testing his character as Troubadour. The short sword,
worn on the left thigh, was for show rather than use."

Besides its "dance and Provençal song and sunburnt
mirth," there is in this country another kind of life,
silent but no less vital. One that touched profoundly
the spirit of young Michel, and which permeates the
Centuries. It is the life of the ancient past. Provence is
an old land where people and races have come and
gone, yet not passed utterly away. Long-dead creeds
and customs, rooted deep in antiquity, survive en-
tranced. Celts, Romans, Phoenicians, Greeks, Goths,
all have left their traces, blended now in the Christian
race.

Nostradamus refers particularly to the long influence of Greece upon Provence in one of his quatrains:

IX—75

From the regions of Epirus and Thracia
People in misfortune shall come by sea seeking help
    of France,
The same people who have left in Provence their per-
    petual trace
In the survivals of their dress and laws.

Across the countryside and in the cities rises the pallor of marble ruins and monuments. Triumphal arches, crumbling amphitheaters, delicate fountains, ghost-peopled by the shades of their builders. In such memory-haunted spots, the whispering speech of the past reaches only ears that are atttuned to its mysterious language. Michel, sensitive even in childhood to the enigma of past and future held in the eternal now, felt the spell of these remnants of a mighty past. He grew up in the midst of two worlds, the living present of his own day, and the majestic dead of the long ago. The first gave him its earthy warmth, its gayety, its sturdy common sense. The other opened to him its secret realm, serene, imperiously aloof, where within its twilight lay dreaming the sword of Caesar, the sails of Greece and Carthage, and the golden bracelets of the Goth.

When Michel was old enough to be curious about the history of the ruins, he liked to go on rambles of discovery with one or other of the grandfathers who could tell him the story of what he saw. It is easy to picture him at the side of the old man stately in his physician's robe and four-pointed cap, a uniform which the boy would later wear with honor. Michel was a little under height, but vigorous, with rosy-apple cheeks, color he kept so long as he lived. His hair was brown above a high, square forehead. His straight, determined features were lighted by large, extremely keen gray eyes.

On a day when the two are rambling through San

Rémy they stop to admire the noble arch of triumph which Julius Caesar built to the memory of Marius and his mighty victory there. Michel is curious about the carvings on the arch. What do they mean, he asks his grandfather.

"They record how long ago the Roman general, Marius, once saved our land. You see," the old man tells him, "the barbarians had poured over the country. Nearly half a million fierce fighting men they had, besides all their families."

"Did the Romans come here to fight on our side?"

"Yes. But longer ago than that, Hannibal had crossed here with three thousand elephants on his way to conquer Rome. Our Celtic folk had fought for the Romans then, and Rome remembered. She sent us Marius, her finest general, in our time of peril."

"Did he bring a great army, grandfather?"

"No, lad, he didn't need a great army. He had great soldiers, the legions of Rome. And he had with him the prophetess Marta, a Syrian woman who had a familiar spirit and could foretell the future. She promised Marius a victory."

"What, sir, is a familiar spirit? How could the prophetess tell that Marius would win?"

"There are such people, Michel. I myself have some slight gift at mind-reading. Some day I will open your eyes a little. But prophecy is, of course, a greater faculty. The Romans called such prophets sibyls, and set great store by them. Marius did. He paid Marta high honor. Even had his wife Julia come on from

Rome after the battle just to meet her. Sometime I will show you the marble stela carved with their meeting."

"Tell me more about the prophetess, please."

"There is not much to tell. Foolish folk believe she still speaks from the cavern of Lou Garagoule where a hundred of the barbarians were thrown to death at her bidding."

"Why? Surely many were killed in the battle."

"Yes. But you see, lad, she was a pagan. Before the coming of our Lord who forbade cruelty, men worshipped gods who, so they thought, must have a special sacrifice of blood to pay for their favors. Marius, no doubt, thought it cheap at the price."

"Grandfather, where is Lou Garagoule? Is it far?"

"Too far for your short legs," grandfather chuckles. " 'Tis some miles beyond Aix, near to the top of Mont Saint Victoire. There is a deep cleft in the rock, with the monastery perching across it like an eagle. Under it runs a cavern so far down that it has never been plumbed. It has a secret passage leading down. 'Tis said the monks unlock it for fools who pay them enough to expiate their sin of consulting Marta, or what they think is Marta."

"But does she really speak to them?"

"Of course not. She is long dead. But they go through heathenish incantations and wait six hours in the darkness. Then all they hear is the howl of the wind in the mountain passages. Never try it, 'tis contrary to the spirit of God, and the monks do ill to allow it."

"Still, I should like to see it, grandfather."

"That you shall. When your mother thinks you are old enough to be up the night, you will go to Mont Saint Victoire on the twenty-fourth of April, the anniversary of the battle. You will see where the legions of Marius stood. You will march in the great celebration of the victory they hold there every year, for folk in these parts will never forget."

"Will there be dancing and music?"

"Drums and trumpets, tambourines and singing. They build big bonfires on the Mont, and all night long they dance the farandole, and shout 'Victory, Victory.' "

"Did you go, grandfather?"

"In my youth. Many times. At dawn there is Mass, and everyone goes to give thanks for the saving of our land."

"Tell me about the battle." Youth is never weary.

"Well, the Roman legions were posted on Mont Saint Victoire, 'tis called so after the battle. Here were the barbarians in San Rémy and stretching all the way across the plain to Aix. Between them and the Mont, Marius had dug a great line of deep ditches, the Fossa of Marius, as men still call them—"

As the story proceeded, the little boy listened enthralled until the final overthrow of the last barbarian.

"The Greek historian, Plutarch, has set down the story of the battle of Marius better than I can tell it, Michel," Grandfather finished. "You will read about it for yourself, and many other interesting happenings, when you have mastered classic language. 'Twill be an incentive to your study. Now, the hour grows late."

One wonders if the tale of ancient battle, heard in childhood, returned in age to mingle its memory of victory with the seer's bitter foresight of the ruin of France, making more desolate the vision by contrast. In the prophet's verses which tell the story of 1940 is a quatrain describing the Maginot Line. In this he uses the word *fosse*, French for ditch, from the Latin *fossa*. Perhaps his vision compared the futility of the greatest defensive ditch ever built with the primitive, victorious one of the Roman general.

IV—80

Near the great river the earth will be excavated to construct a huge Line (*fosse*)
Divided into fifteen parts according to the lay of the waters.
The city (Paris) will be captured, there will be the fires of battle, bloodshed and hand-to-hand fighting,
The greater part of the nation will be involved in the shock.

Alas that Marius should be so long time dead. Gone, too, the ancient Roman friendship. Left, but the sadness which cast its gloomy shadow backwards and touched the mantle of the prophet writing those words four hundred years ago.

But such foreknowledge was yet a long way off

from Michel's joyous boyhood. After such adventure
with his grandfather, he would go home with his head
full of battle and wonder. He would dream over it by
the fireside where the sleepy flames burnished the
copper cooking-pots like a legionnaire's helmet. When
night fell in his small, starkly furnished room, and he
felt the straw of his pallet beneath him, he would pretend, like boys the world over, that he was Marius on
the hillside. The moon, slanting in on the tall ward-
robe in the corner, transformed its dark shape mysteriously into the outlines of the prophetess Marta.

There were a thousand such fascinating stories that
the grandfathers could tell, out of which Michel and
Jean wove their own picture of the ancient splendor of
Provence. Tales of emperors, of lost kings and queens
and popes who had built their castles there. Stories,
too, of the mysteries of the Camargue where giant
flame-colored birds flew high in the mists. Stories of
gladiatorial games, of bullfights, of crusaders who
were sovereigns in the land of Christ. Legends of all
the heroes who had laughed under blue Provençal
skies, and feasted at Pan's rose-wreathed board which
perpetually invites in this land of classic beauty.

As for grandfather's promise to Michel to show him
something of the secret marvels of the mind, it is
written in the record that he kept his word. Michel
would have given him scant rest until he did. "One
day, by way of diversion," it is said, grandfather gave
a little demonstration of the workings of hidden mental forces. What kind of demonstration is not known,

but it was probably a simple experiment in mind-reading. It was, however, a perfect introduction to such mysteries for the boy who was to become an adept in their use. Given casually and naturally by grandfather, it robbed the subject of the superstitions and ideas of devil's magic which permeated the age. It gave the boy an opportunity for a normal attitude toward extra-sensory experience. The incident could take its place, without distortion or disproportion, in Michel's active gathering of assorted knowledge. Its naturalness held a protective significance toward the later development of the prophet's gift, and its influence can be traced in the honesty and fearlessness of his attitude toward his own mysterious power.

CHAPTER TWO

The Education of a Genius

DOCTOR DE RÉMY, Michel's maternal grandfather, took upon himself the early education of his elder grandson. Even today such an education as Michel received from him would be considered out of the ordinary. It was for that period perhaps unique in France. Doctor de Rémy's scholarly prestige and the liberal intelligence with which he guided and inspired his pupil provided an opportunity not often found in any home, ancient or modern. The response of the boy's genius and native love of learning made the relationship between them easy and delightful. How different this was from the usual instruction in the sixteenth century can be appreciated from Rabelais' account of Pantagruel's pilgrimage of learning.

"My will," said Gargantua, concerning the education of Pantagruel, "is to hand him over to some learned man to indoctrinate him according to his capacity and to spare nothing to that end."

"Indoctrination," in the early sixteenth century, meant stuffing the young mind like a Strasbourg goose.

Lack of humane, intelligent methods of teaching was eked out with sadistic technique. Education was driven into the memories of tough-skulled, résistant youngsters with blows and floggings. Rabelais, writing of what boys had to endure for the rudiments of knowledge, said of one especially cruel master:

"If for flogging poor little children, unoffending schoolboys, pedagogues are damned, he, upon my word of honor, is now on Ixion's wheel, flogging the dock-tailed cur that turns it."

There was no idea of home instruction, and public education lacked range and had little that was useful. Fruitless, prolonged study of words, followed by equally fruitless study of interminable subtleties, made a drawnout, bewildering misery of the boy's path of knowledge. Doctor Garencières, telling of his own education in France a century later, says that he and the other children, as soon as they had learned the primer, were set to studying the *Centuries* of Nostradamus. "This book was the first after my Primer, wherein I did learn to read, it being then the custom of France about the year 1618 to initiate children by that book; first because of the crabbedness of the words; secondly that they might be acquainted with the old and obsolete French; and thirdly for the delightfulness and variety of the matter." The picture of babes learning like puzzled parrots the stanzas that have challenged the wits of how many scholars is poor immortality for the man whose own training was so different.

Printing had so recently introduced the curse of schoolbooks to the young that there had not been time to create a pedagogic tradition. Before printing, children had grown up as free and untrammeled as Adam. They learned only to fish, hunt, roam, handle a bow and arrow and, if of good family, to buckle on a knight's armor. If the ways of doing these things improved, the pursuits were still those of the Stone Age. There was, of course, always a class of churchly scholars and a certain amount of mannered culture among the top social families. As a national development, however, few could read and write. But when printing brought books within popular reach, parents everywhere wanted their children to have this strange, new accessibility to knowledge which had been denied to them. So began the painful era of mental discipline for the young.

Doctor de Rémy and Rabelais, almost alone in their period, seemed to have envisioned the kind of education which today is taken for granted. Both believed that youth should be interested, and the book of knowledge unfolded in wonder and delight. Pantagruel, you will remember, spent years learning to say the alphabet backwards, and still more years and years on volumes of Latin commentaries, until Gargantua saw that he was turning out just a daft dreamer. So he chose a master of a different sort who taught Pantagruel the observation of nature and the examination of facts. Eventually Pantagruel returned to his father with a rounded development and an understanding of the relationship of knowledge to living. Rabelais knew this the hard way, Nostradamus learned it the easy way. He had an early joyousness toward study, he never needed spurring, nor had to shrink from what was for most boys a physically and emotionally painful experience that left its mark indelibly on a sensitive nature.

Doctor de Rémy grounded his grandson thoroughly in Latin, mathematics and astronomy, and gave him a general knowledge of nature facts. Ease and fluency in writing and speaking Latin were then of prime cultural importance, for it was the language employed by scholars and public orators. It was much used at court, too, through the reign of Francis I. It is said that the royal family, in hours when they gathered informally, enjoyed chatting affably together in Latin—an accomplishment that is perhaps as difficult for moderns to imagine as anything in the sixteenth century. But children then were put to this study very young to gain the required proficiency. The Provençal tongue still retained more of a Roman heritage than of northern France. This made the study of Latin easier for boys born, as Michel, in the Midi than in other sections of the country. Mathematics went hand in hand with astronomy. Patrons, amateurs and profound scholars of "the celestial science" were very numerous and they had to be able to prepare their own ephemerides, and to make elaborate, difficult mathematical calculations which today are available in published, labor-saving tables. Both of Michel's grandfathers

were ranked as savants in mathematics and astronomy.
Their teaching and his interest soon carried his knowledge far beyond his years.

For frosting on the educational cake, there were,
from both grandfathers, endless memories of brilliant
doings at King René's court, the little Athens of its
day. History and geography took on romantic meanings from these stories. The boy never tired hearing
of the gorgeous pageants and dramas which King
René had never wearied of producing.

"The most splendid of them all," said grandfather,
"was *The War of The Seven Chiefs*. It was a play out
of Greek legend, about gods and men, and all the gods
had golden faces. The king summoned one of the
greatest artists in France to Aix to design the golden
crown, the masque and the sceptre for the sun-god.
The night the play was given, the King and Queen and
all the court had dressed like the ancient Greeks.
'Twas like a country long gone, come back with all its
music and soldiers and ladies and gods."

Another time grandfather would say, "When you
are a man, Michel, you will travel. You will go to
Italy, perhaps you will even see there such a singular
man as Great Beard who came from Florence. Here, I
will show you Florence on this map."

"—and Great Beard, grandfather?"

"A rich merchant who came to trade, and brought
the king a Persian manuscript for a gift. To please the
king Great Beard had gotten himself up in a splendid
Turkish dress. He had on a robe of Eastern silk over a

broidered chemise. And about his middle were girt three belts studded with little jewels. But the joke of it was the king couldn't see his splendid dress unless Great Beard turned his back, and that is never done to a king. His beard was so thick and so long that it covered up the front of him. None of us had ever seen the like before. Amazing vain he was of it too."

Nostradamus sometimes uses the word *étranger* in the *Centuries*, but more often the foreigner is *le barbe*, *les barbares*, and if a foreign tyrant, *Ahenobarbus*. Perhaps his memory kept a picture of the Florentine merchant seen through grandfather's eyes, and gave him a preference for the older, Latin-derived word.

Doctor de Nostradame did not live to see the young prodigy whom he had so lovingly trained grow up. He died when Michel was still in his 'teens. His passing was one of two deaths that marked the closing of Michel's young boyhood. The loss of his grandfather was a personal grief. The other passing was impersonal, remote, yet it ended a period to which he was to look back in later years with nostalgic longing. This was the death of Louis XII, which closed an epoch in the life of France, one which Michel would recall in sadder days as a never-returning patriarchal age of gold.

Michel's life-span saw the rulership of five kings of France. Under the reign of Louis XII, which ended in 1515, France had been ideally united. Never had the country a more popular king than Louis the Well Beloved, twenty-second king of the grand line of Capet.

Louis had guided the government with fewer mistakes than most monarchs and no infringement of the people's liberties. But he was the last king of France whose reign expressed the national unity of a free people. The security of France had seemed at last firmly established. The powerful, one-pointed nationalism for which people and king had worked so long appeared near to realizing the French dream of continental leadership, a dream never to be fully realized, but persisting to Sedan. France never again in after periods reattained this early combination of apparently limitless possibilities combined with balance and simplicity of life, as just before the brook of Mediaevalism became the torrent of the Renaissance.

The kingdom of Provence had come under the sovereignty of France about twenty years before Michel's birth, and memories of its independent realm were still fresh in the minds of Provençals. René, their last king, had long known that with the passing of feudalism, Provence must come under a larger center. Himself a Capet, he wanted France rather than Spain to be his inheritor. But because of the love between him and the people of his little realm he put off the evil day. Louis XI was then King of France. He and René were both very old men, and Louis with an eye always on Spain grew nervous. He invited Cousin René, who always liked to go places, to visit him in Paris. In the interest of larger gain, the stingiest monarch in Christendom unloosed for once his purse-strings. His chamberlain was ordered to go all out with gay and splendid parties, and to be sure to have the prettiest girls in Paris there. The sly old fox successfully lured the gay old dog. René had the time of his ancient life, being then in his eighties, and when the party was over Louis had Provence in his pocket.

In Michel's time, Provence was administered on behalf of the French Crown by a provincial governor, the distinguished soldier Claude de Savoie, Count de Tende. He was a friend of the de Nostradame family, and his name appears with flattering mention in one of the quatrains.

With the death of Louis XII France came under the domination of a new king, and a different branch of the Capetian line—the House of Valois. Francis I, the glamour-boy from Angoulême, was the first of five Valois kings who succeeded to the throne of Saint Louis. Michel was then not quite thirteen years old. Boylike, he thrilled to the accounts of the brave and charming young prince on whom France set high hopes, and who was now his king. That was a year when the annual ceremonial pageant at Aix, which King René had begun in 1448, took on a dramatic meaning from the royal event. The most prized title of the French monarchs was that of *très chrétien*, and René's old festival procession pictured the triumph of Christianity over evil. Michel's parents took the boys to Aix for the occasion. The picturesque, wholly mediaeval solemnity of the procession was as naïve as an illuminated manuscript.

The long procession, which the boys watched absorbedly, winding slowly through the streets of Aix, was intended to show how the heathen gods and their worshipers were driven back into hell by Christ, but the presentation of the allegory would appear to have been as mixed and hard to unravel as one of the *Centuries*. The god Mercury led the procession, followed by the goddess of Night with Pluto attended by a galaxy of flame-dressed demons. Then came walking the huntress Diana and after her, singly, came Love, Venus and Mars. Followed then a gruesome group of lepers, behind whom were the commanders of the city and knights in armor riding proudly, then the dancers and a coterie of musicians with tambourines, lutes, fifes and drums. Now came the Queen of Sheba in silks and jewels on her way to visit Solomon. Next was Moses carrying the tables of the law, and trying to bring back to God a group of mocking Jews who danced around a pasteboard golden calf. Judas followed displaying his purse and counting his thirty pieces of silver while the other apostles belabored his head with sticks in punishment. Now in the distance, Michel and Jean, their heads uncovered, could see approaching the prelates bearing the Blessed Sacrament. Preceding them, strangely enough walked the Abbé of Youth, the Prince of Love, and the King of the Basoche. This last was the head of a guild of law clerks who staged many morality plays.

It should be plain to interpreters of the *Centuries*—though it has not been—that much in its writing which has baffled and perturbed scholars is traceable to the natural impression which such scenes as this procession made upon the imaginative, religious temperament of the boy Michel. The peculiar mixture of allegory, symbolism and historic allusion which abounds in his writings is less cryptic in intention than commentators will allow. Much of this was a normal reflection of Provençal expression in the romantic mediaevalism of the prophet's youth. It is difficult to interpret, mainly because modern scholarship has lost contact with so much in those older modes. When one reflects that with such a background Nostradamus was able to span and summarize prophetically the development of four centuries, it is not the obscurity but the clarity of most of his writing that is amazing.

After Michel's education had been interrupted by the death of his grandfather, his parents were faced with the problem of how best to continue it. They decided to send him to the famous university at Avignon. Jacques and Renée had probably to do some careful figuring of the family budget when they made their plans, for they were by no means wealthy, and a college education, then as now, was expensive for people of moderate means. But scholarship was a too distinguished family tradition for their sons to have anything but the best. Besides, they must have realized by then that Michel had whatever was the sixteenth-century equivalent of a striking I. Q. So to Avignon he went to take his Philosophia, as the course was called which approximated the modern degree of Bachelor of Arts.

Avignon was a proud, powerful old town. Its active student and religious life was carried on within the protection of incredibly massive walls above which reared like guardian swords the stately height of its thirty-nine towers. Here the tradition of learning stretches far back into the past, beyond the true and the false popes, to shadowy Saracenic origins. Here the mistral blows, the cold raw wind which Petrarch bemoaned, against which even the flame of his love for Laura could not keep him warm.

Teachers, with an eye out for promising pupils, quite naturally hoped that young Michel, coming from a family of scholars, would make a good showing. But they must have been a little breathless when, according to old sources, he began at once to display his dazzling memory and amazing information. It is told that he needed to read a chapter but once in order to repeat it with exact accuracy. If, gentle reader, you are visualizing from this something like modern chapters, let it be stated that in those days twenty-five lines of print made a short sentence, punctuation was scanty, and paragraphs were met every few miles. Such ability as Michel's, in an age when all educational emphasis was upon memory, made an impression out of all proportion to its mental value, and was alone enough to give him top rating as a scholar. But he had even more fascinating rabbits-out-of-hat than his memory.

It is said that from the time Michel was able to reason "he was accustomed to decide for himself the meaning of all manner of small, curious facts which interested him." One suspects that it was his grandfather who did the deciding, and that the old gentleman wore himself to his grave answering his brilliant grandson's questions. However that may be, Michel had a vast store of assorted extra-curricular information that soon had his teachers dazed and his enthralled fellow students hanging on his words. Much of what he knew would today be in any child's book of knowledge, but only learned adults had such information then.

When Michel told the other boys how clouds were formed out of vapor, and how they dissolved into rain, he was a sensation to lads who had learned at home that clouds were pumped up out of the sea, as was commonly believed. Shooting stars, he claimed astonishingly, were not stars that had become loosened from the sky. He talked about particles and gases and what made stars shine. And he insisted that the earth really was a round ball, for in spite of Columbus there were still plenty of people who did not believe this. And—incredible idea—he told them that the sun shone on the other side of the world too.

Michel was never a show-off, he had none of that quality. All who have written of him have, without exception, admitted his unassuming manner and quiet modesty. But he lost himself so completely in the interest of study and talked about it so constantly that such absorption had a spectacular effect. His pet interest at this time was astronomy, a subject on which he "gave out" as energetically as a living saxophone, and the college dubbed him "the young astronomer." He was nonetheless, in spite of his superior knowledge, popular with the students, because he was fun-loving and good company. After he had completed his university studies, which included advanced philosophy, astronomy, rhetoric, higher mathematics and Latin, he was put in charge of the astronomy class as student-teacher. This was a traditional honor for such a brilliant scholar.

During his sojourn in Avignon, Michel's devout young mind absorbed more impressions than merely those of academic training. The city was under the dominion of the papacy, as it had been from early days. Religion was emphasized here, as at Rome, by the Church as joint administrator of both the secular and spiritual government. The huge, ancient palace of the popes, though falling into disrepair, was still a potent symbol of this power, and dominated the activities of the town with its brooding, sightless stare. To Michel, it seemed to be forever waiting, somberly watching from dusty windows for the return of its holy tenant. Sometimes the boy watched the moon rise over the enormous pile, making it mysterious with shadows and silver. He thought of it, too, when he walked at sunset near the beautiful church of Notre Dame des Doms, and looked up to the Virgin of the Western Tower, whose famous statue was gold-sheathed like the gods in grandfather's story. At such times a strange feeling would come over him. A feeling of return. As if the popes some day really might come back to Avignon.

He knew by heart the history of the Avignon popes. How the German Emperor had bedeviled Clement V until he had removed himself to Avignon to be free of interference. How this had led eventually to the Great Schism in which three factions had claimed the papal election. How another German Emperor, Sigismund, had then called a great conference that deposed the false popes and then ratified the Emperor's choice, Martin Colonna, the Pope who healed the schism. Could such a terrible situation ever come about again, the boy wondered. Could there be rulers again in Germany who would do wicked things to religion? Would the Holy Father then return to Avignon? And if he did, might it not be that a French monarch would on this new occasion restore peace to God's Vicar? If a new schism ever arose, not Germany but France, he hoped, would name the new Martin Colonna. Half dreams and questions, these, that were to haunt him until the maturity of his mystical vision should give him the answers after many years.

The *Centuries* contain an impressive and detailed block of quatrains dealing with the prophesied return, under persecution, of the schismatic pattern within the Church, and he foresees rhapsodically that a great French monarch will restore a pope to his power in Rome, after Germany had been defeated by France.

He foretells that Avignon will be for a time the headquarters of this king in his struggle to re-establish the
monarchy and the exiled papacy.

Many verses elaborate this situation and the election of "The Great Shepherd," whom he calls "the new
Colonna." These visions, though long distant from his
time, held for him particular appeal and intimacy because of his Avignon boyhood.

When Michel returned to San Rémy after complet-
ing his humanities at Avignon, the next consideration
in his life was the choice of a profession. He wanted to
be an astronomer. To him astronomy was always the
beloved science. But his father is said to have stepped
on this idea. He desired naturally enough that Michel
should be a doctor. In this field his distinguished family background would give him a send-off that would
be almost a ready-made reputation in itself. Besides,
there were always human ills to cure, and medicine
offered a much more secure livelihood than did the
far, bright face of the heavens. His father's arguments
won the day. The opening of the new term saw Michel
entered at the Faculté de Médecin in Montpellier, most
famous university for scientific study in France.

When Michel passed through whichever of Montpellier's eleven gates, he no doubt carried in his light
student's luggage some of the things that had been
part of the professional equipment of his grandfather
and may have been handed down from even older
hands. Perhaps there was a surgeon's antique copper
case complete with gleaming instruments. He would

have no chance to use these in Montpellier's new dissection amphitheater, for dissection was done by the professors, but there was a warm feeling in just having these with him. There also would have been a copper or pewter shaving bowl, very important since it was used for bleeding and shaving the patient, and many a doctor at that time rose to fame through the simple technique of bleeding and purging. And perhaps Michel had a carved wooden box or a leather pouch that his grandfather had used to hold the gold and silver coins that were his fees, and which Michel hoped would one day receive his, too.

The clear air and bright color of Montpellier wore a welcome contrast to gray Avignon. The city, for southern France, was quite modern, too, since it dated only from the eighth century. Michel knew, of course, the legend of its founding. Two sisters, young and lovely, so the story runs, once owned all the land on which the city stands. But they cared nothing for this life, and longed instead for the eternal bliss of heaven. Believing that this could best be secured by giving up possession that bound them to earth, they had turned over to the Church their vast lands. It was a macabre coincidence that the first anatomical dissection ever made in France was performed in Montpellier upon the bodies of two women. Perpetuating the legend, the hills of Big and Little Sister, *Mons Puellarum*, rise about Montpellier. Over them in season, woad spreads a carpet of cloudy blue, and scarlet berries glow in the sun. In Michel's day, sheep browsed in leisurely contentment along their slopes.

Of a certainty, Michel's welcome at the university was a gracious one. Some of the professors had met his grandfathers; all had heard of them. Each teacher hoped that this promising student would enroll in his class. Professors then received no salary at Montpellier. Every student chose and paid his own masters. Naturally competition for pupils was keen among the faculty. The best-known and most popular teachers drew the largest classes, and, in consequence, made the most money. Not that money entered so much into the work of these distinguished men, but professors then as now had to live.

The Church was in active, executive control of the university. Pope Urban V had with high enthusiasm founded this college and made it his favorite project. Since his time it had grown enormously. Many buildings had been added, and the scope of instruction had broadened by taking advantage of new scientific advances. The university's latest cause for pride was its operating amphitheater, recently built and the first one in France. This was not used for operations on living persons, but only for the anatomical dissection of corpses. Yet so daring an innovation was it considered that it was the medical sensation of the moment.

This advance had been accomplished by the tireless efforts of Guillaume Rondelet, foremost anatomist in France and a devoté of the new Greek ideas which the

Renaissance was rapidly introducing. He was idolized at Montpellier and the focus of its most progressive student life. In a journal which Nostradamus kept in later years he eulogized particularly the names of three physicians who were on the staff of Montpellier. These were Guillaume Rondelet, Antoine Saporta, and Honoré Castelin. Presumably these were his teachers. Of this trio, the name of Rondelet still shines with undimmed brilliance on the scientific roster of France as a great pioneer anatomist and naturalist. A man of dynamic enthusiasm and daring courage, he would have drawn Michel like steel to a magnet, and in return would have opened his heart to this unusual student.

A gentle, devout man was Doctor Rondelet, yet vivid too in his ability to dramatize his subjects. Everything he said and did was an exciting expression of the new scientific spirit, and his sacrificial devotion to science had but recently been put to proof. When the amphitheater was opened, Doctor Rondelet had found it all but impossible to procure corpses for dissection. The ban against this had been lifted, but prejudice and superstition were still a powerful handicap. Death took the doctor's son at this time, and in order that knowledge might increase for the saving of others' lives, he had given the body of his son, and had himself performed the dissection before the students in the new hall at Montpellier.

"We have come a long way," he told Michel, "from the days when Charles of Anjou granted this university permission to dissect one corpse a year—and that had to be the corpse of a criminal!"

"Who would have died of hanging, instead of some disease which needed study," Michel observed.

"Exactly. Now we have won freedom to experiment on broader lines. But much more important, science has gained a new approach. Mark you, we do not know any more yet than our ancestors, but thanks to Aristotle we are learning how to go after knowledge, how to observe and study facts—that is what will carry medicine forward."

"You have made a splendid beginning, sir." The young man praised him with formal respect.

"Ah, wait till I get my botanical garden! That is what I am after now. It is what we must have next. More study of the properties of plants, better distillation of essences, and experimentation with rare herbs. If only King Francis were less set on clouting Charles of Austria, and more interested in saving Frenchmen's lives it would be the better for France. I have beseeched him for funds for a plant-garden, but he, forsooth, needs the money for his troops and his new châteaux."

Rondelet did not live to see his dream of a botanical garden for Montpellier come true. But due directly to his efforts, it was eventually realized through the generous gift of that "son of Egypt" as Nostradamus unkindly called Henry IV.

"At least you will agree, sir, that the King has done a fine thing in opening the study of the Greek language to the public in his new Collège de France. "Yes. And we need direct translations terribly. These second-hand Latin manuscripts are a mass of errors. But it will take time. We have to wait now for Greek scholars to be trained, then wait some more for translations to be made. And there is so much to be done!"

"But think you not, Doctor Rondelet, that it is more than a mere change of schools, more than the difference between Greek and Arab medicine? May not the fresh stirring in men's minds develop knowledge that even the Greeks did not have?"

"Of course I think so. And I can foresee trends which may take a hundred, five hundred, years to work out. Sometimes when I think of it, I feel like Moses on Mount Nebo. I shall not enter the promised land of science, but I have seen it from afar and found it glorious. Which reminds me, I shall let you read my new monograph on poisons, Michel. I have just completed it, and it contains material not heretofore presented. It is a case in point. My colleagues will say it is too radical, but the next generation will use it, surpass it, and then it will be old-fashioned. And that is as it should be."

This manuscript, like many others, its use long past, sleeps today on a library shelf. But its preservation records one among the early, patient steps on the long road which Rondelet foresaw.

The coming of the Renaissance had thrown the practice of medicine into a turmoil of transition from Arabic to Greek methods. Galen, Hippocrates and

Aristotle were the new gods, but the dissemination of their ideas was at first badly handicapped by an almost total ignorance of the Greek language, and extreme prejudice in many quarters against its teaching. A fight over the latter was then raging in Paris. Francis I had just established the liberal Collège de France which offered the first public instruction in Greek and Hebrew given in France. The Sorbonne promptly let out fanatical howls of horror and threats of hell to those who studied there, claiming that he who studied Hebrew became a Jew and he who learned Greek was a heretic. In spite of such protests the new learning gained steadily under royal patronage. Montpellier was always in the forefront of liberal thought, but echoes of the bitter quarrel and the persecution of independent scholars reached its halls. Michel, the student, had his attention directed for the first time, hearing of all this, to the hazards with which liberal scholarship could be faced. Anything, he saw, might happen to it from division within the ranks of scholars or hostile authority without. Later he was to experience this in his own work, with jealousy and intolerance toward himself as a physician, and his strange kind of knowledge.

As prophet, he perceived the danger that either a too reactionary or a too revolutionary authority could and would bring to such men as himself, and to such institutions as Montpellier. He foresaw no end to these recurring perils when he later wrote:

I—62

Alas what loss shall be sustained by learning
Before Latona shall complete her cycle,
War and revolution, brought about more through
stupid governments than from other causes,
Will create havoc that cannot for a long time be
repaired.

IV—18

The greatest scholars of celestial science
Will be reproved by ignorant princes,
They will be punished by edict, driven like criminals,
And put to death on the spot.

Memories of the Inquisition, the French Revolution, of great men from Galileo to Einstein crowd to confirm this prophecy. Montpellier suffered in 1792 when its proud Chair of Royal Anatomist and Dissector, which Rondelet's work had established, was suppressed during the Revolution.

Student life in Montpellier was gay, delightful and cosmopolitan. Youths from all over France and from other countries were attracted to its famous universities. Besides its native southern hospitality, Montpellier was expert through long experience in the art of entertaining. Through its gates there was a constant passing to and fro of notables. Prelates, nobles, politicians and scientists who came there were greeted with civic celebrations of simplicity or elaborateness in keeping with the importance of the guest. The festivities included much Latin oratory which was probably as dull as are public speeches today. After that, there had always to be a gala procession in this pageant-conscious land. The students took prominent part in these festivals, which were colorful, and sometimes exciting when some great personage honored the city. Montpellier celebrated with a grand procession the fame of one of her most celebrated students, Rabelais. But it was five hundred years after he had died, when for a day the old town revived the full bloom of its sixteenth-century pageantry. Pictures of this occasion describe all of the bright processions in which he once kept lithe step.

It needs little imagination to visualize Michel or Rabelais in the spirited ranks of marching students which led off the procession. Behind them walked the archers, town lads who made Montpellier famous as the sporting center of military archery. Then came arquebusiers and halberdiers, weaponed and wearing the tin hats of their day. Then pretty, dark-eyed girls swung their wide skirts down the tortuous street, lifting flower-entwined arches in the Provençal trellis dance. Nobles and town-fathers rode on horseback, the feathers, jewels and velvets of the lords set off by the sober richness of the councilors' attire. Scattered through the procession moved the heralds, musicians piping gay airs, and dark-frocked chanting monks. Last, and looking very like a calliope, was the grand car of honor drawn by six horses. Seated aloft in pomp was the guest, with the high dignitaries of Church, State and the university.

Michel had all too short a time to enjoy his student days. He was only twenty-one when a plague broke out in horrible virulence, devastating most of southern France. The Faculté de Médecin for the second time in its long history was forced to close its doors, as were all of the other schools in Montpellier.

What kind of plague it was is uncertain. Those early scourges were of many types, and medicine has little identification for many of them. It may have been, as Forman thinks, the black plague. Or it may have been the mysterious "sweating sickness" which attacked England a few years later when Henry VIII was courting Anne Boleyn. Whatever the nature of these epidemics, the dread word "plague" covered them all. This one appeared in the wake of the brief invasion by the Constable de Bourbon, and is supposed to have been carried by his troops. It swept the countryside like a devil's hurricane of agony and death. So furiously did the Horseman of the plague ride the countryside that burial could not keep pace with him. Unburied corpses lay in the houses and in the streets. So great was the frenzy of terror that gripped the people and so swift the mortality, that many, at the least touch of sickness, robed themselves in shrouds and disposed themselves for death, so that when it came they should not be bereft of this last decency.

The doctors were helpless; some of them as terrified as the victims; others, men of great-hearted courage, died like those they tended, heroic martyrs to the ignorance of the times. Literally nothing was known about these plagues, and the same treatment was given for all of them. Some of the medical men were beginning to get a glimmering of ideas that were the ancestors of modern technique, but they lacked the knowledge to develop them effectively.

They had figured out that contagion was spread by touch or carried through the air. To protect themselves, they wore extra clothing, plugged the nose with cotton and wore goggles, which were in a way the forerunner of the modern mask. They understood the need for prophylaxis, but all they had were "protective" oils with which they soaked their shirts. Garlic, long known for its purifyung properties, was used extensively, but without the least intelligence or information as to its powers. There were no arrangements for isolating victims, and incense was burned to keep down the all-pervading stench of putrefaction. Conditions were exactly the same as when Thucydides wrote his description of the plague at Athens which, he said, killed as many through fear as through infection, because people knew that there was no medical help for the stricken.

Such was the awful scourge against which Michel de Nostradame, just attained to manhood, elected to wage single-handed combat. It was the first of three such battles he would fight, winning victories that are unique in the annals of medicine. But how he accomplished it is a mystery more profound than any contained in his writings.

It is strange that he, a junior medical student, ever thought in the first place that he could cure where the most famous doctors failed. But he did think so, and he had the courage to back his theories. He dared not try these out under the notice of the city doctors who would have stepped on such presumption quickly. He went out into the stricken countryside, where doctors were few or none. He took his rosy cheeks and vital, stimulating personality into the hovels and villages, dispensing remedies that were his own idea. Where he treated, Death withdrew. Devotedly, fearlessly, with the untiring strength of youth he travelled the roads of southern France; to Carcassonne, Nîmes, Toulouse, Narbonne, and west to Bordeaux he went his patient, unswerving way. News spread slowly then, and such news as this was unbelievable. Yet gradually and sensationally the word went out. A young man was curing—yes, curing the plague!

Wherever people who heard of him and could reach his services they did. He was overwhelmed with work. The plague was an exceedingly stubborn one. Its duration was four years, and its cost a multitude of lives. Through all that tragic period Michel fought it, using his skill and energies without stint or thought of self. When, in the course of time, the scourge wore itself out against the immunity of those who had survived, Michel had achieved a reputation that was already legendary. Wherever he went, flowers were strewn in his path, gifts and invitations were pressed on him in cottage and château. Everyone wanted to know this wonder-working student, and thousands had cause to bless his name in gratitude.

How did he do it? No one knows. Definitely not with use of his supernormal gift which had not developed at this time. Besides, medicine and the psychic world were to him always two separate fields, and in medicine he was all scientist. It may be that, due to the influence and opinions of his grandfathers, Michel had not then abandoned (nor ever did wholly) Arabic ideas of medicine. He may have had access to rare Arabic prescriptions, which had come down from his ancestors or via travelers at King René's court. The East was old in plagues and civilization when the West was dressing in skins. Little of what they knew medically ever reached the West, but the crusaders saw their marvels.

But if his remedies came from this source, or from whatever kind of knowledge, they must have been of exceedingly simple nature, easily procurable in quantity, and at little or no cost. There is only one place he could have sought supplies like this, the woods and meadows of Earth. The answer could only be that he found some herb or combination of herbs which suited his need and wrought his miracle.

A legend has come down that he effected his cures with a compound of lapis lazuli and gold. Where would a young student without means have procured these costly minerals, especially in quantity for four years' work, most of which was charity? Such a story is the product of an alchemistic imagination.

Michel, the student, had as yet no right to practice medicine, except under the stress of such an emergency as the plague. He had no diploma, and must now, after this four-year interval in which he had become a celebrity, return to Montpellier to stand his final examinations. The required course there was six years. It is probable that he had been there for about two when the epidemic broke out. His four years of field work with his brilliant handling of the plague would be credited to him, provided he passed the final tests, which were very rigid.

He returned a spectacular popular hero, the focus of so much attention and interest that it is said his examinations were held in public, and a crowd came to see and hear. Examinations at Montpellier were always exciting, because they were oral. The faculty and representatives of the Church gathered in one of the large churches which the university owned. All present fired questions, as searching and inclusive as possible, and woe to the student who knew not the answers. It is said that Michel defended his thesis with vigor and brilliance in this long drawn-out, important ordeal. When all the questions were answered and he was pronounced worthy, he was formally invested with "the four-cornered hat, the ermine-trimmed robe, the golden girdle and ring of the brotherhood of

Hippocrates." From henceforth he is Doctor de Nostradame.

In Michel's graduating class was Jacques Dubois, or Sylvius, as he chose to be known in the fashion of the day. He soon was to become the foremost anatomist in Paris and to advance the knowledge of the human body with distinguished contributions. He was fifty-one years old when he received his degree, side by side with the prodigy of twenty-six. His fellow students no doubt pitied the plodding old boy, starting so late. Yet both he and Nostradamus were in their different ways conquerors of time. One was to look through time, the other ignored age. Both rose to greatness.

Doctor de Nostradame had planned to leave Montpellier after his graduation. But the students, wild over this new idol, demanded him for their teacher. The institution was pleased to have such a drawing-card on the faculty, though he was very young to be given such a coveted post.

Perhaps he did not realize when he assumed this responsibility how much of a strain the past four years had been, and how restless it had made him. He had made dangerous, strenuous efforts in the period when most young men are enjoying life to the full. It came over him that he too wanted freedom to enjoy himself. He did not want to teach. He wanted to travel. He informed the faculty that he was giving up his post. He had no plans, only to be footloose, to go where inclination led him. Regretfully his colleagues and students saw him go, wondering how he could bring himself to toss away so casually a position which not a scientist in all France but would have been proud to occupy. Unlike Rabelais, he never returned to Montpellier to do further work. The strangeness of his development tended to separate him more and more from its strictly hedged fields of thought. Yet Montpellier was proud of him, as she was of her errant Rabelais. She treasured the memory of both the sinner and the wizard. The worn cap and old gown of Rabelais, shabby with much trudging and trotting, hung on the wall at his alma mater, and were pointed out to visitors. And on their register they showed, up to the time of the Revolution, the prized signature of Nostradamus, with the date October 23, 1529.

CHAPTER THREE

Personages and Politics

THE NEW FREEDOM which had lured Doctor de Nostradame from Montpellier's halls was providing the kind of activity he liked best. His success had made him the rage throughout southern France. People were clamoring for him, requesting his attendance on their ills, inviting him to be their guest, for months if he would. Important doors were invitingly open. Everyone wanted to know the current sensation because he was charming, modest and had a great future. Besides, plagues had a way of returning, it was well to stand in with the only man who could cope with them. So Doctor de Nostradame, combining business with pleasure, travelled about from city to city, attending a patient in Avignon, stopping off for a visit in Salon, and moving on to Marseilles to answer new calls.

Everywhere he went he found men disturbed over the international unrest. His own native interest in internal and foreign affairs, dormant since the curiosity of his childhood, responded quickly to the incessant, exciting talk. Some of his new patients were men

54

Etching made by a woman of Salon, from the portrait bust by César Nostradamus, son of the prophet.

in a position to tell him inside facts and give him informed opinions. They enjoyed talking over these matters with the keen, witty young scientist, who listened so eagerly. These conversations bred in Nostradamus a dawning sense of political perspective that led eventually to his study of natural destinies on a plane of perception beyond the senses. Just now his picture of the great, warring forces of power politics was confused, incomplete. Too, he had been for so long in out-of-the-way pest-ridden districts where the only news was a tolling bell, that he was seriously behind on his history, for much had happened in those years.

The high noon of the Renaissance was now shedding its dazzling sunlight upon the most transcendent period-piece ever played by man. Chivalry, antiquity, and the beginnings of a different social order were mingling in a new civilization that was already ornamented with every splendor and blackened with every crime. Conquerors, alchemists, poets, lovers and heretics played their fiery roles in velvets and gems, plumes and armor, scholar's robe and monkish gown, against a background of deep, sensual reds, primeval greens and the blue of Mary's mantle. Chaos, war, unrest drove the scenes forward with climax topping climax. And always wine of violence and the scent of blood flavored the graces, the wit, and the etiquette of courts.

The initial impulse of the Renaissance had united an inherited physical dynamism, an ancestral hardihood, with a fresh, powerful increase in the electric potential of brain and spirit. The vigor was still earthy, and its forces, though far from the primitive, were still natural. It was this new electric urge of the Renaissance, expanding all horizons, which was responsible for the triumphs and tragedies of the grand age of the sword, the lyre, and the printing-press.

The costumes, armor and weapons, so different from ours, seem remote as we read of them. But the political set-up of the age had amazing similarities to what the world is enduring today. If a file of current newspapers could be handed back through time to a man of the sixteenth century, he would be astonished, not because our methods are so different, but because we bring them to bear on the same old situations as of his day. "Persecutions of Jews," "Fresh Axis Threats," "Books Banned," "Massacre of Religious Orders," "New Invention by Scientist," "Communism Gains Ground," "Parliament Asked for More Money"— such headlines would be quite familiar to a gentleman of the Renaissance. Nostradamus knew them all.

Martin Luther was making his bid for power with the new ideology of the Reformation. Sir Thomas More was publishing *Utopia*, the ancestor of Communism. Indeed, Nostradamus in writing of modern Communism calls it "the doctrine of the camel, More." Leonardo was playing with designs for aircraft and hydraulic pumps; Rabelais and other liberal scholars were fighting the ban on their books; and a new star of first magnitude, the Hitler of his day, had risen on the political horizon.

It would perhaps be unfair to call Charles V, King of Spain and Holy Roman Emperor, the first totalitarian, since he was without benefit of national socialism. But he certainly thought that Europe should belong totally to him, and he got his hands on more of it than did anyone else before Hitler. In the matter of real estate, Charles, like Browning's *Last Duchess*, liked whate'er he looked on and his looks went everywhere.

Trouble between France and Spain had started about the time that Michel was entering Montpellier. Francis I had quickly transformed the easy-going government of Louis XII into a cast-iron autocracy. He had flouted Parliament, and he had made the offices of the clergy into a crown benefice, a situation which continued until the Revolution. Francis hoped soon to apply these tactics to the international scene, pick up some spare parts of Italy, and eventually get the best of Spain. But the curtain went up before Francis was ready, on a drama he had not planned.

A Bourbon and a woman opened the scene. They were the Constable of France and Louise of Savoy, mother of Francis. In a short fifty years more, the duel between another Bourbon and another queen-mother, Henry of Bourbon-Navarre and Catherine de' Medici, would ring down the curtain upon the Valois dynasty. Two hundred and fifty years later, the Revolution would begin its drama with the blood of a Bourbon and "the Austrian woman." And shortly, within our own years—so the prophet has foretold—the last and greatest of the Bourbons shall arise to lead France back to power. His reign is to close the cycle of this dynasty which has alternately troubled or glorified France since the time of Nostradamus.

It was a Frenchman, Balzac, who wrote: "To the heart there are no little events. Love magnifies everything. It places in the same scale the fate of an empire and the dropping of a woman's glove. Almost always the glove outweighs the empire." This has been tragically true of France, where passion and politics have gone together from the distant yesterday of Louise and Bourbon to the recent yesterday of Daladier, Reynaud and their plotting loves.

The court drama of the queen-mother's infatuation and revenge which brought the Spaniards on French soil and opened the long conflict between the houses of Valois and Bourbon began while Michel, the student, was listening to Doctor Rondelet lecture on bones and muscles. Except for cynical Paris, the French people had little understanding of what it was all about, nor did most of them ever find out. Palamides Tronc de Condoulet told the story to Doctor de Nostradame over a glass of ripe Provençal wine, in de Condoulet's house at Salon.

"While I was fighting the plague," Nostradamus had said, "I used to think, when I had a moment to think at all, that when it was all over, I would be an old man in a strange world. Such tricks does our time-sense play us that it seemed to me eons must have passed before I returned to the cities. I have still but little knowledge of what happened besides the plague, for at Montpellier they talk naught except science. I saw something of the passing of Spanish troops, before the plague struck. I know that our Duc de Bourbon, Constable of France, turned traitor and brought them here to seize the Crown of France for himself. But why did treachery tempt so great a man? You, my friend, who have news from everywhere, perhaps you can tell me?"

The Sieur de Condoulet, who became a lifelong friend of Nostradamus, was a good gossip. The stories he left about the prophet show that. He was a prosperous Provençal merchant who enjoyed and dealt in the good things of life. He was equipped to bring the physician up-to-date, for merchants often got news ahead of others, and in greater detail, through travelling salesmen and peddlers who went with their wares all over the country. A good salesman's best introduction to a prospective purchaser was a fresh budget of exciting, though not always reliable, news picked up at the inns along his route. Often he displayed his merchandise in châteaux and palaces, the lords and ladies making their own selections. Then the salesman had a chance to talk to the help, and many a juicy morsel was gleaned in this way.

"Bourbon's troops," said de Condoulet, "looted my warehouses and ruined my business. Then the King came rampaging down to drive him out, and his men destroyed the little I had left."

" 'That which the palmerworm hath left hath the

locust eaten,' " quoted the doctor, who was ever partial to the Book of Joel.

"Palmerworm or locust, whichever of the two is the hungrier, that was the Spaniards. You'd think they'd never seen food till they came to Provence."

"A conqueror's appetite is always worse than his guns. An invader brings an empty belly. But you have not answered my question," Nostradamus reminded him.

"*Cherchez la femme*—in this case the King's mother."

"Madame Louise!" exclaimed the doctor. "But, she must be all of—?"

"—forty-five," de Condoulet told him, "and Bourbon was but turned thirty. Some tell it that Madame Louise is arrogant, grasping, but still beautiful. Others say she is arrogant, grasping and fat. The latter insist that of her twin gods, Cupid and Cupidity, the second is so strong that even her flesh seeks gain."

"What happened?"

"She sent Milord Chancellor to Bourbon with the offer of her hand. I had that straight from the palace. Bourbon told him he would never marry an immodest woman, to take back that word to her."

"*Hé, Dieu!* What insult to a royal lady."

"Insult, but understatement. The lady has looked on many a man, and one way or another usually gotten him. But not Bourbon."

"And then—?" asked Nostradamus interestedly.

"Why, then, she wanted revenge. His Grace of

Bourbon, besides being the handsomest man in France, had committed a more serious mistake, he was the richest. His coffers held more gold than the King's. His gentlemen wore three gold chains about the neck, and the King's but one."

"But would the King lend himself to such evil?"

"Madame Louise put the King up to it, but he was willing enough," de Condoulet said cynically. "First they took away from the Duc his command of the armies, which was cutting off France's nose to spite Francis' face. Bourbon was the best general in Europe. Then they stripped him of his last gold écu and most of his land."

"How could even the King do so?" Nostradamus asked, shocked. "There are courts of justice as well as courts of royalty."

"And the chancellor used them. He is a smart man and the queen-mother's creature. It was put over with a nice pretense of legality. And done quietly. Why, people in Bourbon's own domain didn't know what was happening."

"A tale of shame!"

" 'Twas then, they say, that the Duc, with his back to the wall, wrote a letter and dispatched it by secret courier to Spanish Charles. Bourbon's friends deny this, but I had it from a peddler who heard it from a man who is cousin to the courier that carried the letter."

"I pity the Duc," Nostradamus remarked, "but I

still say it was treachery to expose the country to invasion—for a personal grudge."

"It was more than a grudge, it was a man's life. Madame Louise and the King had done Bourbon too great injury to let him live. When the King got wind of that letter, he speeded up plans already made. His soldiers hunted the Duc like a wild boar through the forest. But he got away over the German border."

The physician lifted his wine-glass and quaffed deeply, as if to take away an unpleasant taste.

"King Francis and Emperor Charles had been aching for a crack at each other," de Condoulet continued. "This gave both of them an excuse. The Emperor gave Bourbon a Spanish army and backed him for a try at the French Crown. So, we had Spanish troops and their plague on French soil. And a plague on them all, I say."

"King Francis, whatever his faults, is God's anointed, and the power of Heaven protects him," said the doctor a bit sententiously.

Tronc de Condoulet eyed his friend humorously. "Heaven doesn't always protect its anointed, doctor. The same bishops would have anointed Bourbon quickly enough—if he had won."

"Why did he not, if he was such a great general?"

"The Spaniards fought badly. Their generals were jealous of him, they objected to serving under a Frenchman."

"Why, after the King had driven off Bourbon and the Spaniards, didn't he finish the job?"

"He thought he had. Why, when they fled into the Italian mountains, the Romans put up placards reading: 'Lost—an army in the mountains of Genoa. If anybody knows what became of it, let him come forward and say. He will be well rewarded.' "

"The King should have claimed the reward," the doctor murmured.

"He tried to," de Condoulet smiled. "Our King Francis, is a hero; none doubts that, but glory is too much his god. He thought the way lay open to capture Milaness and Naples, incurable madness of French kings. *Hé Dieu!* he almost did it. He shóuted in the midst of the battle at Pavia: 'Now at last I can call myself Duke of Milan!' "

"The cup and the lip," sighed the doctor.

"True. Bourbon had a whole new army. Germans, Savoyards and Spaniards. In a few short hours our King was not Duke of Milan. He was captive of Charles V, taken by one of Bourbon's own men. He got free of Charles' dungeon about the time you left Montpellier, when you were in the very midst of the plague."

"That was one of the few pieces of news that penetrated to me," Nostradamus said, "that of the King's return to France after two years' captivity. The thought of it made even the sick feel cheerful. But to me 'twas tempered by the sadness of his two small sons having to take their father's place as hostages to Spain. Even though the Spaniards treat them not unkindly, they are too young to be taken from their home. The Spaniards are a dour, stern people, of rigid custom. Who knows what mark such enforced residence will leave upon the tender youth of the future King of France?"

One of those little boys, the younger, grew up to be Henry II, the King of France who honored the prophet Nostradamus. The sympathy and understanding with which the prophet won the friendship of the monarch had its roots in the pity he had always felt for Henry's forlorn childhood. The cold reserve, the almost shy quality of Henry's matured personality, has been attributed to the influence of those early prisoning years in Spain.

"I need not, I suppose, bring you up-to-date as to the sack of Rome by Bourbon's men," de Condoulet said. "All the world knows of that."

"Yes, horrible. I can only surmise that after enduring so much, the Duc fell into a madness."

"Not at all. He was stuck in Italy with a great army, and no gold to pay them. The Emperor promised, but he didn't send it. He, like the others, was afraid of the Duc. He wanted to use him, but keep him poor. Bourbon wouldn't have it. The Emperor had himself just held the Pope up for a mighty sum. There was more where that came from, Bourbon thought."

"He met the fate such an impious act deserved."

"Maybe. 'Tis said that from boyhood he had the prescience of an early death. Before the battle, he told his officers that he had consulted an astrologer who told him that if he went to Rome he would surely die there."

"Why is it people never take the advice of those they consult?" Nostradamus asked reflectively.

"Because they don't like the advice," his friend answered. "Almost the last words of the Duc were that he cared but little for dying there, if but his corpse be left with endless glory throughout the world."

"Ah, glory—tragic mirage."

"And he didn't die in glory. He died of a shot from the arquebus of a common brawler. But perhaps not so common, since he is a metal worker to whom I hear both the King and His Holiness give commissions. A man named Cellini."

"And now, after all that treachery, we have a Spaniard for our queen, the Emperor's sister."

"Power politics," de Condoulet shrugged. "But that too was a cruel jest on Bourbon. She was his affianced, and King Francis took her away from him while he was in jail. Ye God, but our King is ever a great one with women. Another glass of this heartening wine, mon ami."

"No more. The hour grows late."

"What of it? And speaking of women, there are pretty girls in Salon, well dowered too. Let me find a wife for you who will keep you with us always in this town."

"Your wish is dear to me, my friend. Perhaps, some day—I like this town, and the country hereabout is pleasing. Perhaps I shall come back to you. Now, the road still beckons. But my thoughts are lingering on all that you have told me. The House of Bourbon is puissant and able. The Duc is dead, but the Bourbons still remember. A Bourbon may yet one day displace a Valois."

"I never saw such a man for always thinking toward the future. Come, come, you shall take one more glass." And the friends drank a final toast.

It was some time later that Doctor de Nostradame received a call that took him travelling to the haunts of his first school-days, Avignon. The papal legate there, Cardinal de Claremont, had been ill and wished the services of the rising star of medicine. Many were the welcomes and congratulations which greeted the doctor's return to this town where he was so well remembered as a boyhood prodigy.

The prelate gave him his blessing, and brightened up at his visit, as did most of his patients.

"It seems only yesterday," Cardinal de Claremont told him, "that I was hearing tales of how you talked about the stars like an old astronomer. But alas, it is more than yesterday, and my old bones tell me so. Each year I feel the cold of the mistral more. I hope you are not going to bleed me."

"I wouldn't think of it," the doctor replied. "There is altogether too much of that, and purging too. I am going to give you a strengthening remedy in which I have great confidence."

"Good," the legate relaxed with a relieved sigh. "We hear great things of what you can do. Certainly next to the salvation of souls comes the saving of their

earthly tenements. I think mine is in considerable need
of repair."

"Perhaps. But surely the ivy of Christ's spirit grows
ever greener on its walls."

"I would like to think so, especially in these troubled times. Draw your chair nearer to my bedside that
we may talk the better. I want to hear something of
your experience."

It was inevitable that in the course of the conversation the subject of the Lutheran heresy should come
up. The frightening gains of "the religion," as it was
called, were agitating the minds of all Catholic church-
men.

"That renegade monk, that Martin Luther, is at the
bottom of every piece of trouble that afflicts the world,"
the legate railed, propping himself up straighter on his
pillows. "Reform, Luther calls it. May the Holy Son
of God preserve us from such evil kind."

"And does not Your Grace think that the disturbed
state of politics and warring sovereigns play overwell
into the hands of Luther?" the doctor asked.

"Of course they do. When rulers lose all godliness in
pursuit of power, shall ignorant common people do less
than follow them!"

"That is what I mean. Take the sack of Rome, the
most grievous horror the Church has faced since the
Caesars. The army of assault was made up of German
Lutherans, I am told. But they were led by our French
Duc de Bourbon, of the Roman faith, who commanded
for the Holy Roman Emperor Charles. That is what

shocks me so deeply. That men sworn to uphold the Church—"

"Kings and princes are putting lust for power before the love of God," the prelate broke in. "Power politics cares not with what bedfellow it couches, let it be Christian, heretic or Moslem infidel."

"It is that very thing which makes me question the sincerity of these Lutherans. Numbers are no doubt sincere though deluded. But most of them seem as willing to fight under a Catholic banner, if it suits their ambition, as are Catholic kings to employ them."

"Ay. You put your finger on it. Those of the religion are already making their bid for power. It is the kingdoms of earth they want, and already they are tools for leaders of unscrupulous ambition. Proof of this lies in the fact that if the Church had its faults, it has gone a long way to cleanse them, but still the Protestants will have none of it."

"Has His Holiness recovered from the dreadful experience of the siege?"

"You don't recover from a shock like that," the legate said feelingly. "He is as well as may be. Know you that George Freundsberg, Bourbon's Protestant general, had got himself made a great gold chain— and I quote—'to hang and strangle the Pope with his own hand, because since the Pope called himself premier in Christendom, he must be deferred to somewhat more than others.' "

The sack of Rome by the Lutheran *landesknechten* of Bourbon had occurred some two years previously, during the plague. It still holds a record in military savagery unequalled except perhaps by Hitler at Warsaw. The Catholic world had not yet recovered from the horror of this crime against their holy city. The troops, while en route to the assault on Rome, had stopped briefly before Florence where, in the quiet of the Dominican Nunnery, a little nine-year-old girl had heard and trembled at the thunder of their passing. Later she had listened to the nuns tell of the massacre, the looting, rape and burning of Rome. She heard of the terror that drove her own uncle, Pope Clement VII, narrowly escaping death, to barricade himself in the old Castel San Angelo. The little girl was Catherine de' Medici. In a few short years she would be Queen of France. Another span of years would see her also queen of Saint Bartholomew's.

"And yet," marveled the doctor, "men call the Emperor, under whose banner this took place, devout."

"Devout he is," the prelate said bitterly. "Asked his confessor if it was a sin for him to take any thought to his personal life. But his very title of Holy Roman Emperor is in my opinion a trouble breeder when borne by a temporal ruler. The Church is the only Holy Empire."

"Temporal power lasts not long in any man's hands," the physician observed thoughtfully, "but the Church endures. It is the rock. The spread of heresy is a cankerous growth of another sort, far more serious. How menacing are its proportions, thinks Your Grace?"

"Look how its forest fire has swept all Germany!

The sparks are falling now on France. If this fire be not extinguished and quickly, by any means, our country may be next. The intellectuals, the very men who should know better, are taking it up, spreading false doctrine with the aid of the printing-press, which I sometimes think was an invention of the Devil. The king is vacillating. He will adopt no strong policy of extermination of the heretics. Their impudence is even shielded by the King's own sister, Marguerite, a royal daughter of France."

"Strange that there should be so many converts among people strictly trained in the true faith."

"It is all this new freedom that they are demanding. Nobody is willing to submit to authority any more, not even to the discipline of God's Church. They must be free to think for themselves, whether they have any brains to think with or not. They must be free to act as they please, and free to spend their money instead of giving the Church her righteous tithes."

"It sounds as if it were the worst danger since the Great Schism."

"It is more serious." The legate sat upright in his zeal. "Then, at least, there was no argument over the right of the papacy to exist. Luther, if he dared, would deny us even that."

"The seal of Divine authority received from the hand of Saint Peter—Luther has not that."

"True, and the Church will fight to keep that authority. With fire and sword, faggot and rack, the Church will struggle with Satan's armies. 'Blow ye the trumpet in Zion, and sound an alarm in my holy mountain.' "

"But," argued the doctor gently, "is not the special glory of the Church those early martyrs who did not fight back? Was it not the blood of martyrs which made the perpetuation of the Church secure?"

The churchman regarded him frowningly. "That was different. The Christians had not then come into their power. Had a Christian sat where Nero sat, then had Nero been lion's meat as he should have been."

The Church of France drew its descent from prelates who wielded their broadswords beside Charlemagne, and from the embattled bishops who aided Hugh Capet. Sword-clanging lines of Archbishop Turpin in the *Chanson de Roland* flashed across the doctor's memory:

> The good archbishop could not brook
> On pagan such as he to look.
> You pagan, so it seems to me
> A grievous heretic must be.
> 'Twere best to slay him, though I died.
> Cowards I never could abide.

"This time," the cardinal continued, "the Church has the power to fight, and she will use it to the extermination of the last heretic."

> " 'Ha, bravely struck!' the Frenchmen yell,
> 'Our Bishop guards the Cross right well.' "

"You will be giving Luther the martyrs," Doctor de Nostradame told the churchman shrewdly.

"Not all of them I fear," the cardinal answered grimly. This young man was a bit too free-spoken. Cardinal de Claremont opened his mouth to rebuke him. Then he bethought himself of his rheumatic bones, and how much he hoped for from the ministrations of the doctor. Curbing his speech, he pursed his lips and sat glumly silent.

Doctor de Nostradame made his patient comfortable and left with him a tincture and directions for its use. Promising to look in again shortly, he took his leave, his mind full of the cardinal's conversation.

Power! He was beginning to get the picture. They were all playing the same game, inside the Church and outside. He could see that. Still it had to be admitted that right was on the side of King and Church who held their offices from God. Doctor de Nostradame's religion and politics were mediaeval to the marrow, and he had no more tolerance for a heretic than had Archbishop Turpin. His quatrains on the deaths of Coligny and Condé show that. But he was essentially a man of peace, and his life was dedicated to the saving of life. He saw with horror the gentle name of Christ become a trumpet call to violence. And he was too much the mystic not to realize that the true function of the Church must lie in keeping the open road to the house not built by hands. This could not be done in an enlightened age by choking that road with the slain, tor-tured bodies of victims, heretics though they were. Better a thousand times that the Church should suffer fresh martyrdom than confer that crown upon its enemies.

Yet he could see and sympathize with the point of view of the Church—his church. The pattern of Christianity, he reflected, had been a violent one. The forcible conversion of Europe's hordes, the Crusades with their religious orders militant, the constant persecution of Jews, all these had made it natural for the Church to turn in its new hour of peril to the violent methods which had served her so well for so long.

He could appreciate, too, how the Church felt about the uninhibited spread of the new learning. Even while he himself reached eagerly for the long-lost treasures of ancient culture, reclaimed by the printing-press, though he thrilled to the beauty and mirage of the budding knowledge which promised to every man the kingdoms of the intellect, he was alive to its dangers. The influx and spread of knowledge would bring a glory, but already he could perceive how it might also breed a slow madness and frost of disillusion in men's minds. And what would the stake and the rack breed? For the competition of these with the new freedom grew daily more claimant for fresh victims. What tragedies might not all this be setting in train for the unsullied future? Where on the time-road would it end?

Nostradamus later lamented:

X—65

Oh great Rome thy ruin approaches,
Not of thy walls but of thy blood and substance,
The printed word will work terrible havoc,
The point of the dagger will be driven home to the hilt.

Near the time of these two conversations, occurred another which interested the doctor even more because it concerned the East, of which he knew little. This came as the result of a call to attend a celebrated patient, which gave him a boyish thrill of anticipation. It would be, he told himself, like meeting a hero out of an old romaunt.

The dying flame of chivalry was fast being smothered under ideas of the new order. But there were two brilliant sparks, the last, which lighted its final ashes, two soldiers whom history recalls as the last knight and the last Crusader. The former, Chevalier Bayard, the parfait, gentil knight, was gone, struck down not by a noble lance or sword, but killed by a shot, a modern insult, while commanding Francis' troops against the Constable de Bourbon. Nostradamus had never known Bayard, except by reputation, but he had mourned with all France at the news of his passing. Only in written romances would his like be met again.

But that other valiant soldier, the Crusader, still lived and fought for the glory of God and France. He it was, the famous, colorful Villiers de L'Isle Adam, who needed the services of Doctor Nostradamus. His name had recently rung through Christendom as the hero of the siege of Rhodes, the last important outpost of all that the Crusaders had won for Europe.

The sword of Villiers de L'Isle Adam, some three centuries later, was given by Napoleon to Czar Alexander. After the Emperor had returned to Paris from the session on the raft at Tilsit, he sent the ancient steel as his imperial compliment to the ruler of Russia in token that the Czar, as defender of Christianity against the Turks, was worthy of it.

William Stearns Davis, in his *History of the Near East*, calls Adam and his soldiers at Rhodes, "a little band of military monks clinging to a ruined cliff," and tells how that little band fought off twenty assaults by the army of Solyman the Great, and killed a hundred thousand of the flower of the Turkish Army in one of the greatest defenses recorded in history. Of course Rhodes fell to the Sultan in the end, for Solyman's resources were unlimited, and no single galley went from Christendom to help Adam.

The Grand Commander of Rhodes and his fighting monks, for all their courage, appear to have been virtually pirates. At Rhodes they had lived by forays against the Moslem coast, and done themselves so well that the Turks put up loud squawks to Solyman. The Sultan needed the island, anyway, to complete his defenses and further threaten the Western Mediterranean. Solyman, though not a Christian, was something of a parfait, gentil knight himself. When Rhodes fell to him, he permitted Adam and his remnant of men to withdraw with honor. More, he expressed his regret at dislodging such brave men from the island they had for so long called their home.

The Western world, feeling perhaps a little conscience stricken, gave to the returning hero and his order the island of Malta as a permanent home. This was, however, with the understanding that he would earn his board and keep by helping the powers resist the serious encroachments of pirates preying on their shipping.

It was on one of Commander Adam's visits to the mainland of France that he heard of the new medical celebrity and requested his services.

The doctor saw, when he made his call, a powerful man, of the old Burgundian type, grizzled, darkened, and weathered like oaken timber exposed to many suns and seas. His eyes, cold and keen as a blade, were brushed unfathomably with a brooding quality which only long association with the East can give.

"The old wounds ache me, Doctor," the old soldier said. "Days when the wind blows damply with mist, the scars of Solyman's scimitars plague me like fresh wounds."

"That can be helped, though I fear not cured," was the reply. "You have been too hard a taskmaster to your body these many years."

"Do your best. I hear great things of you, sir. By Saint John, my patron, I never envied Solyman his soldiers. 'Twas the other way round. But many's the time I envied him his physicians. The infidels have rare skill in medicine, especially in the poulticing and healing of wounds."

"So my grandfathers held, and taught me something of Eastern methods, which, as I am about to use them in your behalf, may seem familiar. But first, an examination."

The doctor's eye, straying momentarily from his skillful, probing hands, lighted upon the lean, wicked length of an extraordinarily long sword that lay upon the near walnut table. It was the type known technically as bastard, from its unusual proportions.

"Is that, Sir Knight, the sword to which, in your hands, Christendom owes so much?"

"Right, Sir Medic, that is *my* trusty Durandal. Perhaps it has not drunk the blood of as many paynim as did the sword of Roland, but it has not gone thirsty."

"Well I know. I wish, sir, that you would tell me something of the Turks, if you would be so kind as to enlighten my ignorance. What of menace do you think the Turks hold for western Europe?"

"In Solyman they have an abler leader than Christian Europe can boast," the Commander said. "And he has at his beck numbers enough to overflow the continent. Numbers, that was what did for me. And mark you, though Holy Writ may say that the battle is not always to the strong, if the disproportion is enough, any fighting-man knows that numbers do win."

"But surely Europe has men enough for that."

"The trouble is Europe can't, or won't, pull to-

gether. And Solyman is banking on it. Look what has
just happened in these last few years. The Holy Roman Emperor, Charles, takes captive The Most Christian King Francis, and fights Christ's Vicar, the Pope,
at the same time. The Most Christian Francis then
writes post haste to infidel Solyman to protect him
against Holy Charles. Solyman, whose ancestors were
skewered by mine before the walls of Jerusalem, writes
back that the petition of The Most Christian King has
reached the foot of his, Solyman's, throne! And so
Frenchmen put up with the humiliation of being protected by the infidel Sultan of Turkey against other
Christians."

Nostradamus, as he worked with bandages, hummed
to himself:

" 'Blow, Roland, blow,
       That Charles and all his hosts may know!' "

"And don't think that the Turk hasn't a proper
sense of humor," the Commander continued. "He has
laughs a-plenty out of the Christians and he will have
more. His pirates have almost ruined commerce in the
Mediterranean, and he may defeat the navy of Venice before he is through. What sort of madness is it
that grips Europe so that it does not see what lies ahead
of its peoples?"

"The common people know naught of it," the doctor told him. "They have no way to learn, and needs

must trust the guidance of their leaders. But surely heads of state should know if there is really peril?"

"The Turk," said Adam emphatically, "waits until the Christian armies are weakened with slaughtering each other. Then he will attack with all his forces. Europe does not know the Camel of the East, but I have lived beside him long as friend, and fought him as foe. I do know him. Beyond him lie the elephantine hordes of Asia, and there is Africa, which sleeps now, but may some day wake to our sorrow. The one thing that can save Europe is to stop this insane strife, and unite against the common foe. You would think the Pope, as head of Christendom, would be working for this, but he is no better than the rest."

"How soon do you think the Turks will try their hand at conquering Europe?" Nostradamus asked.

"I don't know," the soldier said thoughtfully. "But I would say that there will be a showdown in the next twenty-five years or so. Solyman is still consolidating his gains in his own waters. The East has patience and endless time. They will wait for opportunity to favor them."

"But are not the Turks poor fighters? Judging from the toll you took of them, I would suppose so?"

"No, they are fierce and excellent fighters, though their military science is not yet so good as ours. As for courage, the Moslems rush to welcome death in battle, and why not with their infidel beliefs? Eighty houris, with their keep and jewels guaranteed by Allah, reward each Moslem warrior who falls in battle. 'Tis enough to tempt a Christian, if he could depend on Allah's promises."

"That is all more disturbing than I dreamed of," the doctor told him.

"You cannot shave the Turk so fine but what his beard will grow again," the warrior pronounced. "The West cannot hold the East in final check. Ay, if it takes a thousand years there will come a day—a day of victory for them."

The faultless memory of Doctor de Nostradame registered for the future every detail and impression gleaned from this dynamically interesting, completely informed patient. Later, his vision searching the hinterlands of time for Moslem ambitions, he wrote many prophecies concerning them. A number of these have been brilliantly fulfilled. Not yet has history recorded this one.

II—29

The Oriental will go out from his stronghold,
He will cross the Apennines to look on Gaul,
He will sweep through the sky, across seas and
    over cloudy summits,
His power will smite the countries along his way.

CHAPTER FOUR

Garlands of Fame

DOCTOR NOSTRADAMUS—he had long since adopted the Latin style of name as did most scholars—continued to enjoy the variety of scenes and personalities that made his days a panorama of interest. He felt no inclination to settle down, and prosperity filled his velvet pouch with an agreeable number of gold pieces for his needs and plans. But the bright cornucopia of fortune was not yet emptied of its gifts to him. A letter, delightful as a laurel chaplet, again brought change into his life. Julius Caesar Scaliger, than whom France boasted no more distinguished savant and man of letters, had heard of the marvels of the young doctor, and he had been captivated by reports of the originality and power of his work. He wanted to know him. He wrote to him flatteringly and charmingly that he hoped this might come to pass. Doctor Nostradamus replied at once with such modesty and wit, it is said, that the great man felt in him already a friend. Again Scaliger wrote, this time an invitation to Nostradamus to visit him at his home in Agen. We may imagine with what unaffected eagerness the youthful doctor took his quill in hand to send his acceptance. Here was a man he truly longed to know. A great philosopher with the towering mind of the ancients, a man of medicine, too, learned in botany, and to round out perfection, a poet, an authority and writer on the arts. What inspiration, what rapture of sweet converse would not this visit mean!

Scaliger was one of the most colorful men of letters in the French Renaissance. He appears to have been a mixture of authentic, versatile genius and showmanship, with a dramatic background which his enemies claimed was the invention of his fertile imagination. Be that as it may, he had put himself over in a large way. In his late forties at the time of his writing to Nostradamus, his reputation had reached so great a height that it was unsurpassed in France.

Scaliger's story, as told by himself, was that he was born at the Castle La Rocca on Lake Garda, and that he was fairly near kin of the Emperor Maximilian. A page at the age of twelve, he had fought, so he said, as soldier and captain in the service of the Emperor for seventeen years. During that time, between wars, he had been a pupil of Albrecht Dürer. At the battle of Ravenna, in 1512, his father and brother had both been killed. He had himself performed such prodigies of valor in the mêlée that the Emperor had conferred upon him the highest honors of chivalry. But unfortunately and ungratefully the Emperor had given him no money.

Injuries received in the war and the onset of gout had put an end to his military career. He had then decided to turn his talents to medicine. He had the friendship and interest of the prominent della Rovere family and became their guest during five years which were necessary to take his degree from the University of Bologna. After some years more in Italy spent in medical practice, research and writing, he had gone to France as physician to Bishop della Rovere, who had received the bishopric of Agen.

Scaliger's detractors said that he was the son of a Verona school teacher, that he had got his M.D. at the less important University of Padua, and that the rest of his story was a tissue of lies. Such stories may have sprung from jealousy of the della Rovere patronage. Competition for wealthy patrons was bitterly keen in the sixteenth century. A Maecenas was a practical necessity to a scholar without independent means. Those who were lucky in this respect were natural targets for the envy, malice and undercutting of the less fortunate. It would seem probable that the della Rovere family, knowing Scaliger for so long, would have discovered the chinks, if any, in his armor. The lies were less likely Scaliger's than his enemies. With his own abilities, and the della Rovere backing as a springboard, Scaliger had risen quickly to fame through his critical writings and scientific accomplishments, and in both of these fields he made distinguished contributions.

Doctor Nostradamus traveled in leisurely fashion to

Agen. He stopped off at Toulouse where he had many friends from the plague years, when his work had covered all this territory. There were patients now who wished to consult him again, and festivities planned in his honor. While there he established headquarters in an old Romanesque house said to have had architectural ornamentation of most curious symbols. Succeeding generations pointed it out with pride to visitors as the place where the celebrated Nostradamus once lived for a time in their midst. It was standing until the time of the Revolution.

After a stay of some weeks in Toulouse, the doctor fared forth to complete his journey. The road was brisk with travel in the prosperous exchange of trade between Toulouse and Agen. Had he approached from the Bordeaux side he would have noted the same thing, for Agen, midway between these two cities, was a center for their commerce. It is in the heart of rich agricultural country, and as the doctor neared it, he admired the fine fertile fields so orderly with the produce of the sower's hand. Around the farmhouses ancient trees bent their verdure, and blossoms wove a *mille-fleurs* tapestry upon the earth. He could understand how the Italian-born Scaliger, now a citizen of France, could settle contentedly in this simple, radiant countryside.

Soon he saw the spire of Saint Etienne's Cathedral against the sky and the Romance Tower of the church Saint Caprasius, and knew that his destination was near.

When he halted his mule at the entrance of Scaliger's residence, a servant came quickly to assist him and a moment later his host appeared, moving with slow dignity, limping a little. ₁)ᵢ

"My friend, my friend!" he cried joyously. "Welcome, young Galen, how I have looked forward to your coming!"

The elaborate exchange of compliments in those days partook almost of a Chinese ritual, and each must show the other that he was versed in the art. Nostradamus bowed to the great man, as he grasped his hand.

"*O Micaenus edite regibus,*" he smilingly addressed his host, "the honor of this meeting—"

"Talk not of that," Scaliger broke in. "We shall have more exciting topics for our discourse. You must be tired too with so long riding." He drew his guest into a delightfully furnished interior alive with a sense of art and good taste.

"First, you will want to freshen up," he continued. "So I shall forbear all conversation until I have fulfilled my duty as host. I will show you to your room, and when you return there will be wine to pledge your coming."

"Thank you," returned the doctor. "But might I have a cup of water? When one has come to the Pierian Spring, you know, such a rite is fitting. And I will admit I am thirsty too."

In a trice the servant had brought a tray with a pewter pitcher of cool spring water, and a ruby goblet of Venice glass. The doctor held it up admiringly.

"You do not woo the Muses," he laughed. "You bribe them with such beauty."

"May they grant you their favors," said Scaliger. "The glass is one of a set, a gift from the Bishop della Rovere, who by the way has been as impatient to meet you as I."

And shortly there was the promised wine, and gay pledges from each to the other. Soon there was the sight and laughter of Scaliger's romping youngsters. And there was Madame Scaliger with more greetings. Doctor Nostradamus felt quickly and joyously at home.

"We shall sup *al fresco*," Scaliger said. "I always like to when the weather is fine."

Over the simple, delicious food they talked, and the doctor had a leisurely opportunity to study his hosts. Scaliger was a very handsome man whose vigor and magnetism made him appear much younger than his fifty years. His head was leonine, antique Roman, with broad primitive cheekbones and ridged brows. His deep-set eyes expressed every mood. They could sparkle with enthusiasm, flash red with anger and smoulder sullenly beneath his high philosopher's forehead. His rich full beard was handsomely shaped and curled. His scholar's robe was of fine material draped in classic folds. The doctor did not wonder that the young and charming Madame Scaliger so patently adored this man, though more than thirty years his junior. It was in fact one of the happiest marriages in France. He had been forty-five and she sixteen when they married. She bore him fifteen children, and the

cloudless serenity of their love for each other was un-
marred and lasting until his death, which did not
occur until more than a quarter of a century beyond
this dinner.

Roses strewn upon the board and twining the wine-
cups increased the doctor's illusion that he was the
guest of some imperial Roman. He said so.

Scaliger laughed. "I have been trying to wield my
pen like a sword in defense of Cicero. You shall hear
what I have written and give me your opinion. I call
him imperator of oratory. Would that I had the gift
of Cicero for Cicero's defense. I mean to show up in
all its rank pretense the ignorance of this fellow Eras-
mus. He is making such a loud noise with his bad
translations and worse philosophy that fools are following him. But I shall expose him."

"Is there controversy about Cicero?" asked the doctor. "I had not heard."

"The controversy is a general one of literary criteria. Aristotle is, of course, the supreme criterion,
perfection in every word. And I shall prove it. I intend
to give to the world as my monument a canon by
which men can test the worth of their own and others'
writings. I, Doctor Nostradamus, shall do for letters
what Guillaume Rondelet has done for anatomy."

"Dissector of Literature!" the doctor's eyes glowed.
"It has never been done. I can see the need for it, too.
With everyone rushing into print, and the tremendous
increase of translations, some of which must be very

bad. Yes, it is a wonderful idea, and you of all men
are fitted by your taste and learning for the work."

"There is no question of that," Scaliger agreed.
"There is, in fact, no one else at all."

The doctor winced slightly. It was his first intimation of what Frederick Morgan Paddleford has called
Scaliger's necessity for maintaining the delusion of
his own omniscience.

Madame Scaliger, sensitive to each slightest reaction toward her husband, spoke.

"Is not the last light lovely, Doctor Nostradamus? I
think it is the most beautiful of the day." She rose.
"Do you wish to linger, Jules? I am going in."

Scaliger looked at her fondly. "We shall stay a
while. Until the dew begins to fall."

Her graceful walk, as she left them, the doctor
thought, was like a breeze-swept flower in the pale
light. He remembered Tronc de Condoulet's advice to
him. Perhaps de Condoulet was right. If he could be
sure of finding a happiness like this—

Scaliger was talking again, as the flowing branches
of the trees darkened to black olive in the retreating
light. It was the mystical hour when day is a ghost
haunting the woodland.

The doctor spoke suddenly. "I have the oddest impression about what you have just said—your anatomy of letters. I cannot speak from conviction since
I have not read your opinions on this subject and know
only what you have told me tonight. It is instead a

kind of knowing that I feel." He paused in hesitant silence.

"But what is that you feel?"

"I feel something very distinguished about it that is partly in itself and partly in those whom it will touch. An influence. I hardly know, but my mind is making pictures of foreign countries, men with books, with writings of their own, and you are somehow there too."

The dusk hid the pleasure in the philosopher's face, but the doctor knew it was there.

"You are very flattering," Scaliger murmured.

"No. That is the odd part. It is something more."

Shakespeare, Ben Jonson, whom Paddleford considers singularly akin in mind to Scaliger, Corneille, the writers of the later Italian Renaissance, and many another writer and genius were to heir and benefit from this work of Julius Caesar Scaliger, surgeon of letters. Today its principles are as sound, its reasoning as clear and incisive as when its author wrote. Many a book on the modern market telling aspiring authors how to write but retells in the fashion of its own day the practical wisdom of this sixteenth-century analyst of letters.

This was the first of many talks, glowing with interest for the two men. The doctor must tell all about how he fought the plague, his theories and ideas. In the early mornings and at sundown they walked in Scaliger's garden, where his wife claimed her roses were crowded by her husband's plantings for his botanical study.

"This is good botanical country," Scaliger told Nostradamus. "Anything will grow here. That is why I like it." He stopped beside a small, charmingly sculptured marble of Pan perched on a pedestal, piping away. "Everything that we are or do arises out of earth. Under my trees I feel the reality of Pan come back, and I ask no more than that my thoughts play Echo to his tunes."

The doctor was unconscious that he spoke out loud, as he said, "The earth is the Lord's and the fullness thereof."

The philosopher's lips quirked. "You sound like the Archbishop."

The doctor flushed and stood his ground. "I only meant that in the discovery, revelation I call it, of fresh knowledge, or in the inspiration of poetry you cannot leave that out. It is the danger of the new classic revival that it may do so. When that happens a thread is cut. Power and the road are lost."

Scaliger, who had ever to have the last word, said dryly, "Rome and Athens seem to hold their immortality."

Nostradamus tactfully turned the conversation back to medicine. He had already learned that his distinguished host and senior ill brooked a difference of opinion.

"You do not agree with Rondelet that intensive

study of the properties of plants is what is now needed most?" he asked.

"No. That is all right for the practicer of medicine who must use these properties in his laboratory. But the scientist who makes discoveries for him will never widen the field that way. A pepper is hot and stimulating. It belongs, they say to Mars. I will not argue, I have disputed with Mars on too many fields of battle and come off the worse. He can have his pepper. What I want to do is to show the likeness and difference which a plant has to its fellows. Grouping and classifying them in this way we become acquainted with the structure of plant life, we begin to see the why of things."

"A wonderful purpose. It would give a completely related field forever broadening."

"That," said Scaliger, "is to be the yield this garden makes to science. A flower of knowledge fairer than a rose."

Scaliger was the first who demonstrated the necessity for abandoning the classification of plants based on their properties. and based it on their distinctive characteristics.

The news of Doctor Nostradamus' arrival in Agen had spread quickly through the town. At once a stream of callers came to pay their respects. And very prominent among these were fathers and mothers with marriageable daughters, for it was known that this famous young man was a bachelor. Invitations to fêtes and parties poured in. Scaliger, who had the Latin's love for hospitality and gayety, was eager to show off his guest, though he protested that it was not so.

"The women," he said on the evening that he and the doctor supped with the Bishop of Agen, "are wasting our time with their picnics and dances. I protest that I begrudge so much. I had planned that the doctor and I should sit beneath my green arbutus tree and hold high converse, and I must now struggle to see him at all."

The Bishop's eyes twinkled. "If I remember my Horace," he said, "that arbute tree was planned as shade for Lalage."

His guests laughed, and Scaliger cried, "Then we must find a Lalage for Nostradamus, that we may keep him settled in our midst."

The Bishop lifted his glass. "No fairer girls than the girls of Agen, eh, Scaliger. I pledge their beauty in this wine."

This desire to possess Nostradamus, to annex him to every town where he tarried, was flatteringly illustrated next day. A formal deputation of town fathers came to Scaliger's house with a proposition which would be worthy of the imagination of a modern chamber of commerce. They desired to make some kind of financial settlement on their two valuable celebrities, in return for which they said the two should agree to make Agen their permanent home. It was a smart idea, if it had worked. Both men were supreme drawing-cards. With such a double-bill attraction, Agen would have become a Mecca for all

France. The town fathers would have got back their gold many times over, with fame and increase for their town.

The two doctors listened in silence, somewhat stunned. It was the visitor who spoke first.

"Has the city of Agen no poor?" Nostradamus asked the councillors. "Are there none who are ill, old, infirm, needing your help and support, that you offer gold to us? We can support ourselves, we are strong, able men. Give this money to the unfortunate, we do not want it."

Scaliger gave his great laugh. "Don't you know scholars and artists better than that?" He scoffed at the councillors. "Why, half our travels and half our lives are spent in the country of the mind. Let the gold go to those whom it will help, the hungry, the homeless, the sick."

The councillors were overwhelmed by this unexpected reaction. Practical men of affairs, they did not know whether to be disappointed that their idea had not worked, or to glory in the idealism which seemed to them to lift their idols to new heights of splendor. When in doubt, southern France always solved a problem with a festival. The town fathers departed to tell everyone of the scholars' refusal of their offer and the generous motives prompting it. Immediately a gala procession was organized in honor of the doctors. The town was wild with enthusiasm. They wreathed the brows of Scaliger and Nostradamus with chaplets, and carried the distinguished men aloft through flower-strewn streets to the accompaniment of music, dancing and cheering. It was the high point in the friendship of these two remarkable men.

It soon became apparent to Nostradamus that Scaliger had invited him to Agen in the hope of making him a brilliant satellite to his own glory. Scalinger had no desire nor intention to share that with any man. He was annoyed at the storm of popularity which the younger man attracted, and at every manifestation of it he found it harder not to show his jealousy. Nostradamus could not but notice Scaliger's resentment. He was hurt by his host's unprovoked sarcasm and attempts to take him down. All his tact seemed powerless to change this and he grieved the more because he so genuinely reverenced the older man's gifts. He was having a splendid time in Agen, he didn't want to leave. It would be difficult to withdraw from Scaliger's home and still remain in the town without hard feelings. He was in a quandary. Then Fate, still watching over her favorite of the moment, solved the situation, with her oldest device. Doctor Nostradamus fell in love.

Mystery, which haunts so consistently the life of Nostradamus, clings, too, about this girl of Agen whom he loved and married. Even her name is not known. One writer has given it as Adriete de Loubebac, but that was the name of Scaliger's wife. Was the *demoiselle* fair or dark? Was she of noble birth with a goodly dowry? Was she learned? We only know, from Chavigny, that she was *"très belle, très aymable,"* very lovely and very lovable. Garencières says

of her that "she was a very honorable gentlewoman."
Certainly the doctor could have had his pick of beauty
and dowry wherever he went. Girls had pursued him,
thrown themselves at his head, and match-making
mothers had tried all of their wiles and inducements to
lure this eligible *parti* into the matrimonial net. But
he had remained singularly immune to all this, content with his work and studies.

Much as one would like to know something descrip-
tive of the looks and qualities of this girl who captivated the doctor when his friends had consigned him
to permanent bachelorhood, all that we can be sure of
is that Nostradamus was too much the independent
idealist to marry for less than a deep love. With so
little one must be content.

When he was married and settled into a home of his
own in Agen, the town fathers were delighted. What
their gold had not won, a daughter of Agen had
brought about; they had now their idol well and permanently anchored in their midst.

Nostradamus at some time chose for his personal
motto the serene words of the prior Orvian: "Happy
the first age that was contented with its flocks." One
would like to know if it was at this time, amid the pas-
toral setting of his new-found happiness, that he
adopted the idyllic expression. Or was it in later years,
when, heavy with melancholy of a tragic world, he
looked back upon these his cloudless days as on a
painted picture?

He also assumed his family coat-of-arms, not, it is

said, because he himself cared about it, but as a mark
of respect to the memory of his grandfather. The arms
are described as showing, in the first and fourth quar-
terings, gules and two silver crosses arranged to form
an eight-spoked wheel. The second and third quarter-
ings exhibited an eagle and sable on gold ground.

While Nostradamus was enjoying his peaceful life
in Agen, an event of national interest took place which
was to affect deeply, in time, the fate of France, and
bring to the doctor honors that would crown his career.

In October of 1533 occurred the marriage of the second son of Francis I, the fourteen-year-old Henry, then
Duke of Orleans, to the *duchessina* of Florence, Catherine de' Medici. The Bishop of Agen had gone to
Marseilles, as had a number of other Agenois, to see
the arrival of Catherine and her uncle, Clement VII,
and the great pomp and splendor of the wedding.
Nostradamus accompanied Scaliger to call upon the
Bishop della Rovere after his return from the festivities, to hear his account of them.

"This age," the Bishop told them, "has never seen
so grand a wedding. Splendor enough to blind Charles
of Spain and some others I could mention."

"The *duchessina*, is she beautiful?" Scaliger wanted
to know.

"We-ell, you know how it is at these public weddings. About all you can see clearly is the white robe
and the lace veil of the bride."

"You had better tell us what you can about those,"
said Nostradamus. "We have wives, you know, and

that will be the first question—'Did the Bishop tell you what the duchess wore?' "

The Bishop smiled. " 'Twas a wondrous robe of gold brocade, so bright that you can both tell your ladies, the lace veil seemed like a jealous cloud above it that would, yet could not, hide the sun. Her jewels were, of course, as countless as the stars."

"Report says the duchess is somewhat plain," Scaliger persisted.

The Bishop eyed him reproachfully.

"If she is a thought less fair than some," he said, "she has a spiritual grace. They say, too, that she has inherited the wit, intelligence and tact of the Medici. Besides, it was a great day for France and the papacy. It will strengthen their bonds against Spain."

"How did His Holiness appear?" questioned Doctor Nostradamus.

"Magnificent. His entry into Marseilles was superb. He has had the best artists in Rome working on plans for it from the moment the betrothal was announced. He came in a Venice galley, gorgeously carved. His ship led all the others and as it neared the harbor I could see him plainly, sitting under a golden tent with a carpet of crimson satin."

"Were many with him?" Scaliger inquired.

"Oh, yes. All the cardinals. The Blessed Sacrament was in an ostensory that took the eye, a triumph of the goldsmith's art. It was carried ahead of His Holiness on a fine white horse when they left the ship. And I was glad to see that they had stout fellows with great bulging muscles to carry the *sedia gestatoria* with an even walk. It detracts from even a pope's dignity to be joggled, as so often happens, when carried on the shoulders of bearers."

"I suppose the crowds went wild," the doctor observed.

"Three hundred pieces of artillery, all the church bells and the Virgin knows how many throats made them welcome. The people all kneeled while the Sacrament and the Pope were passing, and received the benediction. The streets were strewn with flowers all the way from the ship to the two palaces the king built just for this occasion, one for himself and one for His Holiness with a covered bridge connecting them, in case of rain, I suppose."

"I paid my taxes the other day," said Nostradamus thoughtfully. "And they had risen."

"People should not grumble about a little taxation," reproved the prelate. "Church and State must have funds for such glorious and necessary occasions." He took up the thread of his description of the wedding, adding more of the sumptuous details.

It was not to be long until the death of the dauphin made Henry and Catherine heirs prospective to the throne of France. Already history was in a train, which, unsuspected by Nostradamus, would draw him within the orbit of the royal pair.

For a time after this, the doctor's friendship with Scaliger recovered, on the surface, its first enthusiasm and cordial warmth. They resumed their long, de-

lightful discourses with the frank enjoyment of men
who have much intellectually in common. Scaliger's
fame continued steadily to mount, as it did, indeed, as
long as he lived. He was worshipped by the *littérateurs*,
and revered by the scientists, even though he made
many enemies by his constant and caustic attacks on
other men's work. He had no cause for jealousy of the
quiet doctor whose sensational reputation had been so
unsought, and who never wanted the limelight. But
the reputation was there, and Scaliger had only himself to thank for bringing its owner into his home territory. All accounts of Scaliger dwell on his enormous
vanity. He wanted to rule alone as uncrowned king in
Agen; now another and younger man shared his
throne. Doctor Nostradamus had resumed his practice
of medicine, with marriage, and now patients were
coming to him from Bordeaux, Carcassonne, Toulouse
and the whole radius of the neighboring country.
Scaliger hated this, and he also disliked the obvious
pleasure which his patron, the Bishop of Agen, took in
the society and conversation of the man he, Scaliger,
thought of as a dangerous rival.

Intellectual differences, too, made their appearance
in the progress of the friendship. The two who had
said they thought as one on first acquaintance discovered later that they thought very differently on many
matters. One of these was literature. Neither man was
an artist, but each man thought he was. Scaliger did
have a profoundly critical knowledge of the basic laws
of poetry, he understood the technique by which words

become the clay and bronze of the poet's sculptured emotions. Nostradamus on the other hand loved a lilting rhyme that raced with a story of derring-do and high nobility, or held a philosophic thought. He admired, and later used, to the despair of his translators, the subtleties of the *rhétoriqueurs*. He did not care for Scaliger's sonnets which Scaliger read to him with huge delight. Man of the world though the physician was, he found them overburdened with sensuality for which there was insufficient compensation of beauty. Few of these sonnets, says Paddleford, have been translated from the Latin in which they were written, partly for this reason, partly for lack of poetic value.

Scaliger was a devoté of Vergil whose writings he held superior to Homer's. Nostradamus, son of the troubadours, was rash enough to say that he thought Homer told a better, faster-moving story about nobler characters.

"That," said Scaliger, "is because you are ignorant of what it is that makes great poetry. When Vergil describes a shipwreck, I am there upon the deck, fighting for my life against the storm. The spray of ocean stings my eyes and salts my lips. Homer had no such art. He did not know the laborious polishing of line and phrase until words became the carving of a living immortality of experience." Doctor Nostradamus still liked Homer best.

Scaliger was a perfectionist. His ideal was the precise word, the studied gesture. His home, his clothes, his writings expressed this with a scientist's thoroughness. He had a certain contempt for the younger man's failure to comprehend the high importance of this chiselled, if cold perfection. Nostradamus, for his part, marveled that a man so learned as Scaliger could not perceive that the universe did not turn on a polished phrase. That perfection, in Scaliger's meaning, was a brittle mask concealing what it was intended to reveal. Nostradamus appears to have absorbed nothing of value from Scaliger's really great power of literary analysis. It is clear, from the writing of the *Centuries*, that if lines rhymed and had their complement of feet, that to Nostradamus was poetry.

What caused the eventual break between the two men is not known. But their quarrel was deep, bitter and final. Nostradamus had put up with a great deal from Scaliger for a long time. Though naturally diplomatic, Nostradamus' tongue was vitriol when he chose. There probably came a moment when, goaded beyond control by Scaliger's jealousy, he let go and told his one-time friend with daggered words just what he thought of him. Then in a cooler hour, too late, he sadly contemplated their cup of friendship, its wine turned into vinegar, its twining roses dead.

The quarrel with Scaliger was the first intimation that Fortuna, the fickle, no longer smiled upon her favorite, Nostradamus. Outwardly all was serene. The pride and devotion which the town felt for its popular and famous doctor were still at peak. The social life of Agen was delightful with the open-handed hospitality of existence under southern skies. The happy marriage

of Nostradamus had brought him further joy in the
birth of two sons. And on these babies the parents lav-
ished the affection and hopes of all fathers and mothers. Then, without warning, a knife thrust in the dark,
death struck. His wife and two small sons were swept
from him by some mysterious stroke of fatal sickness. He, to whose skill and science thousands owed
their lives, could not save even one of those most dear
to him. The green grass of Agen lay above three
graves. Under the skies of careless, sunny blue the doctor stood alone.

Here ended the period of his happy youth. Its doors
were barred behind him. Its days could never come
again. Friends were of little avail to comfort him in
this time of dark despair. Nostradamus was inconsol-
able. Every bright prospect which Agen had held out
to him was blasted. His beautiful friendship with Scaliger—the man whom he had once called "a Vergil in
poetry, a Cicero in eloquence, a Galen in medicine"—
had gone forever. There is no record that Scaliger sent
him so much as a message of sympathy in his sorrow.
His family dead, there was no longer any tie to bind
Nostradamus to Agen. Sadly the townspeople saw him
leave them, for what destination he himself did not
know. Again he was footloose, with freedom now all
unwanted. Once more he took to the open road.

Nostradamus was now just thirty years old. The
next ten years of his life were spent in travel, and concerning this period less is known than of any other
part of his life. Yet these were the years that saw the

beginning and development of his prophetic power and as such hold a vital interest for students of his life. Though so little information about him is written in the record of these years, there are inferences to be drawn which seem rather more than speculative. And there are certain speculations which the meager facts suggest may be true, but of which we can never be sure.

In the story of most great mysteries there is a journey upon the hard road of loneliness and separation. Sometimes the journey is lifelong, sometimes, as with Nostradamus, it is for a period of years. It is during such experience that the spirit is forced in upon itself through suffering and despair until nourishment, purpose and illumination are discovered in the hidden power of the self. This is the symbolic core of all sacrificial rites, Christian or pagan. The sunny warmth of homely joys and comforts is too contenting. These are the sirens that bind the wanderer, Ulysses, with their song, while on seas of mystery the ship is waiting with taut sails and straining figurehead whose eyes look toward infinity.

Nostradamus still had as his interest and refuge his love of science, his study of medicine. Too restless and unhappy to settle down or to practice, he began to travel about southern France and to study the whole field of pharmacy, medical practice and hospitalization, the last having changed little since the days of the Crusades except in the increased size of the hospitals. He may have had some idea or plan which he thought of some day carrying out, some modern, daring innovation. He kept for a time a journal of his findings, which is no longer in existence. Early commentators tell of it and quote a few facts and names from it. They mention his sharp criticism of the greed of the medical men in Avignon. The pharmacies of Marseilles he found excessively bad in their administration. Here and there he found doctors whose work and sincerity he could praise and others whose stupidity or ethics he condemned. How much time he spent in this way is not known but enough to make himself responsible for a great deal of the bitter enmity from which he suffered later on. The doctors and pharmacies that his caustic, blunt speech branded as cheats or charlatans were furious. They missed no chance to hand it back to him when occasion gave them opportunity. They were active from this time on in accusing Nostradamus of being a spy, an associate of condemned secret societies and himself a charlatan.

For three years he settled down in Dauphiny, associating himself with a doctor of fine reputation, but whether this was for medical practice or research is not stated. But his restlessness was still acute. He gave up this work and went into Italy, where he is known to have remained for a while in Milan, Genoa and Venice.

Nostradamus' practice as a physician was always that of a man of science in the strict sense, so far as is known. He did not confuse medicine with his psychic gift. Except for having the advantage of an extraordinarily brilliant mind, he was otherwise on the same footing, scientifically, as other physicians. He had his successes and he had his failures. It was natural that in this period he should be interested in contacting other scientists and getting their point of view, experience, and, if they had it, superior knowledge. That is why, when he had exhausted such contacts in France he turned his steps toward Italy, which had the great tradition in this field. French inspiration in science as well as general culture still drew upon Italy, though slowly emerging to independent progress. No doubt the Italian-born Bishop of Agen and also Scaliger had told Doctor Nostradamus of Italian achievements, which had fired his imagination and given him the desire to go there and see for himself.

Whether news of his own reputation in France had not preceded him, or whether his mood in these years created in him a desire for self-effacement, there are no accounts of his experience in Italy. It would have required considerable and aggressive proof from a Frenchman, at that time, to impress the Italians, anyway. They knew themselves to be the center of progressive learning and culture, and were sceptical toward the development of these qualities elsewhere. Nostradamus would, however, have had full opportunity to study the work being done there. He had, through his own family and important patients, a scientific entrée everywhere. It is said that wherever he went in Italy he sought out and talked with the most learned scholars. The interesting question is, just where did he go besides the few cities mentioned?

Nostradamus' travels in this period covered at least ten years, probably several of these spent in Italy. If he had settled in one city for a lengthy stay, his personality and abilities were so remarkable that almost certainly he would have become spectacular, as he always did, and stories would have gathered about him and some of these would be recorded. He was not a man who could remain unobserved. He had an intensely secretive nature. The *Centuries* with their subtle concealments are evidence of this. He was a man who gave out little concerning himself, and guarded well the secrets of others. Even after his death, so well had he trained his son, that César was careful to tell nothing that his father would not have approved when living, and added little to what was already known. This secretiveness did not develop in Nostradamus' early life; there was nothing to bring it out. But when he reached the deeply introspective period which began after his wife's death, with it went a perhaps protective concealment which still shrouds much that one would like to know.

He was deeply religious, and if in his first grief he sought surcease in active scientific work and travel, it would not have been long until he turned to the cloistered calm of monastic walls and the deep worship and contemplation which his nature perpetually craved. It is said that near the end of this ten-year period he was

to be found at an abbey where the religious observ-
ances were of particularly severe character.

He would hardly have spent much time in Italy
without going to Rome, the holy city of Europe. Nor
would he have been likely to forego a visit to Florence,
city of the Medici. He may, however, for reasons of
his own have gone incognito to cities and countries
other than those the record lists. If he did so, it would
have been because he had become associated with the
pursuit of secret knowledge which was in danger from
the Inquisition.

Italy had long been the center and hotbed of alchemic research. From the East had come a vast heritage of science and philosophy which had never received the sanction of the Church. This knowledge was
bootlegged through the means of secret societies. Some
of these may have provided the background and inspiration for discoveries that were the noblest fruit of
the Renaissance. Some, patterning after these, were
degenerate groups which courted the Devil's favor
with strange rites. A few even exercised a political
influence, as did the far-flung Vehmgericht in Germany, whose ritual was based on old Saxon magical
ceremonies that had come down from pagan times.

The true scientists who worked within these secret
groups, or alone, were for the most part men of profoundly spiritual nature. But they were unwilling to be
bound by the narrow orthodoxy of the current theo-
logical dogma. They had a wider vision in which the
free intellect had its place and its dignity. The search

for the Philosopher's Stone was at once symbol of the chemist's research, which still goes on, and of the transmutation of man's physical nature into the gold of higher forces. Copernicus in these years was hiding his theory of the universe, not daring yet to risk its publication. And many another soaring mind was working in secret with ideas beyond his time. Such men as these would have drawn the interest of Nostradamus, naturally predisposed to knowledge of this kind. Henry James Forman states in *The Story of Prophecy* that Nostradamus knew and used the law of gravitation and Kepler's law of the ecliptic, though Kepler was not yet born. Whether this is more than legend cannot be said, but it may well have been true. Astronomy had been a lifelong passion with him. He may in these Italian years even have known Copernicus and shared his dream of a grander universe.

Could even Italy with its treasure of enlarging thought and its antique beauties content this man who was a dynamo of restless energy, utterly alone and free to go as he pleased? Loving travel as he did, he could have gone in his quiet way to Greece, to Egypt or anywhere. No one would miss him at departure, no one would be surprised when he appeared again among those who knew him. Who knows? Under what secret influences some of these years may have been passed is a fascinating but unanswered question.

Through this old gate traveled Nostradamus on errands of mercy and friendship.

CHAPTER FIVE

The Plague Returns

NOSTRADAMUS HAS SAID, concerning his psychic gift, that it was inherited. Undoubtedly he had been conscious for a long time that he possessed it, and had used it to divert friends occasionally, as his grandfather had amused him when he was a child. During the period of his wanderings, under the emotional tension of sorrow and loneliness, such a faculty would tend to develop even without encouragement. Occult friends and associations, if such there were, would have given impetus to experiment with this perception, and fresh insight perhaps into the laws under which it manifests.

It is said that the first striking experience of his gift came to him while he was travelling in Lorraine. If this is so, it holds a peculiar interest, because Lorraine was the home of that other great French mystic, Jeanne d'Arc. There are two incidents from his early prophetic experiences which have been handed down and are retold by all writers on Nostradamus. These stories date from the period of his travels though the time of their occurrence is not known. One of these is amusing and bears out the idea that he often used the gift to astonish and delight close friends. Had this ability not been known to them and accepted in that way, his host would hardly have been free to tease the doctor as he tried to do.

Nostradamus was a guest of Lord Florinville at the castle of Faim, where he was attending professionally on Lord Florinville's mother. The doctor and his host were crossing the courtyard where two little pigs, a black one and a white one, were running about as was the casual custom of livestock in those days. Lord Florinville said to the doctor,

"I suppose you can even foretell the fate of those two pigs!"

"Certainly I can," replied the doctor. "We shall eat the black one, and a wolf will eat the white one."

Lord Florinville saw a chance for a good joke on his guest. He privately instructed the cook to roast the white pig for supper. That evening, while they were feasting on succulent young pork, his lordship with huge mirth told Nostradamus that he was eating white pig. This the prophet vigorously denied. The pig, he said, was the black one, as he had foretold. The cook was finally called to settle the argument. "Yes," said the cook fearfully, "the pig was the black." The white one had been killed and prepared as directed. But she had stepped out of the kitchen, before putting the pig in the oven, and a tame wolf had stepped in and was do-ing himself very well on the pig when the cook returned. Not supposing that it would make any difference, the black one had then been quickly killed and served, exactly as predicted. This episode occurred long before the writing of the prophecies, and certainly indicates that the doctor's uncanny faculty must have been well known to a select number of his friends and patients.

The other incident happened during his stay in Italy. In the neighborhood of Ancona, along the road, Nostradamus passed a group of Franciscan Friars. Among them was a young lad, a country boy, who had but recently left his father's farm to join the order. On seeing him, Nostradamus dismounted from his mule, went up to him and dropped on his knee before him. The astonished monks asked why he did this.

"Because I must kneel before His Holiness," he told them.

They were probably more astonished than ever, and it seems that little attention was paid to such an unlikely forecast. But it was remembered by those present, and told by them when, years after Nostradamus had died, that country boy, Felice Peretti, became Pope Sixtus V. It must be inferred from his homage that Nostradamus did not confuse principle with personality. He knelt to the symbol of his religion and the office of the Holy See, not to the man, Peretti, who became Pope. Nostradamus did not admire Sixtus V. This is what he had to say of him in one of the quatrains.

The Roman clergy in the year 1609
Will hold an election at the beginning of the year.
They will elect one who comes from the country, and
  wears the black and gray robe,
And never was there one more sly.

The story is that during the election Cardinal Peretti pretended to be a cripple, perhaps to create sympathy or drama. Once assured of success, he threw
away his crutches and sang loudly for joy. That may
have no foundation. Nostradamus disliked Sixtus for
his compromising complacence in dealing with Henry
of Navarre, who in the prophet's uncompromising
opinion was a turn-coat and a heretic. The prophet
had little symapthy with what he thought was the
Pope's weakness. In another verse he speaks of Sixtus
as being "afraid to take off his shirt at night for fear
of its being stolen." Which was a sarcastic reference to
the despoiling of the Church at the hands of the Protestants and ambitious rulers.

The year, during Nostradamus' lifetime, began in
France with the Spring Equinox. Sixtus V was elevated to the papacy in 1585, and the election was
held April 24. If 24 is added to the number of the
year it gives 1609, just one of the prophet's little subtleties which make life difficult for his interpreters! It
is at least an interesting coincidence, and to those who
follow astrology something more, that these three men
whose lives were strangely intertwined, Nostradamus,
Henry IV, and Sixtus V, all had the same birthday,

with the Sun in the second degree of Capricorn. It was to Henry of Navarre that the verses of Nostradamius called *Presages* and *Sixains* were presented after the prophet's death. Henry II, the king who summoned Nostradamus to Paris, had the same degree of Capricorn on the zenith of his horoscope.

When the new dimension of time swung wide its strange doors to Nostradamus, giving upon vistas of the future in extraordinary visions, he must have suffered for a time grave concern, even though long accustomed to slighter manifestations. Such a condition would have, even for the strongest nature, a somewhat terrifying aspect. Nostradamus, too, would have pondered its source, its rightness; his conscience as a churchman would have scrutinized it. For this was the era when there was nothing more dreaded than possession by the Devil. He is thought to have spent a long retreat within a severe monastery. Some believe that it was here that he began the writing of the *Centuries*. It is more likely that he went for the purpose of thoroughly examining his gift within consecrated walls, under a rigid religious routine, and also to take counsel with the Abbot concerning this gift of prophecy. The Church was ever the friend of this prophet; he stood on firm ground with its heads. Although the cry of sorcery was raised madly against him, the Inquisition took no notice of it, and his first Almanachs were dedicated to the Pope. Nostradamus, alert to the dangers of his age, would have made sure of the approval of the Church before he launched himself upon a ca-

reer as prophet. All the more so because his prophecies were not the usual vague cries of woes to come,
but specific information dealing with political destinies.

The Abbot was a very learned man. He would have
questioned the physician closely as to whether there
were any sorcerous phenomena appearing with the
visions. Were there any indications that the Devil was
trying to work through him? Nostradamus thought
not. It was the reason that he had come to the Abbey,
where its strict ritual was well calculated to discourage
any such ideas of the evil one.

"In fact," he told the Abbot, "it is my very love of
God, my fasting, my praise of Him and my prayers,
which seem to draw the visions closer. Surely, such
white and holy light as appears to me then, could come
from none but heavenly sources."

"That is so," the Abbot agreed. "The pure, inef-
fable white flame has ever been a sign of God's favor.
'Tis very well known that the evil one must use the
red flames of hell; he has no other kind of light.

"You say," continued the Abbot, "that this peculiar
foresight is inherited. To what extent did your grandsires experience it?"

"Not to the extent that I have. Their gift was more
personal, they could foresee matters affecting the family or members of the community. But they foresaw
these things less frequently, and never the wide scope
of the world which is opening before me."

The prelate eyed him shrewdly. "My son, I will not

ask you if you have gone further in efforts to develop this gift than did your grandsires. That is a matter between yourself and the confessional. But I am not unaware that there is much dark knowledge in the world."

"And I swear before Almighty God that never have I broken his Holy law touching such matters. I have done only that which I believed to be right. But if God Himself opens a door in my understanding, shall I defeat His purpose, shall I refuse to enter that door? Is not that the meaning of prophecy?"

"Yes," the Abbot said very thoughtfully, "when it is really prophecy." He touched some closely written sheets of parchment on the table beside him. "These visions you have set down touching the near future of France are depressing. I can hope, my son, that in these matters your foresight will be proved wrong."

"It will not be," said the doctor with conviction, "though I hope it no less fervently than do you."

"Well," the Abbot told him, "you have done wisely to set down the impressions that have come to you. Now we shall keep a check on this record. My advice is that you write them down, but do not show them about. Not yet. Many devout men have prophesied for a day, some have been given the sight here within these walls. Later, they are often proved mistaken in what they saw. Again sometimes, even when they were right, the vision left them as swiftly and mysteriously as it had come. That may happen to you. But if you find that over the stretch of years this knowl-

edge continues to come to you, and that its visions are
true, then you may, I think, accept it as a signal token
of inspiration. It is odd, though," the Abbot said
thoughtfully, "I have served Him on my knees these
many years, and never have I had a vision such as
nightly comes to you. It passes understanding."

After the prophet had returned to his cell, the Abbot's mind continued to dwell on this peculiar man.
A goodly soul, he thought, strange, but genuinely devout. There was a power of some kind that dwelt in
him, he could himself sense it, and the doctor had
wrought some wondrous cures among the monks.
True, his prophecies might, in the long run, not work
out. So few did. Still the Abbot believed he was an
honest man. He, as a churchman, could not be too careful in dealing with what might be Satan's wiles, but as
yet he could see nothing in Doctor Nostradamus mer-
iting the condemnation of the Church.

Something besides this new increase in his power
was beginning at this time to make itself felt in the
breast of the prophet. He realized suddenly that he was
homesick. He was tired of the road. He wanted to settle down in Provence in a place of his own once more,
where he could have about him his books and scientific
paraphernalia. Where he could meditate and work on
the knowledge and experience garnered in these long,
weary years. He was now turned forty, time to stop
tramping.

The question was, where should he settle? He could
not return to Agen with its sadness of memories. The

thing to do was to go back to Provence, look about and then decide on a new home. This he did, and no sooner did word of his return get about than it seemed as if every town in that part of the world was begging him to settle there. Friends were active, telling him of just the right house for him, and keeping him busy with kindly advice.

The City of Marseilles thought it would be wonderful if they could get this famous man to live in their midst, and sent a deputation to invite him and offer inducements. He finally decided on the little old town of Salon, because, he told his friends, it was central to Avignon, and to the other cities of Provence, and he would have a radius which would allow him to keep in touch with a wider circle, and see more of his friends than in the other places under consideration. His real reason was probably the smallness of Salon. Just as when he had fought the plague, he had been compelled to go to places that were isolated to carry out his ideas, he knew that in a different way he still faced that necessity. The jealousy and criticism, the constant watchfulness of his colleagues in larger towns would have spelled trouble in short order. In little Salon he hoped to avoid this. Besides, it was a sweet old town, and he wanted peace. Salon was overjoyed, it did its best for him. The old commentators say that "Salon gave him a wife who was well born and wealthy." Her name was Anne Ponsart Jumelle. Whether the lady was a gift from the town's grateful chamber of commerce, or whether the doctor did his own selecting, he did marry again, not long after his return. Settled down comfortably in a house fronting a narrow street, once more prospects for some durable happiness seemed bright. He resumed his medical practice with all of his old-time popularity. Soon, too, there was the first child, a son, to bind him even more closely to his love of home. Life once more was quiet, normal and carefree.

When their boy was born the parents named him César. One wonders if Nostradamus chose this name in memory of his happy days spent in the company of Julius Caesar Scaliger before their friendship ended. He may have thought that such a compliment might heal the breach when Scaliger heard of it. But there is no record that the haughty ego of Scaliger ever softened toward his one-time friend.

It was the month of May, 1544, when a traveler coming from Aix, passing through Salon, brought the disturbing news that plague had broken out in the capital. Wealthy people were already leaving the city, though it was not known yet whether there would be few cases or an epidemic. This time the pest was the hideous *charbon* scourge, so called because its victims turned completely black, so that in death they resembled charred logs.

Then new rumors reached Salon that the plague cases were increasing and conditions in Aix were becoming serious. Nostradamus' young wife spoke to her husband in apprehension.

"Michel, is there any danger that you may be called to Aix to fight this scourge?"

"Probably not," he comforted her. "It is a plague which has occurred before. I have never handled a case, but other doctors have treated it and may have found certain remedies efficacious. There are a number of good doctors in Aix who will perhaps be able to arrest the contagion."

Actually he was not so sure. There was no cure for this pestilence known. The only hopeful sign that he could see was that he had not been sent for. That should mean that the pest was lessening, getting under control so that he was not needed. On the other hand it was just possible that he was needed, and badly, but that professional jealousy was keeping him from being called. He knew too well that there were doctors who would for this reason let their patients die rather than call him in, and he was too proud to offer his services unasked.

In Salon, they were wondering about this too. Strange, people said, that if the plague was really bad Aix did not send for the one man in France who had ever been able to cope with it. True, this time it was a different pest, but still a plague was a plague, was it not? And if you could cure one, why not another? Then came the news that the plague was appalling, that people were dying like flies, and still no call came in for the services of Doctor Nostradamus.

"And for that I give thanks to the Virgin and all

the Saints," said Anne Nostradamus, thinking of her baby.

"Nonsense," Nostradamus told her. "You are married to a doctor. And a doctor goes where he is needed. And they must need me." He walked restlessly about the room. He was worried. Some of his dearest associations were with Aix. He should be there, helping their distress.

Came a day, some weeks after the first news of the outbreak, when a little group of hard-riding men with despair in their faces drew rein outside the house of Doctor Nostradamus. They were men from the town council of Aix.

"We have come to beg your help, Doctor Nostradamus," their spokesman said. "The situation in Aix is completely out of hand. The doctors there are powerless. The whole city is affected, and the pest is still spreading. If it cannot be checked it will spread beyond Aix, and who knows where it will reach? Our only hope is now in you."

"Why," asked the doctor coldly, "was I not sent for before this plague had gained such headway?" Inwardly he was seething with indignation, for in Aix of all places, where his grandfathers had been great, and his family known for generations, he had the right to expect trust and understanding.

There was a moment of embarrassed silence, then the councillors all began to talk at once. They had not anticipated such a rapid, deadly progress of the disease. They had thought the physicians resident in Aix could handle it, they had not wanted to ask Doctor Nostradamus to leave his young wife and child—for these and more reasons they had waited.

Nostradamus refused to spare them. "I know why you have not come before. And if you think that I am Satan's agent, you have done ill to call me now. No—" he raised his hand against their trembling protest. "This must be straightened out now. Otherwise I shall be of no use to you."

"Michel," cried one of the councillors piteously, who had known the de Nostradame family for a long time, "do not reproach us. Help us, and we will bless your name forever."

The doctor's quick sympathy could not withstand this appeal. "Very well," he replied. "Then let us get on with it at once. My servant will bring you refreshment and look to your needs while I get together a few requirements, then we shall ride at once."

"They have come for me," he told his wife soberly.

"Oh, Michel." She held their baby in her arms, and struggled to keep back the tears. Beside these two, to whom happiness had so lately come, there stood a specter now, and each knew that the other saw it. It was the vision of three narrow graves beneath the trees of Agen. What new toll might now be exacted by the grisly visitor of pest? Yet it never occurred to the doctor to consider personal interest and safety. A few simple preparations, a brief, tender farewell to the wife and baby he might never see again, and he was riding with the others at top speed down the road to Aix.

When they stopped at an inn for a quick bite and a change of horses, Nostradamus received more information about the situation.

One of the councillors told him how the cemeteries were choked with bodies. "Even piling them together," he said, "there is no more space in consecrated ground. My wife and daughter lie buried in the open field with the corpses of peasants."

"People die so fast," another told him hopelessly, "the doctors have no time for treatment or study of the remedies. In two days the stricken are dead."

Crime, they said, was complicating the problem, too. The people thought they were abandoned by God, that they had no time left to live, and they must snatch terribly at any pleasure or indulgence that was remaining. Theft, rape and even murder were stalking hand in hand with the pestilence.

"How many doctors have you there, and who are they?" Nostradamus wanted to know.

It appeared from the shamefaced admissions that there had already been a very large corps of doctors, some of them quite famous, who had been called in from outside Aix. A number of these had fallen victims of the plague, the mortality among the doctors being but little less than among the rest of the population. Some, too, had fled the place, unable to stand the horror of the scene. The rest were carrying on as best they could, but utterly helpless to save the victims or arrest the spread. It was the same familiar, tragic situation the doctor had faced fifteen years before.

Already Nostradamus was mapping his plan of campaign. "I want a good laboratory, and some trained pharmaceutical helpers," he told them. "Once I decide on a remedy, I shall want it made up in quantity. I shall give you a list of herbs and essences, and you can check your supplies at all pharmacies against it, and make arrangements to send elsewhere as shortages develop."

"We will do these things while you are resting a little when we get to Aix," they assured him.

"I want no rest," he replied. "There is not a moment to lose."

"But won't you wish to consult with the other doctors, and hear their professional accounts and findings?" he was asked.

"No," he answered with grim positiveness. "I shall not. If they knew anything, I need not have come. I shall get my information from the victims."

"Michel," the councillor who knew him best spoke hesitantly, "what precautions are you using against taking the contagion? I mean, is there something you can suggest to us that we——?"

"Nothing. I know too little as yet to recommend precautions. Of what good to plug up the nose and deprive yourself of air when the contagion may come from food or some other carrier? A clean body, internally and externally, is a general measure at all times. But the one important thing at this time is to control your fears, for fear is a killer. Put your trust in God, have courage, and pray as never before."

Nostradamus knew that these were brave men, but they had been under a terrible strain for weeks, they were exhausted and near the breaking point. It would not do to sympathize with them. His calm, matter-of-fact attitude took hold of them. Some power seemed to go out from him and reach their spirits. They were conscious of being at the same time relaxed and strengthened by his personality. Each breathed a sigh, as if a heavy load had been shouldered by another and stronger. In this man, they felt, was help. They rose to resume the ride and finish the journey, which was a full day's ride.

Along the rutted roads, where they were making all speed possible, sweet buds were bursting into blossom, framed in the fresh green leaves of the year's loveliest season. The rustle of brook-song and the notes of birds were carried on the woodland breezes. Sheep and cattle browsed content under ancient trees. Here was Nature upsurging in all her vivid beauty, with the rose of Spring at her breast. And beyond, at Aix, the stricken children of Earth were dying like the seared boughs of lightning-struck trees. As the group approached the suburbs of Aix, the doctor noted increasingly the processions of burial carts heaped high with human clay on its way to fields already thickly pitted with newly dug graves. Soon he breathed the fever-foulness weighting the air. From the town came the mournful sound, faint at first, rising in volume as they drew nearer, of the church bells tolling unceasingly their terrifying dirges.

Doctor Nostradamus preferred to stop at an inn to becoming a guest of one of the councillors. He would have more freedom at a public hostelry. Most of these had closed, but one was found which was willing to admit him to its empty rooms.

"Everything is dead, Doctor," the innkeeper told him hysterically. "The palace is closed, all the shops and every kind of business. Of course, places of amusement shut down first of all. Now even the money-lenders have put up their shutters. When that happens," he spread his hands in a weary, cynical gesture, "then truly there is no life left."

When Nostradamus had washed and put on fresh linen, he found a member of the council waiting for him accompanied by one of the Aix doctors.

The physician greeted Nostradamus cordially and said he had come to offer his services, he would be glad to work under Doctor Nostradamus, since there had seemed little that he could accomplish working alone. Nostradamus looked at him in pity, for his appearance was enough to frighten a beholder without the plague. He looked utterly exhausted, white and sunken as death itself after his long bout. He was bundled up in so much clothing that no one could say how much was man and how much wrappings. Since it was hot weather, and he was sweating profusely, perspiration mingling with the medicinal oils had soaked through his coat. Garlic added to these made the odor which he

had brought into the room nearly unbearable. Nostradamus said that he was ready to begin work, and
that he would like to go first to the hospital and pest-
houses. He wanted to see the arrangements for handling the cases, and then settle down to a study of the
symptoms and progress of the disease. He could not
say how long it would be before he could begin to im-
provise and experiment with remedies, since he was
entirely unfamiliar with the *charbon* plague.

When Nostradamus stepped from the cool, shadowed
interior of the inn once more into the blazing Midi
sunshine of the deserted streets, it was to begin his
first of two hundred and seventy days of fierce and un-
remitting battle against the plague, days filled with
unending sights of black, twisted agony, and heavy
with the stench of putrefaction which no breeze could
freshen. Along the way to the hospital, he saw how
many of the beautiful old houses, empty now, had suffered injury from vandals and looters. There were, the
other doctors told him in answer to his comment, no
magistrates sitting, no pretense of the administration
of justice or the apprehension of criminals. Everything
was being looted, he said, and live stock driven away.
People of good repute were too disconsolate to take action, those, that is, who had remained in the city. Several
times in the course of their progress the doctors were
forced to dodge quickly to escape being hit by corpses
tossed callously from windows to lie hideously in the
streets until the burial carts picked them up. Nostra-

damus saw that hope was indeed an exile from this ancient and opulent city.

The churches were as empty as the rest of the buildings, Nostradamus' companion said. No one, he thought, believed any longer in prayer. As for the priests they were as confused as rabbits, they ran around in utter helplessness, accomplishing little even in the way of solace.

Nostradamus found the hospital staffed by gaunt, utterly weary men. The stamp of terror was on every face there as elsewhere in the city. There was the disorganization caused by insufficient attendants and the crowding of patients far beyond hospital capacity. Sanitation, food, attention of every kind was suffering from neglect or lacking. The woebegone staff of doctors and nurses greeted him with joy and thankfulness. Hope stirred faintly in his wake like a salt sea breeze. Fear slackened in the presence of this man for whom it did not exist. Serenely he made the round of the hospital, studying conditions deliberately, questioning, now and then making some practical suggestion. He sat for a time at the bedside of the victims in various stages of the disease, observing symptoms and conditions, leaving some blessed ray of comfort where he passed.

One disadvantage in the study of this and other plagues had been the fear of contagion, which was so great it prevented the doctors from spending enough time with the victims to study properly the course of

the disease, its character, and the patients' reaction to
the remedies that were tried out, though the latter
were still for the most part cordials, bleeding and
purging. Nostradamus began by spending hours at
bedsides, observing. Forman thinks that he studied
excreta and may have been the father of modern ideas
of antisepsis. One of the old commentators, Astruc, says
that he paid careful attention to arrangements for
patients, their transportation by whatever was the sixteenth-century equivalent of ambulances, and the disposition of corpses. This undoubtedly was an effort to
limit the carrying of the disease.

Only after prolonged study did Nostradamus begin
to try out some remedial ideas. How much trial and
failure was necessary we have no record. Evidently,
from the length of time the plague persisted, a great
deal. Here was no easy success such as had been his
youthful conquest of the plague. This bears out the
idea that he had some inherited, little known and un-
tried *recepte* which, in the first experience, he used
with brilliant results. In the plague of Aix, he had no
such assistance, he was face to face with a contagion
of which he was ignorant, without theories, and on
the same footing with all of the other doctors in
charge.

The peculiar remedy which he at last evolved was
a kind of troche to be held in the mouth. That is all
that he used. Eugene Bareste, a scholarly and highly
intelligent French commentator, writing in 1840 tells
of his discovery of a rare little volume by Nostra-

damus. He found it, lying ancient and dusty in the Library of Saint Geneviève, such a rarity that not even the Library of France possessed a copy. It is entitled *A Collection of Numerous Receipts For Perfumes and Lotions For Beautifying The Face and Preserving Bodily Wholeness. Also Various Liquid Confections And Other Receipts Not Hitherto Presented.* It was originally in two volumes, but one, alas, had disappeared. The remaining volume, however, contained Nostradamus' description of the plague at Aix, and his formula for the troche.

Nostradamus says in this account that neither bleeding nor medical cordials had the least efficacy. "Nor was any found but this (his own remedy). All who carried it in the mouth were preserved." Here is the receipt, as given by Nostradamus himself.

"Take of the distillation of the branch of the greenest cypress-wood, one ounce; of Iris of Florence, six ounces; of cloves, three ounces, of sweet-flag, three drams, of ligni aloes, six drams. Reduce these to a mixture not overly evaporated. Then take of blood-red roses two or three hundred, completely fresh and gathered before dawn; pound these thoroughly, then blend them with the mixture. When the whole has been well mingled, make it into small pats, like troches, and set them to dry in the shade. In addition to the excellence and fragrance which this prescription affords, when held in the mouth it sweetens the breath for an entire day and relieves gaseous stomach conditions."

How, one ponders, could such slight, fragrant, medicinal pot-pourri afford resistance to the mortality of a deadly contagion? Perhaps in several ways. All historians of plagues, from Thucydides down, stress their accompaniment of destroying terror. The rose-pats of Nostradamus, considered only as bread-pills backed by his sensational reputation, would have helped enormously to relieve the fear. Anyone who could obtain something that this celebrated doctor said would save them, had already conquered fear and acquired resistance. But there is more to this old *recepte* than just that. One of the first symptoms of the *charbon* plague was frightful bleeding at the nose. Nostradamus must have believed that the infection entered through the mouth or nasal passages. This pungent, delightful little cake was designed to both stimulate and relax the nerves and passages of nose and throat, and perhaps give a mild antisepsis. There is a close connection between these nerves and the brain, so that terror in itself tends to congest them, lessening resistance to infection. His troche would have affected both physically and psychologically the particular head-area which appeared most vulnerable to the contagion.

Nostradamus, in the infinite subtlety of his mind, may have considered, too, that the red rose has been from time immemorial the symbol of life and happiness. Its fragrance and flavor would carry that message and symbolism to patients even though they were unconscious of it. It was the substitution of the idea of life and hope replacing that of death and despair. Roses are becoming a rarity in modern life;

a grouping behind the plate-glass window of a florist's shop, or a few in the vases of the fortunate. They were a more vital and plentiful treasure of the ancient world, and put to many uses. Marvelous rose cordials were made by carefully guarded family receipts sometimes centuries old. The bloom was also sacred to the making of odorous pot-pourri which gave summer fragrance to the house through the winter. And confitures of rose leaves were a frequent delicacy. It would be strange if in the ancient world these glorious blooms should not have been used in some remedial way that old scientists might believe infused something of their vivid life into the fading vitality of illness. Nostradamus was fortunate in being summoned to Aix in the season when roses were abundant. The picture of him, which history presents, calling those who stood in the midst of the whirlwind of death to go into the dewladen dawn and gather the red roses of summer for healing, is in itself symbolic of the way in which the skill and spirit of this great man touched the lives of those who turned to him for help.

For the efficacy of Nostradamus' prescription there is testimony of the most practical kind. When the plague had been at long last conquered, the city of Aix gave him the highest and most grateful credit and praise. They paid him in full for the nine months of his service, and in addition, the parliament voted him a substantial life pension which was paid to him as long as he lived. Nostradamus writing of this, says: "And it is true that in 1544 I was chosen and received

compensation from the City of Aix in Provence, where
by the parliament and the people I was entrusted with
the preservation of the city . . . Toward the end of
the plague it was clearly demonstrated that I had preserved a world of people."

Wealthy citizens, besides all this, made him rich
presents of money. These he distributed with his customary generosity among families victimized in the
plague.

Weary with the long pull, laden with glory, he returned to Salon and his family. He had been away
almost a year. The small rural town is now almost
bursting with pride in their star, and richer than their
wildest dreams had ever imagined. For Nostradamus,
after this triumph, more than ever means business to
the little place. The nobility from all the country
around are pouring in to see and consult him. The
nobles from Arles, Avignon, Aix, Marseilles, choke the
street leading to his home with their horses, coaches
and litters. These educated, sophisticated people of the
great world were enchanted with a doctor whose skill
could cure them while he diverted them with his learning and witty conversation. But in the background
there was always the enmity of his own profession,
insanely jealous of a man who could do what other
doctors could not, and accomplish it by means they
despised, envied, and could not comprehend. It was
openly said in regard to medical innovations generally,
indeed it was the credo of the old-line physicians,
that it was much better for people to die under treat-

ment approved by the majority of doctors than to have their lives saved by unorthodox methods. The only trouble with this theory was that the man whose life was at stake wasn't likely to agree, not until he got well, anyhow.

Nostradamus was now openly accused by the doctors of using bootlegged knowledge gained through association with secret, heretical societies and outlawed alchemists. These accusations were not without effect. The times were so deeply superstitious, so rent by all sorts of hatreds, that many listened, though not enough to jeopardize his position. But the snapping at his heels continued.

Nearly a year went by in which he was peaceful and happy in his home life, popular and sought after. Then came the news, once again, of the coming of the *charbon* plague. This time the outbreak was at Lyons, and on this occasion Nostradamus was early called on to help. When he arrived at Lyons, however, he found Jean-Antoine Sarrazin already in the field and directing the work. Sarrazin, according to the history of both Lyons and Montpellier, was considered one of the great medical figures of his day, his reputation was of the highest. He was extremely ambitious, and eager to make a record in stamping out the plague in Lyons that would equal if not surpass the work of Nostradamus for the city of Aix. He had the devotion and the courage to do this, but lacked the science. The coming of Nostradamus immediately roused his jealousy, and he stated that he intended to work alone.

Nostradamus, always a modest man, having no desire except to save those whom he might, agreed at once. He said that he would gladly share with Sarrazin what had been learned about the plague in Aix, and then he and Sarrazin would take separate routes which were not in conflict. This was done.

The situation at Lyons was somewhat different from that at Aix. Lyons was one of the largest and most important cities of France. It had a long medical tradition, for it was there that the first hospital in France had been established by Childebert in the sixth century. An interesting description of a sixteenth-century hospital which may be taken as typical of the best institutions, such as that at Lyons, exists in a document sent by the Hospital of Santa Maria Nuova, at Florence, to Henry VIII. This was written at the request of the king for information which would aid him in improving the hospitals of England. The hospital staff, according to his letter, comprised a number of internes who lived in, and a larger number of visiting surgeons who paid daily visits, just as today. The hospital maintained a dispensary for the treatment of ulcers and slight disorders. This was conducted by the foremost surgeon in the city who, with his assistants, gave their services without charge to the poor, and supplied them with free medicines from the hospital pharmacy. The modern clinic continues this tradition. The large hospitals were all independently wealthy, owning extensive vineyards and other properties and industries. Revenue from these was supplemented by taxes. But since then, as now, there was never as much money as was needed, wealthy patrons endowed beds, gave annuities, and assumed responsibilities for particular comforts and various needs of the patients. All of which sounds surprisingly modern.

The Church administered the hospitals, and appears to have done so in a skilled and highly responsible way. Even Martin Luther confessed that under the papacy generous provision had always been made for all classes of suffering, while among his own followers no one contributed to the maintenance of the sick and poor. Architecturally, the hospitals were constructed on the religious pattern of the cross as established by the Crusaders. The beds were arranged in rows in one enormous room, the long section of the cross. There was no such thing as private rooms, or separate wards. Some of the hospitals provided screens which could be used to partition off the beds. But this was in the interest of privacy when religious rites were administered, rather than any consideration for the patient at other times. In times of plague, the accommodations of even the largest institution were but a drop in the bucket of need, though they served all they could. However, the hospital was the focal agency from which all plans and effort were put forth.

In the Lyons hospital Nostradamus found a trained efficiency and order, even under plague conditions, far beyond the limited facilities he had worked with at Aix. The institution had two thousand beds and a large staff of well-known doctors. Association, as doctor or interne, with the Lyons hospital carried a certain prestige such as the great medical institutions of today confer upon their chosen staffs. It was also a hotbed of gossip, hatred and controversy over new techniques and theories, and watched over with a malicious eye by the fanatics of the Sorbonne. But a few years previous, Rabelais had been a member of the staff, when his friend, the distinguished physician, Etienne Dôle, was burned at the stake by order of the Sorbonne. No liberal scholarship which was boldly acknowledged could consider itself safe here, for there were always spies. Nostradamus braved more than the plague when he excited the enmity of Sarrazin.

In the pestilence at Lyons it soon became apparent that Doctor Sarrazin, with all of his zeal, was killing a great many more people than his methods were helping. Citizens from Sarrazin's territory began rushing pell-mell to Nostradamus, who wanted no trouble with his jealous *confrère*. Crowds threw themselves at his feet and implored him not to abandon them. Nostradamus finally said to these groups:

"I want to help you, but you must let me experiment in my own way. I honor Doctor Sarrazin, who is my colleague, but our remedies are different. So you must choose which one of us you want to remain as medical director of the city. You must decide at once for one of us, myself or Doctor Sarrazin."

The whole deputation cried out, "We choose Doctor Nostradamus, the deliverer of Aix." Sarrazin left, discredited and furious.

One month later the plague at Lyons was completely stamped out and over. Once again the little roseleaf cakes had done their work. Once more Nostradamus took his leave heaped with glory and gratitude. A deputation of members of the city government as an escort of honor accompanied him on his return to Salon.

The municipal histories of Aix and Lyons report in detail the work of Nostradamus in these two plagues. Whatever room for controversy there is in minor matters of the physician's life, these medical achievements are incontestable. Sarrazin immediately accused Nostradamus of magical practice and spread evil rumors far and wide. This was followed a year later by a book published in Avignon bitterly attacking him, branding him as a charlatan and worse. It was the hatred of the man of today which almost invariably pursues the man of tomorrow. It is said that in later years Nostradamus was deeply wounded when, on a visit to Lyons, he found that he was no longer popular there. This was after the misrepresentations through imitations and pirating of his writings. The doctors, too, who were his enemies had no doubt reminded the former patients of Nostradamus many a time that if they had been left to die, they would by then be enjoying the delights of Paradise. That having been cured by sorcery, they might have forever forfeited those delights. A potent argument in the sixteenth century.

CHAPTER SIX

A Prophet's Eyry

NOSTRADAMUS HAD FOUND, up to this time, that a settled home life was about the most unattainable of his ambitions. Yet each time that he returned from his absence it had been with more acclaim and a wider, if bitterly controversial reputation. Now, once again he settled down to live quietly in Salon, surrounded by the people and things he loved. More than ever he sought an uninterrupted family life and pursuit of the profound studies that were beckoning him to their secret fascinations.

He fitted up the top floor of his home as a study and laboratory sacred to himself, and prepared to enjoy long hours of solitary concentration in the late hours of evening when the day's professional duties were done, and his dearly loved family were abed. Here in this eyry he could arrange his books and instruments, placed to his liking with scientific nicety. His library must by this time have been considerable. From his grandfathers he would have inherited *incunabula*, old treatises on medicine, mathematics and astronomy. He

had added to these with books and manuscripts picked
up here and there in his travels. He watched the printers' lists for new scientific works that seemed worth-
while, and editions of the classics. Greek, Latin, Hebrew and French, they stood in orderly array upon his
shelves. Among them was a large, square Bible, its
pages softened with much handling.

Near a window of the study, where the light fell
most clearly, was his long work table on which were
writing materials. Against the far wall there was a
bed which he occasionally used when the few hours
before dawn were all that was left of a night spent in
study. Nostradamus, like Edison, is said to have needed
but little sleep, and to have found five hours or less
always sufficient. A small, but for its time, modern and
well-equipped laboratory occupied part of the space in
this private haunt. Its charcoal brazier, alembic, re-
torts, and chemicals permitted him to compound some
of his prescription needs, and if he wished, to carry out
some research. Hour-glasses in several sizes stood
about, including a large twelve-hour time-keeper and
a small one registering the half-hour, useful in timing
chemical experiments. A fine astrolabe spoke elo-
quently of the doctor's continued interest in astronomy. Nostradamus could afford to indulge his taste for
the best in scientific equipment. His patronage had
been for a long time very large and wealthy. He gave
liberally to charity and to the Church, but he lived
simply by preference, and had plenty of income to indulge his interests and hobbies.

Inconspicuous in a corner, though startling to a beholder, stood a tripod of solid brass which might have graced the mysterious rituals of the Pythoness of Delphi. This was the *"selle d'airain"* of his first quatrain, upon which, he tells us, he sat when in prophetic trance. On the wall hung a mirror of soft-toned old glass in a gilded Italian frame. Some said it was a magic mirror in which he saw his visions. Others said he saw them in the large, gleaming copper bowl which was also a part of the room's furnishings and which, the whispers told, he filled to the brim with water for his occult ceremonies.

Among all of these practical furnishings there would have been, as there always are, little personal things which he liked having near him and looking at sometimes when he worked. Such as, perhaps, a childish drawing by young César, who turned out in later years to be a very good painter and sculptor. Perhaps there were also mementos of his grandfathers. Some of the things in this room would be gifts from wealthy patients. He had received many handsome presents from the time of his young days when he first fought the plague. After he became famous as a prophet gifts multiplied *ad infinitum*. From Delphi to Nostradamus, all great oracles have been loaded with gifts, the general idea being the hope that the favors of destiny might be commensurate with the offerings.

About the study clung the dry, pungent odors of blended herbs, of which a few clusters were visible. The rest, powdered or distilled for use, filled a variety of decorative earthenware jars. Sometimes a fresher fragrance gave its odor to the room. This was when Anne Nostradamus would climb the steep flights of narrow stairs to bring a jar of roses in her arms from her garden.

Here in his high retreat Nostradamus began enjoyably to burn the midnight oil to the scandal of the town. Late hours have long been associated in simple minds with sin and sorcery. The country town of Salon, where all knew that the Lord made the night for sleeping, to say nothing of the high cost of candles, was early and suspiciously conscious of the strange nocturnal habits of its celebrity. Nostradamus had come to this town, in part, to escape from the enmity and envy of powerful personalities in the large cities. Here he had thought that he would be entirely free. But he found out that life had its drawbacks in this place too. Because he was the one illustrious personage in its small midst, everything he did and all that could be found out about him fascinated the townspeople. Their desire for excitement fed on his doings and, as in all little towns, they watched and pried and gossiped. Who were his grand visitors, how many litters and blooded horses stood outside his house, what did he eat, where did his wife go, what did she pay for her clothes, and WHY did he sit up all night? Why couldn't he go to bed like a Christian? Was there truth in what some people said, that he trafficked in magic? One should not, of course, say too much, for he had brought prosperity to the town.

The talk and rumors kept up, in spite of the fact that the town was both fond and proud of him. Nostradamus is said to have been not too happy over all this. He had endless patience over anything related to his work, but he was psychically thin-skinned and he had an irritable side. He was hurt over the suspicions and gossip of the townspeople who owed him so much. After the vicious accusations spread by his enemies, he became more taciturn, though he still talked brilliantly in sympathetic company. There were in Salon some charming, cultivated families, such as that of the Sieur de Condoulet, with whom he and his wife were on terms of intimacy. But he felt increasingly drawn to solitude and research.

His growing family, too, demanded more of his time and interest. Five children, two boys and three girls, were born after César. The dates of their births are not known, but Michel, Charles, Magdeleine, Diane and Anne arrived in due season to add their charms of childhood to the home. In his will Magdeleine is favored above the other girls to the extent of a hundred écus above their portions. No reason for this is given, but there must have been some ill health or handicap which required particular provision. It would not have been like Nostradamus to play favorites.

One pleasant day among the calls the doctor received was a social one from the scholarly magistrate of the town of Beaune, Doctor Jean-Ayme de Chavigny. He introduced himself and mentioned a number of mutual friends in Provence, and expressed his deep admiration for the doctor's achievements and all that he had heard of him. Nostradamus was delightfully impressed with his visitor's dignified manner and intelligent talk.

"Doctor Nostradamus," Chavigny said, "I have come for something more than the great pleasure of meeting you. I want to study with you."

"To study with me!" the doctor echoed in surprise. Not since his days at Montpellier had he taught. "To study what?" he asked.

"I should like to learn something of your wisdom which seems to me to be beyond that of other men," Chavigny told him. "I have my degrees as Doctor of Law and Doctor of Theology. I have been a student all my life, which should be some preparation. I desire to continue studying, particularly those things which will give me a deeper insight into the mysteries of existence. I have never studied astronomy, except superficially. And I think that I might also find the higher branches of mathematics interesting. But if you will become my master, then I shall leave the guidance of my studies to you."

Pleased, though hesitant at first, the doctor was gradually won over to the idea, because he already liked Chavigny. The doctor agreed to plan and supervise some studies for the magistrate who was to see him reporting progress and receiving instruction from time to time. It was the beginning of a fine and lasting friendship. How deeply Doctor Chavigny penetrated into the mysteries of Nostradamus' gifts, or if he had some psychic flair of his own, is not known. But the prophet's eyry soon became familiar territory to him, and more than any other friend he was received into his confidence. Unlike the friendship with Scaliger, no disagreements marred the even tenor of the association, unbroken to the death of Nostradamus.

It is supposedly in this period of his life that Nostradamus took up for the first time the study of astrology. Garencières says that he did so because he thought it might throw some additional light on the diagnosis of disease. This would seem to be an unlikely reason. Medicine had all too lately begun to emerge from its long bondage to superstition in which a misapplied astrology had played its part. The pathology of the humors, so recently blasted by Paracelsus, had its foundation in the elemental divisions of astrology, as did many ideas of treatment then being discarded. Nostradamus was too modern, too much the scientist alive to the trends of the times to have taken up this study for medical reasons.

From Belshazzar to Hitler, astrology has been the esoteric science of courts and kings. Its oldest traditions are linked with governments and their rulers. This was still true in the sixteenth century when there was no monarch of importance but had his court astrologer. Where royalty led, the courtiers followed. What the nobles did, the common people imitated. The sixteenth century was permeated with astrological belief and practice. No picture of the Renaissance is complete which leaves out the overwhelming desire of the age to penetrate the laws of destiny, to discover and manipulate fate through prevision.

Astrology as much as astronomy was then the science of intellectuals. It had not become "The unwise daughter of a wise mother." The two were still sisters in prestige. Scholarship in one was incomplete without knowledge of the other. Nostradamus had come to the study late because his life had been filled with other activities. But keen astronomer that he was, he would quite naturally have wished to round out his education with knowledge of the sister science. Not to know it was a reflection on his scholarship.

Nostradamus, no more than a man of today, could not be invited to dinner without having his neighbor at table complain of what Saturn was doing to him and lament that it would be another year before Jupiter helped him financially. Someone, too, would be certain to ask what did Doctor Nostradamus think of the political effects of the oncoming eclipse. Doctor Nostradamus might choose to discount astrology, but it did not do for him to be ignorant of it.

Nostradamus did not need astrology for his prophetic work. The completeness of his extra-dimensional vision gave him what no astrologer could ever find in his charts. There is no record of any horoscopes cast by Nostradamus, although he may have occasionally made such charts at the request of patrons and as a personal hobby. His patients may have asked him for decumbency charts, for much was made of these horoscopes through the seventeenth century. They were horoscopes of illness, erected for the time when the person was first taken ill. From such a chart the doctor or astrologer deduced not only the nature of the illness, but its critical period, duration and chance of survival. People liked the charts because they flattered their egos and they could talk about them. "My astrologer said he never before saw anyone live through such a frightful position of Mars." It was just the wav people talk of their operations today.

Nostradamus, besides his desire to be acquainted with astrology, to test it and see for himself how much truth it contained, had another reason, a very practical one, for establishing a reputation as an astrologer. This motive was self-protective. He was already deep in the psychic experiences which were to result in his written prophecies. Perhaps he was even then toying with the idea of eventually publishing some of them. He knew he would be treading on dangerous ground, and that he might risk the accusation of sorcery by the Inquisition. Astrology was more respectable than other kinds of prophecy. It was called The Celestial Science. It was patronized by the best people and the most learned minds, many of whom were high within the Church. If Nostradamus could launch his prophecies under the protective coloration of astrology, he had a better chance to escape persecution than if he put them out as revelation only. Such would be the wise course to follow, at least until he had tested public and authoritative reaction. Which is exactly what he did.

Queen Catherine was a sincere believer in astrology

and came of a family who had employed court astrologers for generations. She had brought Ruggiero, the son of her father's astrologer, to France to act as her adviser. Later, after the king's death, he had apartments in the palace connected with the queen's by a private stairway, and still later she built an observatory for him at Blois and erected a column to honor him in Paris. Canny Catherine was herself an expert astrologer. So also was Renée, daughter of Louis XII, and Duchess of Ferrara, who was considered one of the most cultivated women in Europe. Pope Julius II had been known as a fine astrologer, as was Clement VIII later on. Old Doctor John Dee, the English astrologer, planned Queen Elizabeth's coronation and advised her throughout her tenure of the throne.

Seldom has an astrologer changed the course of history. Kings did as they pleased, not as they were advised. But they kept the astrologers on the pay roll because the good ones were usually right. Monarchs, even the richest, were invariably short of cash for their needs, and a good astrologer came high. He had to have a laboratory, expensive instruments, and de luxe books. Sometimes he had more worldly tastes for which he expected the king to foot the bills, as had Angelo Catho, astrologer to Louis XI. Monarchs who employed astrologers at least believed that they had value received for their money, for not one of them was keen about giving away gold. Acceptance and use by royal and powerful personalities conferred dignity upon the old science and kept it in the limelight of fashion and practice. Everybody of importance had horoscopes cast, if they did not do them themselves. Notable collections of the birth-charts of all important personages of the times were compiled, and have been handed down to the present day. These may in some future age be considered as precious as written histories. Forman says that when Kepler cast horoscopes, a generation later, "To have a nativity cast by Kepler was like having one's portrait painted by Rembrandt."

Nostradamus reiterates in both his letters, to César and to King Henry, which preface the *Centuries*, that he has made use of astrology in combination with his prophetic gift. But as a matter of fact the *Centuries* show little use of it. A prophet who could casually identify James I of England and Cromwell by the planets rising at the time they were born, which was long after his own death, had no need of astrology. Nostradamus, however, had to use a certain amount of the terminology of the science and some of the trimmings to back his assertion of its influence. What he really did—and it is a marvel of marvels, utterly unique—was to *foresee clairvoyantly* the kind of horoscope under which the two rulers just cited would be born.

For the rest, he used his knowledge of the heavens as an astronomer would. Instead of giving dates, he often, in the *Centuries*, times events by astronomical positions. Sometimes he mentions a grouping of planets, and again only Mars or the Sun. One of the great outcries against the reputation of Nostradamus came from the ranks of the astrologers themselves, after he had published his astrological Almanachs. They well knew that his prophecies transcended their limitations, and, echoing the doctors, shrieked, "Sorcery!"

No previous analyst of Nostradamus has inquired as to the precise place astrology occupies in his writings. The attitude toward this has seemed to be that in verses so cryptic, anything which puzzles the commentator must be just part of the general oddity of expression. Whereas much light is thrown on many prophecies by an understanding of how Nostradamus used his knowledge of the stars.

Nostradamus may have been influenced to take up this study at the time that he did through having seen and heard discussed a book published by Jerome Cardan at Nuremberg in 1543. Cardan was one of the great mathematicians of the epoch, and for this reason entitled to respect. He was also a famous astrologer. His book was a collection of nearly seventy nativities of public personages and a number of predictions concerning those who were living at the time. Among his horoscopes was that of Martin Luther. Nostradamus, passionately interested in all that concerned the Church and contemporary religious conditions, would have had his attention particularly caught by what Cardan had to say from an astrologer's point of view. What Cardan did say, (as quoted in Manly Hall's *Story of Astrology*,) was:

"Incredible is the vast number of followers which this doctrine has in a brief space achieved. Already the world is on fire with the wild struggle over this madness, which, owing to the position of Mars, must ultimately break up of itself. Countless are the heads which desire to reign in it, and if nothing else could convince us of its futility, then the number of its diverse manifestations must convince us. . . . Nevertheless, the Sun and Saturn in the position of their future great conjunction indicate both the strength and the long duration of this heresy."

In his book Cardan predicted the hanging of the Archbishop of Saint Andrews, one of the remarkable forecasts of the period. Nine years later, this English prelate, ill of a puzzling malady, sent to the continent for the assistance of Cardan. The astrologer, after making a diagnosis which brought about a cure, told the churchman that, though he had been able to cure him, he could not change his destiny nor prevent him from being hanged, as was eventually his fate. Cardan also correctly predicted that his own son would be beheaded.

Nostradamus, mathematician and descendant of mathematicians, would have been impressed by the authority of this book and the reputation of the author as a mathematician. He would have said to himself, "I shall look into astrology—when I have the time." It was not until after the plague of Aix that he had this leisure, in 1547.

Another stimulant to his interest in the subject was the death of Francis I, which occurred in 1547. This event brought to the throne a new king, the son of

Francis, who now reigned as Henry II and whose
queen was Catherine de' Medici. Whenever there was
a change in the government it always was, and still is,
.the signal for the prophets to burst into print. Prophets have an advantage over the "now it can be told"
groups, because the latter have to wait for whatever
happens, and spill the secrets afterwards. But no such
limitation binds the reader of the future. He "tells
all" before the event occurs. His disadvantage is that
usually nobody believes him. Prophets of all ages have
seemed to love and specialize in gloom, the motto appearing to be the opposite in most instances to the sun-
dial, which records only the happy hours. It must have
been a little hard on Henry II, the new king, to have
the astrologers working on the details of his death before he had time to put his crown on straight.

Everybody in prophetic circles knew that Henry
and Catherine both had afflicted nativities. Lucas
Gauricus, a learned, competent astrologer whose fine
collection of charts has been handed down, had published in his *Tractatus Astrologus*, 1542, the horoscopes
of both sovereigns. He had predicted that Henry would
be killed in a duel, and warned him against any kind
of single combat in his forty-first year. This prophecy,
like that of Nostradamus concerning the fate of Henry,
is a famous one because it was an accurate forecast.
Two stories are told about it. One is that Catherine
gave the birthdate to Gauricus under a false name,
and that he made the prophecy not knowing whose
chart it was. This would have been impossible. Royal

births are timed and witnessed, information was immediately and widely accessible to astrologers. Gauricus would have recognized the horoscope at once. The other account, which the Duchess of Cleves related in her memoirs, was that the king told her that he visited Gauricus in disguise and that the prophecy was made to him. He commented on it by saying that kings did not fight duels except with equals, and he had just made peace with Charles of Spain.

Interest in his forecast centers in the fact that Gauricus could not, by the nature of astrology, have specifically predicted a duel. The violence of Henry's chart, with its Aries planets afflicted by Mars and Saturn, might have meant illness affecting the head, or war, or any number of things. Catherine, born in the same year and just two weeks later than Henry, had a chart as dangerous as his, yet her life was different and nearly twenty years longer. So that if Gauricus really predicted death through single combat, he was using the same extradimensional sense, combined with astrology, which made Nostradamus great.

There seem to have been no dramatic public forecasts about the Queen, who was to be so much more fatal to France than the short-lived husband. The French had never expected that Catherine would be their Queen. When she married Henry, he was still the second son. Then the sudden death of the Dauphin had put Henry in line for the throne. The match was considered quite a step up for the Medici, who were, in the eyes of the French aristocracy, trades-people, no matter how glorified. Had Henry been Dauphin at the time, a more patrician alliance would have been planned for him. Perhaps, thought the seers, studying these two fatalistic horoscopes of their rulers, neither one would live very long, and maybe Catherine would go first.

From the time of Henry's accession, the forecast of Gauricus seems to have been known generally and talked around. With the works of Gauricus and Cardan published in successive years, attracting the attention and discussion of scientists, scholars and court circles, it would have been strange if Doctor Nostradamus had not felt that he wished to be conversant with this much debated branch of prophecy.

The leading astrologers, whatever their limitations, were for the most part honest, high-minded scholars, with many dramatically fulfilled predictions to their credit. They were in their way a picturesque ornament of the sixteenth century. But there was another and a darker side to the century's "lust of knowing what shall not be known." Magic, the black art of witch and sorcerer, flourished surreptitiously, offering its secret, propitiatory rites to Satan, and attracting large numbers of people in all ranks of society. Whereas astrology was acknowledged by science and tolerated by the Church, the hidden ritual of Devil-worship required of its votaries a willingness to make a compact with Satan, and a little blood drawn from the worshiper's veins wherewith to seal it.

Religion was the only form of mass production

which the century knew. From the time that Clovis had presented Christianity to the Franks, saying take it or else, to the Renaissance decree forbidding any other religion within France, belief and conversion were strictly compulsory. The Inquisition was there to see that they remained so. In those days of the tremendous certitudes when, as Heywood Broun once said of the past, "heaven had a mighty low ceiling," both heaven and hell were well-mapped countries whose inhabitants, customs, flora and fauna were a matter of exact knowledge. The Devil and his minions had for many, if anything, a more omnipresent reality than had the beings of divinity. He was always prowling. Few were the peasants who had not seen on starless nights a flash of scarlet flame against black branches, and smelled the Devil's sulphur. Nor could the rustling sounds from the heart of a dark wood always be distinguished from the sinister witches' chant, by a man plodding home on a lonely road. Sometimes, even in broad daylight, he might come upon the clear track of the print of a cloven hoof, when woe betide his flocks and herds. From Egypt and Carthage, from Greece and Rome, from the Druids and all the people of the forgotten lands, the old spells lived on, woven by Satan to affright the heart and tempt the soul to its damnation.

The blessed saints wrought miracles for the benefit of mankind, but the evil one worked his magic through man and could not accomplish his works except with the aid of human co-operation. When strange misfor-

tunes befell Jacques Bonhomme and his pious wife
Marie, they knew that Satan had found his like on
earth to do his bidding. If the flocks sickened and died
for no reason, if the harvest was blighted, or Marie's
fresh cream soured in the pan, and a child broke an
arm, then someone in their community had sold out to
Satan and was working mischief.

"Thou shalt not suffer a witch to live."

Stark terror and primitive fear were the witchery
that drove people of the Renaissance into a kind of
madness. To this, color was given by the very real
number who sought Satanic contact with pentagram
and incantation, incense and sacrifice in the hope of
gold and power, the ancient promise of the kingdom
of the world, never fulfilled.

There was only one way to protect the righteous,
that was to fight the Devil with fire. So the witch-fires
of the stake were lighted and burned high over Europe
for more than two hundred years. While Nostradamus
was a boy preparing for Avignon, five hundred of the
piteous creatures accused of witchcraft were burned in
Geneva. This was typical of what went on throughout
Christendom. Nor was there any more tolerance among
Protestants than among Catholics. It was Martin Luther who said that the Devil caused children to dis-
appear and placed his own minions as changelings in
their place to be reared, all unsuspectingly, by honest
parents. Since Luther found a great many people
whom he did not like, it was easy for him to spot, as
he did, such changelings. Not without reason has Doc-

tor Victor Robinson, in his *Story of Medicine*, called
the sixteenth century the world's darkest age. The
very brilliance of its blaze of glory and enlightenment
made blacker the shadows that it cast.

Among the common people, such medical practice
as they had sustained the belief in witchcraft. The
two went hand in hand (as with the hex doctors of
present-day Pennsylvania). The herbalist and the
"wise woman" were the doctors in country districts
and among the city poor where there was no free
clinic. Here old magical ideas of the sympathetic virtues of plants were as strong as ever. These had all to
be gathered in certain phases of the moon, and their
distillations made under proper magical conditions.
The witches' brew was a part of such beliefs, and the
charlatan's decoction of the Elixir of Life.

In the upper classes, the spread of the new learning
stimulated, if anything, the interest in magical practice, because the writings of Greece and Rome are
filled with the most intriguing stories about it. The
seeker after occult information could get from the
classics new ideas and techniques with which to experiment. One of the books accessible to the times and
apparently much consulted by the "evil folk," as Nostradamus calls them, was the work of an early writer,
Michael Psellus, entitled provocatively enough *Concerning Demons*. If there was one thing above another
that was adored by the sixteenth century it was the
sinister doings of demons, and also with many, how to
get hold of one and put him to work. Psellus gives full

details of the way to do this. He also gives descriptions of degraded orgies in connection with such rites, which were once the ceremonial of the old fertility magic. Nostradamus wrote this curious quatrain about the followers of what might be called the Psellus method:

The tenth of the Calends of April, by the pre-Gregorian
   calendar,
Is again revived by evil gentry,
The light extinguished, the group of evil-worshipers
Seek to rouse the ancient Demon of Psellus.

No one can say today whom the prophet was accusing. The magic rites had greatest power when used on the night of Good Friday. It is supposable that he referred to a group who were experimenting in a year when this day fell on the twenty-third of April.

"Sorcery and sanctity are the only realities," wrote that English master of mystical prose, Arthur Machen. The distinction between the two is sometimes fine drawn. If the difference is to be based upon the means employed, then Nostradamus, judged by sixteenth-century standards, was, as his enemies claimed, a sorcerer. But if the distinction is one of motivation, then in his deep religious faith, in his long record of charity and good will toward men, his life followed better than most the pattern of sanctity. It is indisputable that he came deeply under the old pagan methods of divination. That is written in the record, and by his own hand. But he truly believed that the agencies which he invoked were heavenly ones.

It must be assumed that the Church also took this view. His work and his life were known in their completeness to the Church. Only acceptance by the papacy of his inspirational claims can account for the fact that throughout his life no rebuke nor interference ever came to him from the Inquisition. Had he not been sure of it he would never have dared to publish the *Centuries*. The hue and cry against him from the enemies within his own profession, their constant accusations of sorcery, would, at the slightest notice from the Inquisition, have carried him to the stake. Nor could the King and all the prophet's courtly patrons have availed to save him. Nostradamus was always on terms of friendship with important prelates and he may have rendered secret and valuable services to the Church, for which it was grateful. The published prophecies are but a small part of the predictive work which he carried on after he became known as a prophet and possibly before that. It is said that Europe is strewn with his forecasts made privately to noble and royal families, and never given out.

I—1

Seated at night in secret study,
Alone, at ease upon my tripod of brass,
From out the low flame of solitude
Comes realization of that in which it is not empty to
   believe.

I—2

Holding the bough with my hand where the branches
  fork,
The Branch seeking the Ripple moistens (with a
  spatter) the hem of my robe and my foot,
Fear and a voice make me tremble in my sleeves,
Splendor divine, the Divine Being is seated near.

In these opening lines of the *Centuries*, Nostradamus gives a clear, specific picture of his lone, late evenings when all the world was quiet and sleeping. He shows himself to posterity engaged in the ancient rite of divination by water, an oracle so old and universal that its origin is one with the lost river that first ran by the feet of the first man dreaming beside its banks. Nostradamus, in his letter to César, has told something of the books which were the source of his knowledge of the water-ritual. which he considered too dangerous to keep.

"Although many volumes have come before me which have lain hidden for long ages, dreading what might happen in the future, after reading them, I made an offering of them to Vulcan. As the flame caught them, the fire, licking the air, flared in unaccustomed brightness, clearer than natural flame, more like the explosion of powder. It cast a subtle illumination over the house, as if it were filled by the reflection of the conflagration. So that you might not at some time be harmed by alchemic research for the perfect lunar or solar transformation, or the hidden, incorruptible metals of earth or sea, I reduced these books to ashes."

There has been much speculation over what these books were and how Nostradamus came by them. Some commentators have thought they might have been inherited. Those who would have Nostradamus of Jewish descent have concocted the fantastic theory that the books were part of the temple treasure salvaged at the time of the Diaspora. There is no evidence for such ideas. It is most unlikely that the books were inherited. Grandfather de Rémy, be it remembered, initiated the boy Michel into some slight exhibition of extra-sensory perception. Having done this, the old man would hardly leave within the reach of a boy whose curiosity he had aroused, works which might spell danger, and even his doom at the stake. He would have withheld them for the same reason that Nostradamus destroyed them, to protect the child he loved from possible harm. Grandfather de Rémy, too, was too wise for anything else.

Europe was full of ancient books on magic; some were spurious and some authentic. When Constaninople fell in 1540, many Greeks fled to Italy and France. They brought with them all they could rescue of their written works. It was said that invariably beneath the rags of the refugee could be seen the parchment edges of some treasured rarity of manuscript. The Greeks sold many of these; they were forced to in order to live. Nostradamus almost certainly acquired his magic books during the years of his travels, and found them in either Marseilles or Italy. Both were gateways for all the world, and many strange, lost secrets of antiquity drifted in at their ports.

The particular work on water-divining was in all likelihood a Greek manuscript and one of the priceless *incunabula* which the refugees brought with them. Probably the manuscript contained an accurate account of the divinatory ceremonies practiced in ancient Greece in the temple of the god Branchus. Since Nostradamus mentions "long ages" in connection with these magical books, they may have been of the time of Alexander the Great, or even as early as Xerxes. The priests of Branchus were said to have sold out to the Persian invaders and fled, to escape popular anger. They were later destroyed by Alexander. The work on water-divination must have been something very special, for there is an account of the rites of Branchus in *The Mysteries of Egypt*, by Iamblichus, in current circulation in Nostradamus' day. His own books must have contained knowledge far more prized and secret.

The word "Branches," which Nostradamus printed in capitals to emphasize its significance, has reference to the forked branch of laurel or hazel used in this divinatory art, and also stands for the name of the god, Branchus, from whose name are derived "branch" and "bronchial." The myth of Branchus makes him the son of Apollo and a mortal. The sun-god entered the mother's mouth in a dream, and impregnated her. Branchus means throat and branches. The ancient

oracle of Branchus was very famous, and it is easy to
see the association of prophecy with this god of the
throat. It is not so easy to see his association with
water, except that speech is difficult with a dry throat!
Even so it would seem more reasonable for the priestess
of Branchus to take a drink of water than spill a little,
as she did, on her foot and the hem of her dress. However that may be, it is undoubtedly Branchus whose
ritual Nostradamus describes.

Did Nostradamus really believe in the worship of
Branchus? Of course not. Nostradamus says more than
once that his prophetic faculty was inherited. This
ancient method of the vision by water could have stimulated, perhaps developed his gift to greater scope, but
it never could have conferred it.

This man, whose intelligence was universal and of
tomorrow, understood that the laws of attunement between the world of the senses and the realm beyond
their range were in themselves unrelated to creed or
dogma, nor were they inconsistent with the Christian
life. The same force has animated the prophets of all
ages, only the methods, the technique by which the
psychic accord is established are different and indi-
vidual. Nostradamus had found in the old Greek ritual
one that suited his faculty. Mantra, incantations,
chants, all such have only the purpose of attuning the
prophet. That Nostradamus was familiar with the
spoken words of magical ceremonies and probably
used them in just this way may be judged from the
passage in which he warns the frivolous and the char~

latans to keep hands off his *Centuries* or consider themselves "cursed according to the rites of magic." Such curses were like the chants, oral pronouncements, and evidently the prophet knew their literature.

And what happened next in this strange night-life of prophecy? Let Nostradamus describe it. Writing to César, he says:

"Through some eternal power, and epileptic Herculean excitement, celestial causation is made known to me . . . But the perfect knowledge of causes cannot be acquired without divine inspiration. All authentic prophecy derives its first principle from God the Creator, next from favoring conditions, and last from natural endowment."

This passage is the answer to those who call Nostradamus pagan. In his letter to Henry II, the prophet writes concerning the *Centuries:*

"The entire work has been composed and calculated on days and hours of best election and disposition . . ." That is to say, he began his work and carried it on under favorable planetary conditions. The choice of a desirable time for beginning any undertaking is called, in stellar parlance, an election, meaning that a time has been elected. "Disposition" refers to aspects favorably disposed. Such elections have in all times been considered of the utmost importance by astrologers. This has been particularly true of the coronations of royalty, their marriages, wars and important affairs. There is no knowing if Nostradamus did use elections or if their mention was merely part of his insistence on the importance of astrology in his work. But perhaps he did consult his ephemeris for the positions of the Moon and Mercury, watching the import of their transits upon the clarity and expression of his vision. Perhaps, too, while studying astrology he cast his own nativity, curious to see this celestial blue-print of his own destiny.

The curtains drawn, the candles lighted in his study, on some evening when the oracle is silent, he may have drawn the twelve-rayed circle upon a sheet of parchment and placed precisely the symbols of the Sun and Moon and planets.

Interestedly he studies the chart. In the eighth mansion of the chart, in the mystical water sign of the Scorpion, a waning, secret Moon is setting. The eighth house is the house of death, and of interest in all that lies behind the veil. Nostradamus sighs as he thinks how truly that portent of the Moon's position has been fulfilled from early years. But the Moon is in trine, a benefic aspect, to the powerful conjointure of Jupiter and Saturn in the Moon's own sign, Cancer. These grave planets rule the hierarchy of the Church, of the political and economic conditions, and, placed in a water sign, are a splendid augury for success as a physician and for psychic matters. "And here is my success." His finger touches the Mid-Heaven Sun. "I should not fear to dedicate my work to king or pope." Longest his eye lingered on Mercury in the sign of the Centaur, for Mercury, planet of brain and speech, is the celestial prototype of Branchus.

"Mercury," he whispered, "27 degrees of Sagitta-rius, it touches the Mercury of Jeanne d'Arc in the same sign. Oh, Branchus, speed the Archer's arrows, let my words be winged—for France!"

On other nights when the prophetic spirit was upon him, the candles would flicker on the forked laurel branch as it bent from the prophet's electrically sensi-tive hand to the clear water filling to the brim the great, gleaming copper bowl. As the seer bent above the water undulant to the laurel bough, a listener might have heard his low chanting in an ancient tongue, words that once wove a spell amidst the splendor of a long-razed temple.

The phenomenon of illumination which has always been an accompaniment of great prophets, which is mentioned in the Bible, and which has given its name, the illuminati, to those of advanced spiritual percep-tion is referred to by Nostradamus in the letter to César in these words:

"Though everlasting God alone knows His eternity of light, yet I speak frankly to all whose long, mel-ancholy inspiration is informed by the revelation of His immeasurable greatness. It is through the hidden source of divine light, manifested in two principal ways, that the understanding of the prophet is in-spired. One way is the intuition which clarifies vision in him who predicts by the stars. The other is proph-ecy by inspired revelation, which is practically a par-ticipation in divine eternity. In the latter, the proph-et's judgment is according to his share of divine spirit

which he has received through attunement with God
the Creator, and also according to native endowment.
The complete efficacy of illumination and the thin
flame is to recognize that what is predicted is true and
of heavenly origin. For this light of prophecy descends
from above no less than the light of day."

Did Nostradamus see history flow before his sight
in a bowl of water? Did the "Divine Being" dictate
his writing as he sat in trance? None knows. Research
can pursue no further these "nocturnal studies of
sweet odor." Within the prophet's study the candle
and the "thin flame" burn low in mystery.

King René, the minstrel monarch of Provence.

CHAPTER SEVEN

Purpose

TIME WORE ON. The fruit of the prophet's nocturnal
visions multiplied enormously as the history of events
to come unfolded its vast stretches before his eyes.
Nostradamus, in common with most men of genius,
began to feel the urge to share his vision with the
world. Yet he knew he would have to move very cau-
tiously in presenting his work to the public. Its peculiar nature made necessary all possible safeguards
against suppression or destruction not only during his
own lifetime but in the future centuries with which his
prophecies were concerned. His plans must be carefully made, there must be no mistakes.

He had shown some of his prophetic verses to close
friends, and already some of these forecasts had been
fulfilled with impressive exactitude. Those who had
been privileged to read them wanted to see more of
them. A whole bookful, they told Nostradamus, could
not hold enough of such fascinating inside information on destiny.

"Why not publish your prophecies?" his friends

pressed the question continually. This enthusiasm was a good augury for the popularity of his work, Nostradamus thought, and he wanted to present it as soon as possible. Yet there were difficulties. He talked it all over with Ayme de Chavigny, who says that Nostradamus kept his prophecies by him for a long time, reluctant to bring them out because of the risks which the times made so menacing to scholars. Chavigny, himself a lawyer, scholar and theologian, saw the difficulties clearly, but he, too, was eager for the world to know the marvelous work of his teacher and friend.

"*Mon ami et maître*," he said to Nostradamus, "you believe that your foreknowledge is divinely inspired. Well, then, does not that carry its own obligation to reveal it? Had the prophets of Scripture dwelt only on their dangers, we should not have the guidance of Daniel, preserved from the lions, nor Jeremiah, who was rescued from a dungeon."

"True, Ayme," the prophet smiled ruefully, "but you can see there are my wife and children to think of. They would not like either lions or dungeons. Perhaps it would be safest to wait until after my death to have the prophecies published."

"But think of your splendid horoscope," urged Chavigny, who loved to dwell on this chart in admiration of its power. "It promises great preservation."

"Yes, but you and I both realize that though valuable in certain ways, astrology cannot be too heavily relied on. You have only to follow its public prophecies to see that."

"But the astounding accuracy of what you foretell will confound your enemies."

"Oh, no." The prophet's voice was bitter. "They will say that only the Devil could supply such knowledge. You see, Ayme, if they could ever have dismissed me as a charlatan, they could forgive me. But that they will never be able to do."

Chavigny was troubled. He did not know what advice to give. It was true that there was a constant martyrdom of great scholars. Nor was the Inquisition responsible for all of it. The Protestants, when not too busy protecting their own skins, could show the zeal of Torquemada, and their numbers were increasing in Provence. Both sides were lavish patrons of the stake. For Etienne Dôle, burnt by the Catholic Sorbonne, there was Michael Servetus, burned on the order of John Calvin, with the torch applied to an imitation crown of thorns made of straw and set upon his brow.

"But the Church, Michel, is your friend," Chavigny urged. "The fanatics at the Sorbonne, the physicians who hate you, all the rest—they cannot hurt you if the power of the Church supports you. Why not talk to some of the bishops and cardinals who know you well?"

"I have," Nostradamus told him. "They are not against my publishing. Some were encouraging. But I must feel more sure."

"I do not seek to probe unduly," Chavigny said, "but back of your hesitation I seem to sense some other, unpoken reason which is influencing you."

"You are right," Nostradamus told him gravely. "There is another reason for my caution." He rose and walked restlessly about the study, the long black velvet folds of his robe swaying in sculptural rhythm to his movements. When he spoke again, it was with passionate emphasis. "Ayme, my work must live. Must, I tell you. When I think that some agency might compass its destruction, fear lays a hand on my heart."

Chavigny looked at him in astonishment. He silently waited an explanation. Nostradamus turned to his long work-table heaped with parchments. Searching among these he withdrew one and handed it to Chavigny. "Read this."

Chavigny took the screed and read it carefully, first to himself, then slowly aloud.

VI—4

The Capital of France will change from the bank of the river,
No more shall the City of Agrippina hold dominion there,
Everything will be transformed, only the ancient language shall remain unchanged,
Saturn in Leo will pillage Mars in Cancer.

VII—34

The people of France will be very decadent,
Their hearts will be filled with vanities, they will put faith in irresponsible rashness,

There will be scarcity of bread and salt, of wine and
ale and all kinds of brewage.
Their leader will be captive of hunger, cold and necessity.

I—8

How many times, O Paris, City of the Sun, shalt thou
be captured!
While thou art changing thy empty, barbarian laws,
thy great misfortune is drawing near, bringing dire
slavery.
But Great Henry will see to it that your vanities are
buried.

"My friend," Chavigny said distressfully, "except
as you interpret them to me, I do not understand these
clouded words. Only I perceive that a disaster of
mighty extent stretches an evil hand toward Paris and
the nation. Will it be soon? Is it the Spaniards who will
conquer in spite of all?" Spain was the ever-present
menace of the sixteenth century.

"No, not Spain, *mon ami*. Nor is it soon. To you it
would seem a great way off. To my vision, telescoping
time as it does, beholding now this distant tragedy, it
affects me as if it were tomorrow. As a matter of fact it
is nearly four hundred years away."

Chavigny released the long sigh of a man reprieved
from instant calamity. Nostradamus looked at him
with a smile half sad, half amused.

"You are in no personal danger, Ayme. But you do not see now what I mean? Why my work must live?"

"But of course!" Chavigny's Gallic vivacity quickly rallied. "That you may warn the country! They will know you for a true and great prophet, they will believe you, they will be saved as Jeanne d'Arc saved France. Oh, what a destiny of grandeur!"

"No. That is not it either," Nostradamus said somberly. "No prophet can contravene the laws of destiny. Would God some word of mine could save France. It is impossible."

"But that makes no sense—"

"Destiny, a man's or a nation's," Nostradamus told him, "is according to divine plan; it is the cross upon the shoulders of humanity. The prophets of Scripture did not utter to change that plan, but through perceived truth to lead men closer to God."

"But your writings pertain to affairs of state, not religion," Chavigny objected.

"That is true. If I have really any mission, it is a humble one," Nostradamus sighed. He was silent for a little, then he took up the thread of his explanation. "There will be in the years to come many crises which France must meet. Two of these will be terrible. In the first one France will for a while seem to be without her soul, but," he added a little cynically, "she will not lose her lands. In the second disaster, which will occur about a hundred and fifty years later, to which I refer in the verses you have just read, her soil will be ravished, her spirit crushed, and her people in bondage.

For a time there will appear to be nothing left. There will be famine of bread for the body and of bread for the soul."

"Horrible, unthinkable," murmured Chavigny.

"These distant calamities," the prophet continued, "will come because the people shall have forsaken spiritual law and are like lost sheep." From memory he quoted one of his verses.

IV—25

The heavenly bodies, visible in their infinite courses,
Shall cloud eventually man's judgment,
Then shall man's forehead, which is body's throne of
    judgment, lacking its invisible leadership,
Little incline to bend in sacred rite of prayer.

"Ah, Chavigny, could man but realize of how little worth is pride of intellect. And they will call this strange period The Age of Reason, not knowing that when they lose heaven they lose all."

"You paint a dreadful picture," the lawyer commented. "Yet because it is so far off, I cannot somehow feel it as I should. It has no reality for me. And if you cannot avert this disaster with your warnings, what is it, my friend, that you hope to accomplish?"

"Very little, I am afraid," Nostradamus answered mournfully. "My great desire is to write something that will reach France across the centuries. I was a physician before I was a prophet. My hope is that in

her day of disaster some word of mine may administer
to the people the caustic of pride, the stimulant of
courage, and bind about their wounds the healing
salve of hope. If I could but do that much, I would ask
no greater boon of God."

Emotion choked Chavigny's voice as he said, "Jeanne
d'Arc did no more. I see what you mean, my friend.
In the last extremity, a people must help themselves.
All that can be done is to arouse them to the effort."

"Yes," Nostradamus agreed. "And here is my message to them. He handed Chavigny another piece of
writing. The lawyer read:

III—24

When impotence and violence shall have bred the great
    confusion
Born of loss of thy people and thy innumerable treas-
    ure,
Thou should not then permit thyself to weaken,
France, this is my word to thee, remember thou thy
    past.

"I have not spared the faults of France. I have reported what I think are the self-wrought causes of her
downfall. Do you think," Nostradamus asked anxiously, "that she will listen and heed?"

Chavigny's curiosity had reverted to the earlier
quatrains. "Who is there that can conquer France if it

is not Spain?" he asked belligerently. "You speak of moving the capital—how could that be? And what is the meaning of that reference to the planets, Saturn in Leo, wasn't it?"

"Slowly, my friend! In that period of lost judgment, which will cover quite a long space of years, some of which will be rich and prosperous, there will be no king in France, the government will be a republic."

"Like Venice and Florence?"

"Well—no. It will be more extreme. You have read *Utopia* by that misguided camel across the Channel, Thomas More. It will be more like that— at least they will have similar ideas. They will say that all men are equal."

"What folly!" cried his friend. "Men can grow in grace, if they would. But a peasant cannot equal a king."

"All political ideas will have changed," Nostradamus replied, "except the greed for power."

"But you still have not told me—"

"Germany," Nostradamus cut in with his answer, "will be the dominant power. Twice it will conquer France, and the second conquest is the time I speak of as so desperate. You know, Ayme, that I like to date and to identify events by means of the positions of the heavenly bodies, which cannot lie, nor are they subject to change as is the calendar. In the chart of this Republic of France, the position of Mars will be in the sign of Cancer. There will, in the final disaster, be no real leadership. It is the government which will be both criminal and victim. That is why I designate particularly the government. Nor do I wish to give exactly the year of this downfall, but only to indicate under what constitution of the government the event will occur. But the German, the one man who will tear down the realm of France, I have identified him by the position of Saturn at the time of his birth, for in that day he *is* the government of Germany. In another verse about him, I have even given the precise degree, Saturn in the thirteenth degree of Leo."

"Then the meaning of this line is," said Chavigny, consulting the verse, "that this powerful German, one who has Saturn at birth in the thirteenth degree of Leo, will ravish that government of France which will have Mars in Cancer. Is that it?"

"That is correct," said Nostradamus.

In the last tragic days of June, 1940, the current astronomical position of Mars was exactly transiting the position Mars held in Cancer at the birth of the Third Republic, September 4th, 1870. Saturn was in thirteen degrees of Leo when Adolf Hitler was born.

"Will this German be of the religion?" asked Chavigny in concern.

"No, there will be a new and far worse heresy which will then arise, resembling more the pagans of the Northland." Again he quoted from his prophecies.

III—67

A new sect of Philosophers will arise
Who scorn death, gold, honor and wealth,
The mountains of Germany will not set their limits,
A following and the printing-presses will support their
movement.

II—76

Germany will give birth to diversified sects
Which will approach a prosperous paganism,
But such beliefs will collect scant profits,
Eventually they will return to the payment of the true
tithe. (of religion)

"Grand Dieu!" cried Chavigny, "but this is all horrible. I begin to feel its sorrow like a black shadow. Is this to be the end of France? France without her robe of glory—it is unthinkable. Is there no hope?"

"Hope! Ah, yes, take heart, my friend! Hope and splendor such as France has never known. But this will only come after a long and cruel wounding. A crucifixion of all that she holds most dear."

"And what is the nature of this great hope?" Chavigny questioned.

Nostradamus' fine features kindled to quick enthusiasm. "A king. The greatest and most glorious of the kings of earth. A son of ancient France and of the lineage of the *fleur-de-lys*. A prince who will restore the monarchy of France."

"Our own Capetian monarchy! It will not then have died out?" Chavigny exclaimed in surprise.

"No, indeed. The coming of this king will carry the memories of Frenchmen back to that other ancient day of darkness when all seemed lost. I mean the times of Charles VII whom the Maid of Orleans restored to his throne. The king who drove out the English and built a greater France. His name will be on men's lips again and they will liken the conquests of the new monarch to those of Charles VII, buried half a century. I will read you some of my verses about all this." Gathering up some sheets of writing in his hand, he read:

III—94

For five hundred years no accounting will be made
Of him who was the ornament of his time, (Charles VII),
Then there will come a sudden burst of brilliant light,
And the age will be made very happy.

S—49

From the dark realm of old Charon the Phoenix will be reborn,
The last and greatest of the firebird's sons,
He will relight in France the ancient flame, he will be loved by everyone,
Long shall he reign with greater honors

Than ever had his predecessors
In whose name he will achieve a memorable glory.

V—41

Born into shadows of the times and secret effort,
He will be sovereign in his rule and kindness,
His lineage will be that of the lily flowering from its
   ancient vase,
He will transmute the age of bronze to gold.

III—100

He will be the last reigning king whom France shall
   honor,
He shall be victorious over him who is the enemy,
He will put to the test his own power and his country,
With a thunderbolt he shall destroy the man of hatred.

VI—3

The river where will be the scene of his effort
Will be in great discord with the Empire,
The youthful prince with the assistance of the Church
Will offer the crown and scepter of concord.

V—6

The Pope will place his hand on the king's head,
He will implore him to establish peace in Italy,
The king will change his scepter to his left hand (the
   symbol of peaceful intention)
And emerge from his kingship as the peaceful Emperor.

I—80

In the great reign of the great king reigning
He will open by armed might
The great bronze doors (Rheims Cathedral) ; he will
unite in himself the qualities of king and leader.
When the harbor is free, its defenses demolished, he
will escort the barque of the Church to its font,
(Rome) and day shall be serene.

VI—28

The great Celt shall enter into Rome
Leading the masses of the exiled and banished,
The Pope, great shepherd of the flock, will give asylum
to all
Who for the fighting Cock (of Orleans) united in the
Alps.

I—97

That which fire and sword knew not how to achieve
His gentle speech will accomplish in council,
The king will develop his ideals through repose and
meditation.
There will be no more enemy, nor sword, nor blood
shed in battle.

VIII—38

The King of Blois shall reign in Avignon,
Once more he shall be the sole ruler of his people,

He will build his walls on the land that is bathed by
the Rhone.
Fifth of his name, and last of his rank before the second coming of Christ.

"Will not that give them hope?" the prophet cried.
"And there is more that I have seen, but it is not yet
shaped into verses. There is still an immense amount
of work to be done on my prophecies."

"It is magnificent," Chavigny exclaimed. "There is
the glory of Charlemagne and Saint Louis both about
this Prince Capet. I wish that I could see his like on
the throne of France today. Tell me, have you seen
him, actually looked upon him?"

"Yes, I have indeed," Nostradamus said smiling.
"And searching his face I find there justice, sympathy
and the wisdom to serve his people. Four centuries
separate him and me." A whimsical smile touched his
lips. "By such standards of time I become a very ancient man compared to him. So I hope that he would
not, if he knew, take it as an unbecoming liberty that
I should love him as a son."

"This message of yours should mean all the world
to him, 'born under shadows,' as you say. Will he recognize it, see it as himself?"

"That is my hope," Nostradamus told him. "My
purpose is that he shall read it, and feel the ancient
royal strength of Hugh Capet flow through his sword
arm. My hope is to give him confidence of victory, of
freedom for his people—our people."

"Now I understand your anxiety for the preservation of this work," Chavigny said. "But can you not foresee its fate?"

"Yes," Nostradamus answered, "I know that it will live, and that it will avail. But I cannot be sure how much. It is harder to foresee those matters which concern oneself. What I fear is that the work may be mutilated or changed, or that others may imitate it so that people will be hard put to tell the true from the false."

"What I would fear more," his friend told him candidly, "is that people will not understand its meanings when they read it. These verses are clear enough to me now, but many that you have shown me, I frankly could make nothing of, lacking your help. In a matter so important you should write with the utmost clarity." It was the lawyer in Chavigny speaking.

"What you are pleased to call my clouded words," smiled Nostradamus, "have a purpose. Books too often survive because time forgets them, they are safe because unread. My prophecies must be read by every generation, their flame must be fed by constant interest, so that in the day of their need they will not be on musty shelves, but in the hands of the people of France." The prophet's grave eyes twinkled at Chavigny. "Can you, my learned and legal friend, think of a better way to set the generations reading than by giving them a puzzle, of which each age solves some pieces of its truth, and none ever solves it fully until the time of its fulfillment?"

The lawyer thought it over. "I see your point," he

said, "it is a good one. But even, if, as you say, people
cannot change their major destinies, still they have to
wait for the fulfillment of a prophecy to know if it is
a true one. And each accurate forecast will make them
pay closer attention to what is foretold as coming
next."

"And also bring them greater suffering in anticipation," Nostradamus reminded him. "No. Life holds
more of sadness than of joy. Many things are better
not revealed in advance. But my prophecies are not all
obscure. That would not do either. Many events are
clearly described, with names of persons given, and
dates of occurrences. Men will know by these that
there is truth in my words, and they will never leave
off searching for more of it in the difficult passages.
That is how I would have it."

Chavigny's mind had gone off on a tangent. "I suppose the world will be a very different kind of place in
four hundred years. I doubt that I would recognize it."

"Outwardly different," Nostradamus told him.
"The nations of that day will, as Scripture says, have
sought out many inventions. But man himself will be
the same. Unfortunately." Chavigny got up from his
chair, shook out the folds of his scholar's gown and
carefully adjusted them. "If I had not studied with
you so long," he observed thoughtfully, "I could not
credit a vision of such immensity as yours. But because
I know you, know the already fulfilled prophecies that
you have made, I must believe you. Yet it staggers the
imagination. Four hundred years!"

"And far beyond that," the prophet told him dreamily. "My eyes have beheld the oceans of time that swirl their mighty tides against the gates of God." He too arose. "You are leaving, Ayme?"

"Yes, I must be getting back to Beaune. Besides, my mind is incapable of digesting more wonders. You are right, there is something about prophecy, even when it does not touch one's own life, that is somehow shattering."

After Chavigny had gone, Nostradamus seated himself at his table. He spread a parchment carefully before him, selected a quill, and began to write:

III—79

The fatal order of destiny is an eternal chain
Forever looping on itself in cycles consistent with its
    own order.

He threw aside the quill, the verse unfinished, and began to think. His friends were right; if his work was to be published, it was time to make a beginning, to try it out. Time to conquer doubts and misgivings and to get on with it. He realized and faced the fact that what he most dreaded was the fresh cries of sorcery, the calumnies and vituperation that would be heaped upon his head by the very men who should be his friends. His nature, as unselfish and affectionate as it was deeply sensitive, shrank from this ordeal. But there would be, surely, a preservation from harm. Not as Chavigny had said because of the power of his horoscope, but because he held his prophetic gift from God. Certainly, he thought it had been given to him for a divine purpose. He had never misused it. God would look after him. He would trust in that, and act with confidence.

His decision made, he began to think of details. How many verses should he publish at first? Not too many. Better see how it went. If there were interest and demand, a new edition could be quickly run off with more of the quatrains. As soon as he could leave Salon, ill patients permitting, he would go up to Lyons and look for a publisher. Macé Bonhomme was reputed a good printer of excellent standing. He would see him and make arrangements.

There was also the matter of the dedication to be planned. Chavigny, de Condoulet, all his friends would, he knew, urge him to select a powerful patron to whom he could flatteringly address his work. This would have the double advantage of protection and publicity. Moreover, it was customary. Well, he would break the precedent. He had always stood alone. Not so many men in France among the ranks of scholars or artists could say as much. Most of them couldn't exist without the gold and prestige of a patron, and fought like wolves among themselves to attract the help and protection of great prelates and nobles. But with him, Nostradamus, he proudly thought, the shoe had been on the other foot. Patrons had supplicated him, begged him to save their lives and foretell their destinies. He owed no man for gold or favors.

The dedication, he decided, should be to César, his oldest and dearly loved son. Between father and son there was a fine sympathy and understanding. César was going to make a good man and one who would do well with his gifts. He thought wistfully how much he would like to see César's young manhood, and guide it. But whenever he should be called to leave the scene of his labors, he wished to leave behind something of himself that should belong exclusively to César. It should be the letter of dedication and the first book of his prophecies. In this letter he would reveal something of his gift, how it manifested itself, how he differed from other prophets of the time. And in particular he would warn his son against the danger of alchemic research and all the forms of black magic. It should be a document which César could keep always by him, recognizing therein his father's true self. César would value it and be proud of it when he, his father, was gone.

He had told Chavigny of his plan to complete the work in twelve divisions, each one a century containing a hundred quatrains. He liked the arrangement in centuries. It suggested such periods of time and caught the imagination. Yet it really meant nothing in this sense, because he intended that the verses should be so well scrambled that only with difficulty, and usually after the event, could the prophecies be assigned to their proper dates. He decided against publishing an even number of verses, such as five hundred. Everyone would be searching for hidden meanings, and he wanted to pique interest and curiosity as much as possible. If there were but, say, four hundred and fifty odd verses, people would wonder why. They would speculate on whether those were all he had ready, or if there was a secret reason, perhaps a hidden clue to his dates—well, that might be true too, though unlikely that anyone would find it.

He had already set aside a large number of the completed verses which he had chosen to go in the book. But these must again be carefully checked, with perhaps some changes, additions and omissions. There must be enough verses about current personalities, who were immediately identifiable or in which the events predicted were of not distant occurrence, otherwise interest would languish and die at the beginning. And there must be other verses which people would think they had identified and which would work out differently, and these would keep them puzzling their wits.

Chavigny had at times wondered why he, as a scientist, did not prophesy more about future developments in this field. It was hard to make Ayme understand how he felt about it. Man's works passed away, but man himself went on. What he was, and in particular how he governed himself, was the important thing. Under a good government and wise leaders ideas expanded, invention and discovery flowered in multiple forms. Given long wars and fools at the head of things, such works disappeared, had to be rediscovered, the work done over again. And, too, there were plenty of men besides himself then living who, if they dared, could give almost as precise a picture of what science would develop in coming centuries as those men of tomorrow themselves. Leonardo had known that some day men would fly, he had foreseen many other inventions they would use. Copernicus had understood that his discovery was but the prelude to vast knowledge of the heavens that would be unfolded. Farther back, the Englishman, Roger Bacon, had written in secret of the principles that would be commonplaces of chemistry one day, but were still too dangerous to mention openly. Plenty of men had this kind of knowledge, better than himself. But these men did not have what he, Nostradamus had, the vision of men and times, the chord within which all else must work.

But, he smiled to himself, he *was* telling some things about science. The men of tomorrow should see that at least he had not omitted such forecasts because he was ignorant of them. Certainly he was saying enough about "gnats" and "locusts" and "strange birds." The men of the future should recognize exactly what he meant by these terms, because their flying machines looked just like that. He had watched them, in pictures of the future, swarming against the sky, blackening it like a cloud of locusts. Like insects, too, was their weird humming. In time of war they would be an insult to heaven, fighting close to its blue vault, and worse than all the plagues of Pharaoh. Man would pay for such invention; he, Nostradamus, had nothing good to say of airplanes.

He had told, too, about the strange air-bag with a hole in it—another one of those flying-devices. He had set the time quite closely for this. It was the kind of picturesque bit that he knew appealed to readers, as was the gun-part with the amusing name which Frenchmen would give to it. And for those of his own profession, he had described the strange case of an abnormal birth. People took great interest in such things and he, as a physician, did himself. Many thought such births were Devil's changelings. As a scientist, he knew that there were unknown biological laws at work in such cases, but he had often wondered if there had been a soul inclosed in such hideous shapes as he had seen and prayed God's pity on. The child of which he had written would fortunately not be born alive. It was an extraordinary case and would make talk, not only as a wonder but because he had predicted it.

Doctor Garencières, who was, like Nostradamus, a doctor of medicine, and whose translation of the *Centuries* first introduced Nostradamus to England, was, a hundred years later, fascinated by the prophecy of this unique case. He investigated the circumstances and interviewed one of the medical men who had to do with the preservation of the freak and could tell him all about it. In his translation he devotes considerable space to the account. This quatrain is Nostradamus' prediction.

I—22

That which shall have life, but no intelligence,
Shall have the perfection of its form injured by the
    steel instrument.
Langres, Autun, Chalons and the two towns of Sens
Will suffer greatly from strife and ice.

Here is the story as told by Doctor Garencières.
Speaking of the verse he says:

"This is a great riddle which was never found out
till now; and had I not been born in the Country where
the History did happen, it might have been unknown
to this day, and buried in oblivion.

"In the year of the Lord 1613, which was that of
my birth, there lived in the town of Sens a Taylor's
wife, named Columba Chatry, and who presently after
her marriage conceived and for the space of twenty-
eight years persuaded herself to be with child. She had
all the signs of it, and after having gone her compleat
time, began to feel the pains of a woman in labor.
Then her breath failed, the motion of the child ceased
and the pains subsided. For three years the poor
woman kept her bed complaining of a hard swelling
and griping. She frequently spoke of bearing a child as
being the cause of her death. After her death her husband engaged two prominent chirurgeons to make an
autopsy. On making the incision with a razor, their
knives encountered a horny substance and they had to
exert their full muscular strength. Within the womb

was a child, perfectly formed and partly petrified, its skull shining like a horn. The wrist was broken in removing the child ("perfection of the form injured by the steel instrument") which was so grown to the mother, nor did the doctors realize what they had (in time to prevent the injury). The little body was perfectly developed and of such hardness that to this very day that little body defieth all kind of corruption. The child was kept by a Mr. Medill, a chirurgeon of Sens who kindly showed it to all strangers who came from far and near to see it."

Doctor Garencières goes on to relate that the fame of this wonder was so great that doctors in particular travelled great distances to verify the happening and see the child. A prominent English physician urged Charles I to buy it for England, but this was not done, and Venice, instead, obtained it. Of the last two lines of the quatrain, Garencières says:

"Autun, Chalons and Langres, and Sens, the Town where this did happen, did in that year suffer much damage by Hail and Ice which did come to pass, as many persons in that country may testify that are alive to this day."

César de Nostradame says in his *History of Provence*, that his father predicted "astronomically" the birth of a two-headed child, and that this occurred, as foretold, in 1554, in February, and was brought to Salon for his father to see.

Comets were another source of perennial appeal in older times when as portents of doom their appearance

provided gloomy excitement and much agitated speculation as to where the blow would fall. Not much was
known in the sixteenth century of the erratic orbits of
these wanderers which were a never-failing source of
astonishment and dread. Nostradamus had enough
showmanship to know that comets were always good
for arousing interest. He has reported a number of
them in the *Centuries*. While he was organizing his
quatrains for the first edition of the prophecies he was
pleased that one of these eerie visitors could soon be
expected. There was a verse about it that must certainly be included because it would only be a year
until its fulfillment.

II—43

While the star with the hairy tail is visible,
Three great princes will become enemies,
Peace will receive a blow from the heavens, there will
      be earthly upheavals.
The Po and the Tiber will be in flood, and there will
      be a serpent on the shore.

There was a verse that, from the popular viewpoint,
had everything, comet, royal quarrel, disturbance of
the earth, and a sea serpent! Nostradamus delighted in
confounding his readers by using the same words for
a political upheaval as for an earthquake. This verse,
it transpired later, meant some kind of actual disturbance within the earth. In March, of the following
year, and less than a year after publication of the

prophecies, a great comet appeared and could be seen, terrifying in the night sky, for three months. Truly enough, the new truce between France and Spain was quickly broken when the French king went to the assistance of the Pope, who was fighting the Spaniards. To make the forecast perfect, the Tiber and the Arno for no known reason, unless it was some underground disturbance, overflowed and flooded the surrounding land. When the Tiber receded, sure enough there on its bank was a very strange, large serpent, just as promised. Nostradamus knew that a verse such as this would linger in the minds of people, making an impression where events of graver import might be overlooked or forgotten. He counted on such prophecies to increase his fame and serve its continuance.

Not long after this, his letter of dedication to César finished, his verses chosen, he journeyed to Lyons and gave them into the skilled hands of the printer, Macé Bonhomme. Thereafter in due time in this same year, 1555, a slim volume containing four hundred and fifty-four prophetic verses by Maistre Michel Nostradamus was offered to a wondering world.

CHAPTER EIGHT

On to Paris

THE SUCCESS OF THE BOOK was immediate and enormous—adjectives which seem to keynote the life of Nostradamus. People were fascinated by the cryptic novelty of the verses which became the sensation of the moment. Everybody was reading, puzzling, spotting, quoting and arguing over them. Some of the verses were daringly easy of identification. Some semed to point to certain public personalities but were debatable. These were shuffled among quatrains that no one could pretend to understand, or even guess at the persons referred to. Since the baffling prophecies were decidedly in the majority, the detractors of Nostradamus, who said that here was no prophecy but only incomprehensible gibberish, had, it must be confessed, much on their side.

When one remembers that it has taken "seven men with seven mops" working diligently all these intervening years to decipher the meanings, some of which are still controversial, and others yet not understood, it is no wonder that the derisionists of that day refused

194

to be shouted down by the chorus of enthusiasts. Everyone who had known the prophet personally chanted his praises. From Provence to Paris people talked of him, relating the successes, legends and accusations that had grown up about his history. More than ever the narrow lanes and crooked streets of Salon were choked with the crowd pouring in to consult the new authority on destiny. Patients needing the doctor of medicine were now jostled by patronage seeking the doctor of destiny.

Paris was in those days a long way from Provence. Nostradamus' fame had hitherto been local. With the publication of the book, reports of his astonishing history reached the capital. It is not surprising that Catherine de' Medici desired at once to meet Nostradamus. Her interest in occultism was well known. What is surprising is that the King, who had no such interest, was the one who summoned the doctor to Paris. His curiosity was on this occasion at least the equal of the Queen's.

It is probable that before he extended an invitation to Nostradamus to visit Paris, he sent a cautious inquiry to his Provençal governor, seeking reliable information about this strange subject of his. A king had to be careful not to excite ridicule and criticism in such a matter.

The King could have asked no one who was better fitted to extol the prestige and abilities of Nostradamus than was Claude de Savoie, Count de Tende et de Villars, Governor of Provence. He had known Nostra-

damus all his life as friend, physician and seer. He
knew his background and family history. He and the
prophet had both been young together. Both had
fought their first great battles at the same time. When
Nostradamus had left Montpellier to wrestle with the
plague, the Count de Tende had been holding at bay
the Spanish army under the Constable de Bourbon.
He had defended Marseilles and defeated the Spaniards with a valor which had established him as one of
the first soldiers in France. As Governor of Provence
he had endorsed the life pension with which the city
of Aix had rewarded the doctor's second battle with
the plague. He knew how Nostradamus' prophetic gift
had come down to him through inheritance. He had
seen many illustrations of its uncanny power and authority. These were all things which he could write to
the King, adding that the greatest princes and prelates
in the south of France called Maître Nostradamus
friend.

All this he set down in his letter to the King. Then,
before he closed it with the customary salutations, he
sat back in his chair and nibbled his quill thoughtfully. This writing was a chore for a soldier. He would
be glad to get it done. But there was one thing more
that he wanted the King to know. Again his quill took
up its scratching rhythm as he wrote a concluding
paragraph.

"Maître Nostradamus has also honored me with a
prophecy concerning the future of my line. Inasmuch
as my ancestors served those of Your Majesty, and

since it has been my privilege to wield my sword for Your Majesty's late father, and holding it always in readiness to strike for his most puissant son, the Very Christian King of France, it is a comfort to my declining age to learn from the inspired vision of this true prophet that in the future of times to come the sword arm of Villars shall still not fail in its valor to defend the crown of France on behalf of Your Majesty's descendants."

He added the final compliments, his signature and the date with a satisfied flourish. That did it. Now perhaps the King would ask Nostradamus what this prophecy was, and his friend would tell the King the tale of the future about the line of Villars which in a rare mood he had unfolded to him one evening when they had supped together in Aix, and had sat late by the Governor's fireside afterward, talking of many old experiences.

A Frenchman, perhaps more than men of other nationalities, is concerned over the continuance of his line and the maintenance of the prestige established by his ancestors. The Count de Tende et Villars had spoken of this to Nostradamus. The prophet had gladdened his heart by saying that there would come another Claude de Savoie in time, who would even surpass all former military achievements of his house, that he would rescue France from desperate peril, and fight his battles on a far-flung field. The Governor had begged the prophet to tell him something of this coming soldier, his namesake. It meant so much to him that his own name would be carried on to greener laurels. He felt such an old fogy in these days of new artillery, and odd gadgets on guns, all so different from the weapons he had used to defend Marseilles. That, too, had been a great fight; it had preserved France from Charles V, and made him, Claude de Savoie, famous. But that had been thirty years ago, and the world forgot so quickly.

The prophet had smiled at him quizzically. "You have," he told him, "already read without knowing it something of the battles of the coming Claude de Savoie."

"Where?" asked the Count.

"In my new book," the prophet told him. "There are several verses about him, and I have still more to foretell, perhaps in another volume."

"Tell me, old friend, I implore you." The Governor sat forward excitedly. "When is this to be? How long before it happens?"

"That I shall not tell you," answered Nostradamus, "but it is sometime off. You and I won't be here."

"I hope Saint Peter will let me see the fight. By God, I'd snatch Lord Gabriel's trumpet and sound a blast for victory!"

Nostradamus looked shocked. He did not relish the profanity of camps.

"Which are the verses, man? I must know them," the Count cried. "Don't stand me off with your puzzles. I won't tell anyone. I can keep my counsel, as you know. I understand how everyone would be at you if they found that you had broken your precedent and explained a little from that book, though I can't see why you are so unwilling. But my word as a soldier, I will not tell of the verses to anyone. Do you mention my name?"

"Yes," the seer assured him, "both names, Tende and Villars. And since I wish the men of that day to say 'like ancestor, like descendant,' I mention also Provence, so that it shall not be forgotten from what place and what fighting stock this soldier comes."

"He will be born here in Provence, I suppose?" the Count said.

"He will come from Narbonne. Your namesake will be a Gascon."

"Pah!" the Count exclaimed disgustedly. "A Gascon is a braggart who fights with words. Why can't he be born right here?" He looked at the prophet in naïve hopefulness as if it were possibly not too late to do something about it.

"I have called him 'the heroic Villars, the man who is more like Mars than Narbonne.' He will be a boaster, but he will make good his boasts when he saves his country," Nostradamus assured him.

"More like Mars than Narbonne," quoted the Count with relish. "I like that conceit, 'tis clever. Martius Narbo was the old Roman name for the city of Narbonne. Yes, it is a pretty play on words, and means, I take it, that this young Claude de Savoie will be a better fighter than a boaster. I begin to think well of him. By Saint Denis, I do!" The Count smiled broadly.

In his many verses on the War of the Spanish Succession, Nostradamus has described its hero, Marshal Villars, and told a great deal about his long struggle. It is not on the record how much he related to the Count de Tende et Villars concerning his illustrious namesake, but the verses which he left for posterity are given in Part II of this book.

In due time the Count de Tende received the royal invitation summoning Maître Michel Nostradamus to Paris as the King's guest. The Count was requested personally to make all arrangements for the trip and to expedite it in every way as His Majesty was impatient to meet the prophet. Here was a breath-taking compliment. Kings had always used prophets, but not since the days of ancient oracles had they paid them any particular honor. Paris was then filled with seers of one kind and another. Some of them were good, and a few were famous. But such a public invitation as this from royalty was an unheard-of thing. It was the crowning honor of a sensational life.

Salon buzzed with the excitement of the news. Quickly Avignon heard about it, and soon Marseilles. All Provence, except the enemies of Nostradamus, was thrilled and proud. Wherever Nostradamus was known, wherever he had patients from as far back as the first plague, the conversation was all of a piece in marketplace, cottage, château and council hall. The King had bidden their great man to Paris!

Preparations for the journey got under way at once. Maître de Chavigny, the Sieur de Condoulet, the town fathers and a host of friends and patients poured in to offer their congratulations, give practical advice about the long trip, and tell what they knew or had heard about the customs and personages at the court of the Valois. The housewifely instincts of Madame de Nostradamus came immediately into action to look after the details of her husband's travel needs. There was brushing, steaming and airing of the doctor's best robe of Lyons velvet. Two costumes were the limit, even for the affluent in these days, and they were expected to last, if not unto the third and fourth generations, at least unto the second. There was baking and roasting to be done, a flaky loaf and a tender young fowl for the hamper in which would also go the leathern bottle of vintage wine, which a grateful patient had contributed. Perhaps the children, being French, may not have surged around shouting, "My Papa is going to Paris!" but they and the whole household would have felt the excitement.

Only the doctor was unaffected and moved about in his usual serene and casual fashion. He prepared and labeled tinctures and essences which some of the sick might require in his absence. He packed his inkhorn, his quills and writing-tablets. He might want to do a little writing in the evenings at inns along the route, since his travel would be all done by day. He would probably be too tired when night came for much effort, however, so for company he chose his well-worn copy of Aristotle to take with him, and the latest volume of poems by Ronsard, the celebrated and fashionable poet who had just received the Toulouse award and the silver statue of Minerva. Perhaps Ronsard would be at the court, and he might have the privilege of meeting him.

Nostradamus was now fifty-three years old, and no longer in good health. He had used his splendid energies throughout his life without stint or thought to himself. Premature age was taking its toll, and he was suffering from that so common ailment of the time, gout. The long trip to Paris was a great undertaking for him, even under the best conditions which the Count de Tende could arrange. There is no account of his mode of travel. But it was probably, as he had always travelled, on the back of a sturdy mule. He may have made part of the trip by coach, but coaches were still a rarity, and their build was so cumbersome and their springs so joltingly hard that they offered, outside of their impressive appearance, little relief.

Nostradamus left Salon on the 14th of July, 1555. This date, looking forward in time, and told by another calendar, would one day be pregnant with meaning to France as Bastille Day, an event of the future which the prophet sadly chronicled. Looking backward in time, it was the date when Frenchmen, fighting valiantly for their God, had seen Jerusalem fall to the Crusaders, rescued from the infidel. Nostradamus had not forgotten that page of history, now made melancholy by loss of the Crusaders' gains which his writings mention as Christendom's disgrace.

All of his friends had gathered with his family to see him off on his trip. A waving, smiling crowd from in and out of town had assembled to wish him Godspeed. The Count de Tende had ridden over from Aix to supervise the details of departure. He found a moment to whisper in the prophet's ear, while giving him his schedule of travel.

"Tell His Majesty about young Claude de Savoie, if opportunity permits. I think the King would be well satisfied to know of him."

Nostradamus smiled indulgently. "Yes," he said, "and Claude, the elder, too. A thousand thanks for all your kindness."

Since he was on the King's errand, the prophet no doubt made top speed for the times. But the roads, though more numerous, were often no better than in the days of Clovis. They were full of deep ruts, which became small ponds when it rained, and great stretches of mud. Travel at best was appallingly slow, though never having known a swifter mode, it doubtless did not seem so to Nostradamus. Besides, he was an experienced traveller and liked the road. It was his first trip of any length in a good many years and he was prepared to enjoy it. He savored the character and charm of each locality that he passed, drawing in the perfume of its herbs and flowers as a connoisseur savors a vintage bouquet.

Travelling northward through the valley of the Rhone he watched Provence roll past him, slowly receding. Its panorama never failed to enchant him, its gardens, its cypress and olive, its thyme and lavender, rosemary and rue. Besides their beauty, these held for him, as physician, the deep meaning of the soil, the healing power of earth's plants for earth's children. Across the countryside at intervals his ears caught the joyous shrilling of a flute or the tinkle of a tambourine, and occasionally there was a flash of Moorish color, or the glimpse of a festival procession.

In two weeks he had passed Lyons, and left behind him the *langue d'oc*, "that beautiful Provençal language, more than three-quarters Latin, formerly spoken by queens, which shepherds alone now understand." Once across the Rhone, he had entered the land of the *langue d'oïl*, or modern French, which had been the official language of France for some twenty years. He was now moving through the beautiful landscapes of Lorraine, drawing closer to the country of the Maid of Orleans, and the fields and blossoms bright with summer celebrated by Ronsard's verses. The prophet's memory, "almost divine," did not need to consult the volume of Ronsard's poems. Softly to himself he quoted:

"Sky, air and winds, and naked hills and plains,
  Tapestried woodland halls, and green morass,
  And river-shores, and pools of sombre glass,
  And viny slopes, and shivering gold champaigns,
  And moss-mouthed caverns' shadowy domains,
  And buds and blossoms and dew-glimmering grass." *
  * Translation from *Ronsard* by Morris Bishop.

And about him he saw lordly châteaux topping the hills, their arrogant towers lifting in conscious elegance above the half-screening woodlands. Cottages in the deep heart of bowering trees, foot bridges over streams dancing across valleys of emerald velvet, offered their northern loveliness in substitute for the high color of Provence.

While he was traversing the long road, Nostradamus had ample time to ponder the personages and conditions he would meet in Paris. He had heard a great deal about the King and Queen. He reviewed it now as a guide for his successful approach to royalty. How different, he thought, had been the lives of these two, and yet there was a pattern of similarity, too, especially, in their early youth. Both had experienced a loveless, prisoned, dangerous childhood when each had been a helpless, political pawn in the hands of savagely warring powers.

From his seventh to his eleventh year, Henry had spent shut up in a gloomy Spanish monastery, hostage, with his older brother, for their father, King Francis. When he had finally returned to France, it had been necessary for him to relearn his own language, forbidden him in his imprisonment. A shy, alien boy, he had come home to a Spanish stepmother and a country which, though his own, seemed a stranger. He had not been the dauphin then, only the second son. He had been lonely and ill adapted to the gay court. The prisoning walls had not been wholly left behind, something of their barriers was now within himself. Then

when he was only fourteen, they had married him to
the pale little Italian girl from Florence, with whom
he had found nothing in common, not even a child for
ten years. In all the carefree glitter of his father's
court, there had been only one who had taken an interest in the diffident boy growing up within his shell.
Only one who had understood him and concerned herself with his boyish life. This was the gloriously beautiful Seneschal of Normandy, now Duchess of Valentinois also, Diane of Poictiers. The adolescent heart of
the boy, still yearning for the mother he could not remember, had attached itself with passionate fidelity to
this woman twenty years his senior. Now, all France
knew and accepted its two queens, Catherine the
crowned, whose diadem but scarcely gilded the indif-
ference of her husband, and Diane the uncrowned,
whose power dispensed the patronage and spent the
revenues of France with arrogant assurance.

The King at this time was enjoying the first period
of peace that he had experienced in some years. Six
months before, he had signed a five-year truce with
his enemy, Charles V. That monarch had then betaken
himself to a monastery to consider his soul's salvation,
after first dividing up his empire. Austria he had bestowed upon his brother. Spain, the Netherlands and
possessions in Italy he had given to his son Philip.
No one expected the truce between Spain and France
would last. Philip II was as bitter a foe of France as
his father had been, while Henry's warlike nature
and inherited glory-dreams bided only an opportunity

to strike at Spain. Nostradamus well knew the kind of
questions that the King would ask him about all this,
and he realized how little his answers would affect the
course of events. For had he not seen those events
transpiring in his visions?

His thoughts turned to the Queen. An intelligent,
agreeable woman, by all reports. Deeply interested in
occultism, too, but desiring, like all ambitious people,
to profit by it rather than to live according to its laws.
It was going to require more adroitness to meet and
parry her questions, and at the same time satisfy her
than would the inquiries of the King. He felt a vast
pity for this woman, even though he knew what tragedy she would one day bring to the country. The
French had never been enthusiastic over "the banker's
daughter," and they remained indifferent to her. Not
the least of the reasons for this was that "the three
pearls," which Clement VII had optimistically mentioned as her dowry, Genoa, Naples and Milan, had so
far proved uncollectible. The money she had brought
from Italy had been negligible. Her wealth, and it was
large, had come to her from her French mother,
Madeleine de la Tour d'Auvergne. It was through her
mother, too, that she was cousin to both her rivals, the
older siren, Diane de Poictiers, and the young beauty,
Mary Stuart, the enchantress of her son the dauphin.
Not until Catherine could rid herself of the power of
these two women would she have her turn.

Nostradamus, who knew her history fully, understood how Catherine's whole life had been spent in

trying to hold her own—just that. And it would always be so. From the time of her birth her ears had been assaulted by the sound of trampling. First, it was the Horseman of Death, taking both her father and mother within the month of her coming into the world. Ariosto, touched by her fate, had written then of her babyhood, "A single branch grows green again with a little foliage. Fearful and hopeful, I do not know if winter will spare it or tear it from me."

The heavy tread of armies, trampling the lives and fortunes of the family great Lorenzo built, had menaced all her childhood. "Put her in a brothel so the Pope cannot marry her to a noble." "Bind her to the ramparts and see how straight the Prince of Orange aims his bullets." These were the outcries of soldiers and demagogues at the siege of Rome, when she, a child, was hidden in a convent.

At fourteen had come marriage and the transplanting to the colder soil and grayer sunlight of Paris. Then a new kind of trampling had begun. This time it was her pride and her heart that were beaten into the dust. The men and women of Europe's haughtiest court scarcely permitted her to forget that they counted their noble lineage by centuries, while she, the Medici, counted hers by years. Nor did they disguise their careless pity for her lack of beauty. Catherine had been ill equipped to compete in this new field, but she had tried. However, she soon found out that fine clothes, the grave grace of her beautiful leg flung boldly over the saddle-bow, defying convention, and the supplicating gesture of ivory and exquisite hands, were not enough. Not in that court where every woman was hand-picked for beauty.

Catherine, like Henry, had turned to age for sympathy and companionship. She had attached herself to King Francis and won his genuine affection. "She prayed the King," wrote Brantôme, "to allow her to be always at his side." Francis liked her love of sports, the wit and maturity of her mind. Always a connoisseur of women, he was the only one of his court to appreciate that his daughter-in-law was a girl of unusual interest. Then Francis, her one friend, had died. Never did life give to Catherine de' Medici the opportunity to love or be loved. Always there was defeat and frustration for her affections. Even maternity was so long denied to her, and then so continuously thrust upon her, that love for her children was never a part of her life. Ruggiero, her astrologer, whispered to her of future power through her long years of repression, sustaining her with this dark bread, while what should have been her heart turned slowly and terribly into stone.

Such were the royal pair whom Doctor Nostradamus was so soon to greet.

A month and a day had gone by from the time he left Salon until he sighted the walls and spires of Paris, ancient Lutetia. It was the feast day of Notre Dame when he arrived, late in the afternoon. There was no one to meet him, since the time of his arrival could not be known. Travel-worn and very tired, he looked

about for an inn to rest his weary bones. The sign of
the first hostelry that he came upon bore the name of
the Inn of Saint Michel. Here were two omens, the
day and the inn, which had spelled his own name,
Michel de Nostradame, in silent, pleasing welcome to
the city. Already he felt the friendship of Paris, how
could his visit be other than successful? After he had
eaten, he dispatched a messenger to the King, an-
nouncing his arrival, and holding himself at His Majesty's disposal.

Next morning he had scarcely breakfasted before he
was attended by the Constable of France, Duke Anne
de Montmorency, who brought the King's greetings
and word of his eagerness to see the prophet. He was
also there to escort the prophet to proper accommodations.

"His Majesty has provided suitable quarters for
your visit, Maître Nostradamus, in the hôtel of the
Cardinal de Bourbon. You will be comfortable there
and under a pious roof in keeping with what is, we
hear, the divine source of your inspiration."

In lodging Nostradamus in the residence of the
Cardinal de Bourbon, Archbishop of Sens, the King
had rather cleverly served notice on scoffers that the
man of prophecy was under the approval and protection of both royalty and the Church. It was a tacit
warning to sceptics to hold their opinions in leash. On
the way to the Hôtel de Sens, prophet and soldier
chatted enjoyably. The constable was then about sixty-
five years old. He was the last of the old guard who

had fought with Francis I at Pavia, who had been the friend and companion-in-arms of such men as the Chevalier Bayard, the Count de Tende, and, before his downfall, of his predecessor in office, the Constable de Bourbon. He was at this time, next to the King, the most influential figure in France. Head of the Catholic party, high in favor with the Seneschal Diane, and commander of the army of France, he wielded enormous power.

He inquired affectionately after the Count de Tende, recalling their old comradeship when together they had fought the Provencal invasions of Charles V.

"Touching this matter of prophecy," he said, "I don't know much about that field. A soldier usually makes his own destiny, and carves it out the hard way. There have been times when I could have used your vision to know what the enemy was up to, but never have I been in doubt as to how I should speak and act."

The constable was noted for his blunt, forceful words and autocratic opinion, even in the presence of the King.

"I am an old man now," the constable continued, "the prophecy of my life has about reached its last fulfillment, when other and younger hands will carry on my work. And I can make my own prophecy about that. As long as there is a Montmorency to bear the name, he will be at the forefront to defend his king as I have been. Knowing that, I am content."

There was a grand sincerity to the soldier's words that touched the seer. He was suddenly very glad that he had not included in his book a quatrain mentioning the house of Montmorency. For Nostradamus knew how much less fortunate in his famous descendant the constable would be, than his friend the Count de Tende. A future Duke de Montmorency, whom history would call "the great," would meet his end on the block, for conspiracy against the King, Louis XIII, a tragedy some seventy-five years away. The verse describing it is one of the most celebrated of the prophet's forecasts, and a favorite with commentators because it is so specific. It appeared in the later, completed volume of his prophecies.

IX—19

The dauphin shall carry the *fleur de lis* to Nancy
And even into Flanders to the elector of the German
    Empire.
A new prison shall confine the great Montmorency
Who, far from the customary sites, will be delivered
    to the well-known punishment. (Clerepeyne)

There was an interval in which the use of the title of dauphin was allowed to lapse, and Louis XIII was the first to revive it after the time of Nostradamus. Louis did make a triumphal personal entry with his troops into Nancy, not then a part of France, in 1633. Two years later he marched into Flanders to aid the Elector of Trèves, who had been imprisoned by the Spaniards. It was just before this, in 1632, that Henry

Montmorency was taken in rebellion and conspiracy, as were a number of important nobles during the reign of Louis. It was the old fight to retain feudal powers against Richelieu's work for national unity. Montmorency was imprisoned in a newly completed building at Toulouse, and privately beheaded in the courtyard instead of one of the customary public places of execution. The soldier who beheaded him was named Clerepeyne, a name which strangely enough comes from two Latin words, *clara poena*, meaning well-known punishment. Nostradamus has been criticized for his double-talk, but here it was not he, but history which did the double-talking. The ironic, amazing coincidence of the executioner's name and its actual derivative meaning was merely noted with the exactitude of Nostradamus' prevision, and set down with an accuracy which history has attested. Fortunately the constable was unaware of this distant disaster to his house, as he piloted the prophet toward his new quarters.

The fine old Gothic-Renaissance Hôtel de Sens, at the corner of the Rue de Figuier and the Rue de l'Hôtel de Ville, the town house of the Archbishop of Sens where the constable established Nostradamus in comfort, was built about the year the prophet was born, and at the time of his visit was one of only about fifty such palaces in Paris. Because of the scarcity of such establishments, and the overcrowding and cramped quarters which even wealthy nobles coming to court from out of town had to endure, it was the occasional custom for the owner of a town house, when not in residence, to place it at the disposal of the King. One infers from this, that the archbishop was not himself in Paris at this time, and that the hospitality of his mansion was under the stewardship of the King's household.

Nostradamus was quite used to being stared at. It never bothered him. The mixture of deference and intense curiosity with which the staff at the Hôtel de Sens regarded him, the half-awed, half-mocking eyes of the street crowd which had gathered outside when the Constable de Montmorency returned to conduct him to the King, concerned him not at all. On the way to the Louvre the constable remarked that the attendance at court was unusually large.

"News of your arrival has brought them all out," he told Nostradamus. "I fear they will make your visit to us a very strenuous one. All hope to consult you," he smiled cynically. "The ladies hope that you will foretell vases of gold to hold their roses of love. The men hope to savor in prophetic anticipation the rewards of ambition. Some of them, I think, will savor it no other way," he finished grimly.

Outside the Louvre more citizens had gathered, watching for the prophet's arrival, curious to see what he looked like. Another crowd confronted him when he entered the square courtyard which the palace enclosed. A colorful throng, all jockeying for position to get a front-line view, turned their battery of eyes toward the black-clad figure beside the constable. Nostradamus, smiling in pleasant salutation to the crowd, picked out with his lightning perception its carnival variety. King's gentlemen, cardinals and lovely ladies were in the forefront with the best points of vantage. Back of them pages, lackeys, servants, priests and a nondescript assortment of persons who had made business at the palace an excuse to get in, all elbowed each other and craned their necks to the utmost. Even the narrow windows that looked down on the court were filled with faces.

The constable acknowledged the salute of the gaudily dressed Swiss guards as they entered the building and directed the prophet to the stately new staircase which bears Henry's name. Upstairs there were more people, eager to catch the constable's eye. Montmorency gave a brief nod here and there but he did not slacken his long-legged stride which Nostradamus had, with his ailing foot, some ado to keep pace with. Through unfamiliar doors and corridors they swept to halt at last outside a closed door, which a gentleman in waiting swung open to them. Inside the room a man seated beside a table was reading in a small volume. He looked up as the door opened. The Constable de Montmorency announced:

"Maître Michel Nostradamus."

The prophet was in the presence of the King.

"Ha! At last!" Henry exclaimed, rising with a smile of welcome. "We are pleased that you are safely here. It has seemed a long time." He extended his hand for the kiss of homage and graciously asked

Montmorency to place a chair beside the table, near him, for the prophet.

Nostradamus murmured his thanks for the privilege, to which the King answered that his guest having come so far, he would scarcely ask him to tire his body more when there was so much to ask of his mind. The constable did not linger. He quietly withdrew, leaving seer and sovereign to their talk.

Nostradamus gave a glance of swift appraisal, and understood the man who was King. The monarch studied the prophet intently, slowly, carefully adding up in his mind the sum of his observations to give him a conclusion. Each recognized in the other authority and the quality known as presence. Nostradamus saw a tall, blond, splendidly built man of thirty-seven whose bold blue eyes and handsome features were amiable but somewhat inexpressive. Threads of gold and jewel-fires made points of brilliance in the silk-on-silk of his sumptuous dress. Below his clipped beard, an overturn of fine lace half concealed his high, built-up collar. A heavy, elaborately wrought gold chain made a double loop about his neck with a beautiful medallion of gold and jewels, pendant.

The King observed a short, ruddy-cheeked man severely robed, whose extraordinary eyes somehow held him, interested him, gave him the feeling of confidence that he had wanted to feel.

What these two may have said to each other in this confidential interview is not in the record. But we may imagine that the talk ran something like this:

The King gestured toward the book which he had laid down on the table, and which Nostradamus recognized as a volume of his prophecies. "We are interested in this matter of prediction," the King said, when the amenities had been further disposed of, "yet much that is foretold never comes to pass, so that there has seemed to us to be little of guidance in it. The Queen leans more on prophecy than do we. But it is not the Queen who makes decisions; she has not our responsibility to decide for France."

"Your Majesty's valor and wisdom—" began the prophet, but the King broke in.

"No pretty speeches, Maître Nostradamus. Our court is well versed in those. Men say that you have foresight divinely inspired and therefore true. What we desire from you is truth."

"Sire," the prophet answered, "I would not demean this honor with less."

"You have written some things," the King continued, "in this book that seem to touch our family and certain persons of the court. But we shall not speak of that yet. Our personal fate is subject to God's will. It is of France that I would have you prophesy. What of our claims, what of our enemy's ambitions, how shall the glory of France be best advanced?"

"The lilies," the prophet told him, "will bloom for a great while and fill a larger garden. But I will not hide from Your Majesty that there will be troubled times and much bloodshed. But from each time of peril France will emerge greater, more powerful."

"A brave prophecy!" said the King. "The blood will no doubt be shed by Spain. Well, we expect that, though God be our witness that we have striven for peace."

"Not for long shall Spain hold her power," the prophet told him. "Her time is drawing to a close, though she will trouble France until she has passed her zenith, but her power will be surpassed by the English."

"England!" said the King in vast surprise. "An heretical people, whose rulers do not scruple to intrigue with those of the religion in France to foment sedition. The worst troubles in the history of France have been with England. I wish we might get Calais out of their hands!"

"Ah, that you will," Nostradamus told him, "and shortly. Calais, I promise you, shall return permanently to France."

Henry's eyes sparkled. "That is a forecast which tickles my ears. Now we are getting somewhere. Spain put down, and Calais back. Give us but Italy, those portions which rightly belong to France, and we shall be well content."

The prophet was silent, as the King looked at him expectantly.

"Well, Maître Nostradamus, shall we gather in Milan, Naples and Sicily next year?"

"No, Sire. Success will not crown the war in Italy."

The King's face clouded. "What! You contradict

yourself. If Spain is to weaken, nothing can stop France."

"Spanish power will not vanish in Your Majesty's lifetime, but in the lifetime of one of your sons. The Italian venture will prove costly and unprofitable."

"We shall change that forecast," said Henry aggressively, "and sooner, perhaps, than we shall take Calais. The Italian lands *must* come to the crown of France, and we shall lead Frenchmen to take them." The King's bold blue eyes challenged the prophet's reflective gray ones. As the prophet sat silent, the King said imperiously, "Such a matter touches the honor of the crown, and it is one which only the crown can decide."

"The future expansion of France," said Nostradamus, "will be toward the Rhine, toward which Your Majesty has already made a strong beginning." The great fortress of Metz had fallen to the French under Francis of Guise but a few years before.

"You think we shall get still more of that territory?" asked the King.

"I do, and that too is not far off. Those who now speak the French tongue under foreign sovereignty will be returned to their motherland."

"There is already enthusiasm for that policy," Henry remarked. "It is intolerable that men having this bond of our language should be subject to another rule. We have taken the matter greatly to heart. We rejoice to hear what you have to say of it."

It was during the reign of Henry II that the idea

was born that people speaking a common language
should be united under one flag. France used the argument to justify her conquests toward the Rhine and
Belgium. It was the same argument with which Adolf
Hitler opened his campaign to seize Europe.

"How long shall England hold her power?" the
King desired to know.

"More than three centuries," the prophet told him.

"Body of God!" cried the King, "and what will
France be doing? Will there be no French kings to
wrest the strength from England? Dare not to tell me
of another Agincourt."

"There will be no Agincourt," the prophet assured
him gravely. "France, too, shall be an empire of far-
flung grandeur. Yet there will be one time when a
great soldier will arise out of England and overflow
the continent. France then will be in great danger.
But there will be another Claude of Savoie to rescue
France."

"The Governor of Provence so wrote me." The
King rose and walked about the room, pleasurably excited. "I shall enjoy telling the Queen that. Her
Majesty admires the teachings of her countryman,
Machiavelli. She thinks I treat my nobles too well and
will pay for it in their conspiracies for power. But I
will not believe it of them. Men who not only give
their lifehood to France, but unasked melt the white
and the red from their tables, and take the last coin
from their pouches for my needs! I prefer to rule such
subjects through friendship, not severity."

"A feeling which does great honor to Your Majesty's character," said the prophet warmly. "And God will preserve his anointed kings of France who have Your Majesty's strength and goodness."

"I suppose there is no future danger to the continuance of the Capetian monarch," the King said questioningly. "Can you tell me how many more kings of France there will be?"

"There are twelve more to come of the line of the *fleur de lis*. The last of them shall be greater than Charlemagne. His glory shall light the firmament, and be long remembered of man."

"Only twelve!" cried the King. "And after twelve?" The King leaned forward in his chair.

"The whole world shall then greatly change, and for a long time there will not be peace between God and man."

The King was silent for a time, thoughtful. Then his mind reverted to the royal obsession.

"Tell me, Maître Nostradamus, touching this thing that men call fate, how far do you think it can be changed? You say that we shall not regain Italy. Well now, if I accepted that and made no effort, then we ourselves should be furnishing the cloth to make the cloak for your prophecy. But suppose we are unwilling to be so accommodating."

"The outcome would be the same in either case," the prophet said firmly. "Only in the former circumstance, Frenchmen's lives would be saved. As to your question about fate, it is my humble belief that prophetic visions, when true, are not subject to change. I hold that they can only be perceived by the prophet because they have already transpired within the mind of Almighty God. Touching, however, the times, events and climates of which there is no prescience, these may perhaps be changed according to the will of man. God has given volition to man, and a measure of freedom in using it. Only when man misuses it does God deprive him of it and send disaster upon him."

"And have you seen our defeat in Italy?" persisted the King.

"With sorrow, Sire, I have."

"You may be right," the King admitted. "But I still shall not accept it." The prominent royal jaw set stubbornly. "To do so would make me a coward, traitorous to the just claims of my ancestors."

The King rose, this time in token that the interview was at an end. The prophet's gaze dwelt admiringly for a moment on the beautiful tapestries which covered the walls with their pictured story of the labors of Hercules.

"Were Hercules not a tapestry," he said to Henry, "but a living hero, what could he not learn with profit from a monarch whose tasks are greater and more glorious than were his."

The King smiled. "Hercules, at least, finished his work. I often despair of that. We have many more questions to ask you, Maître Nostradamus, and we look forward to more conversations. Just now, though

I count myself a man of courage, I quail at the thought of how I shall be chidden if I keep you longer. The Queen, the Duchess of Valentinois, and Madame, my sister are all impatience to meet you. The Constable of Montmorency will continue to have you in his care. He will see that you have refreshment, and will then conduct you to other interviews. For the present, *adieu.*"

CHAPTER NINE

The Court of the Valois

THE ARRIVAL OF THE PROPHET in Paris had stimulated afresh the popular interest in his book. Everyone
who had not seen it before was reading and talking
about it now. Speculation centered particularly on a
few of the quatrains that seemed to yield more promise of immediate fruition than the rest. There was one
which spoke of a new king, crowned at Rheims when
Saturn was in water, who would "slaughter the innocents." It would be in a water sign, Cancer, again
in 1561. Was that the end of Henry II, and who
were the innocents? Of course if 1561-3 went by and
nothing happened, then the prophecy couldn't take
place for another seven or eight years. But maybe
something *would* happen, because there was that other
verse about the old lion being killed, fighting in a
golden cage. The astrologers had said Henry II would
die in a duel, and only a king was privileged to wear
gilded armor. Henry II didn't have long then, did he,
they gossiped.

There was the verse, too, about the Bailiff of

224

Blois, setting of royal splendors and tragic destinies.

Orleans. Would that be Jerome Groslot, the present bailiff? Condemned to die, deserving to, but saved from death—what could bring that about?

Then there was that wicked verse about *Bossu.* Everybody knew who that was—young Louis de Bourbon, the hunchback Prince of Condé. Well, the gossips said, he wouldn't be the first Bourbon to turn traitor and get shot for it. Already he was of the religion, like others of his family.

Bossu was then in Paris. While the fanfare of the prophet's arrival was being noised abroad, he dropped in at Admiral Coligny's quarters fuming with anger.

"You would think that God Himself had come to town," he raged. "The entire court, I hear, are making complete fools of themselves over this charlatan."

Coligny, his brother Francis d'Andelot and some other Protestant gentlemen who were present gave Condé ready agreement. D'Andelot said,

"The old sorcerer ought to be tied to the stake and a very slow fire lighted under him."

They spoke of what they considered the outrage of the quatrain about the Prince de Condé. One of the gentlemen had not heard it, and Condé repeated it:

III—41

The Hunchback will be elected by the council,
A more hideous monster never appeared on earth,
A deliberately fired shot will pierce the eye
Of the traitor who had accepted the obligation of
  fealty to his king.

A shocked silence greeted the words. Coligny's stern face was dark with pity and resentment as he looked at the brilliant young prince already important in Protestant councils. Louis de Bourbon, though hump-shouldered, was a very winning, virile figure. Women felt the charm of his merry blue eyes and clever, sensitive face. He was far from being a monster in appearance or character. The verse, mentioning his deformity in such bitter words, is the most bitingly cruel that Nostradamus ever wrote. Inasmuch as the young man was living and could not fail to see and recognize himself in the lines, it seems nothing short of vicious. Yet one has always to bear in mind that Nostradamus was a mediaeval Catholic, fanatically against the new heresy. He was, besides this, a political prophet who saw in the ambition of such men as Condé and Coligny the blade that would cleave France in twain, and he foresaw that the cleavage would never be completely healed, but would lead to untold tragedy and horror through the years. Condé had become to him the symbol of all that was twisted, hideous, and, from his point of view, false in the politico-religious scene rapidly developing into a death struggle between the Protestant and Catholic creeds. Nor did he see Condé as the gay young courtier whom others in that room saw and loved. He saw the later Condé, elected general by a council of Calvinist nobles. He saw the menace of his military genius, and he was glad that he could see the shot that put an end to him at the battle of Jarnac. Nostradamus could view psychically with pitiless satisfaction this gallant fighter, his leg broken by a horse's kick, helpless on the ground, deliberately shot through the eye by Henry of Anjou's captain of the guard, just as the verse described it.

Francis d'Andelot thought Nostradamus could do a great deal of harm. Coligny took the opposite view. He said:

"What can he do but feed the hopes of those who are already doing all the harm they can? Francis of Guise already thinks himself the coming Charlemagne, and is out to crush us at the first opportunity. Besides, the more the court indulges in such superstitious, ungodly nonsense as this Maître Nostradamaus purveys, the more quickly the intelligent masses will rally to our side."

"Has any of you seen this man?" asked one of the other gentlemen. It seemed none had.

"My dear uncle of Montmorency is shepherding him around," said Coligny disgustedly. "And my kinsman the Cardinal of Châtillon is like to burst with curiosity. I shouldn't be surprised if he paid his respects. Faugh!"

"I wonder if he has brought a vial of the Elixir of Life to Madame Diane," sneered d'Andelot.

"Does she need it?" asked Condé mockingly.

Nostradamus did not include in this first volume his bitter verses on Coligny; they came later. Coligny was at this time in no danger. He was the brave admiral of forty, needed and valued for his services in spite of his religion. But Nostradamus had seen a vision of Coligny whitened by age, watched for three nights by the murderous thugs of Guise as he sat reading his Bible. He had seen, without a qualm, the old man murdered, his body insulted and mutilated. He believed that it was the ambition of these Protestant leaders rather than the faults of Church or Crown which would precipitate the nation's tragedy.

Naturally during Nostradamus' visit Protestants were conspicuous at court by their absence, except a few drawn by curiosity to join those who gathered at the Louvre, or called to pay their respects and ask for consultation at the Hôtel de Sens, though Nostradamus had as yet no time except for royal audiences.

Next in order, after his interview with the King, had been his reception by the Queen. Catherine was accustomed to prophets. She had been brought up with them as a family tradition of the Medici, and she usually, since her marriage, patronized those who had a reputation. With Nostradamus she was calmly gracious and, as to the matter in hand, most practical and businesslike. There were certain definite things which she wanted if possible to learn. If Maître Nostradamus knew them and could tell her, Catherine was not at all concerned with whether he got his knowledge from God or Devil.

She received the prophet in company with the dauphin and Mary Stuart, his betrothed, to whom she presented Nostradamus.

"This is our son who will in time assume the royal

burdens of his father. And this is our dearly loved royal daughter of Scotland who will, as my son's wife, adorn the crown with her character and learning."

Nostradamus saw a frail boy of twelve, with a kindly, ineffectual face that showed neither mentally nor physically the making of a king. He felt his heart contract as he looked into the pure, sensitive face of the fair Scottish girl whose fate he foresaw. What awful troubles beauty could bring to nations! Mary smiled at him charmingly and greeted him with a brief salutation in Latin. She was nearly two years older than Francis and her poise and assured bearing were already that of a queen. There was little curiosity in her frank regard, and the prophet was glad to see that she was too young and too happy to be as yet mistrustful of fortune's favors. Francis looked bored with the meeting. Catherine sent them away after the introductions, explaining when they had gone that she had thought the meeting might make it easier for the prophet to frame their forecasts.

Old commentators have indulged in dramatic speculation as to what went on at the sessions between Catherine and the prophet. It was said by some that he "bodied forth the angel Anael" to predict for her, others said that he made the future pass before her eyes in a magic mirror. Such suggestions of midnight spells and mystic incantations are arrant nonsense of course. Catherine was too intelligent to expect anything of that kind.

Just as Henry's interest was in the extension of the

kingdom and in winning victories over other nations, Catherine was concerned with her particular problems which were of a different sort. Catherine's questions pertained to her personal power; there lay her difficulty. Her concern was on how to acquire power, which she had never possessed, what were its instruments which she could use to best advantage, and how could she most securely hold the power once she had obtained it. Undoubtedly she had accepted and thoroughly believed the prophecies of Henry's death, and she knew it might not be far off. As a practical woman she was making her plans to be ready, plotting her moves and policies that would pave the way for her ambition. Already she foresaw the coming struggle. She dreaded the influence which Francis of Guise and his brother, the Cardinal of Lorraine, would be able to use through their niece, Mary Stuart, when Mary became queen. If on the other hand, she, Catherine, played in with the Protestants to offset this, there was the predicted threat from the house of Bourbon-Navarre which the astrologers said would supplant the line of Valois. She saw herself between the frying-pan and the fire. She wanted a prophet who could show her a way out. She wanted assurance that the power she had waited for and dreamed of for years would be hers.

There had been plenty of prophecies made, and Catherine had written records of them all. Ruggiero she trusted, because he was from her home, and her family had long employed his family. But she wanted a check-up on his predictions to see where this new man would confirm and where he would differ with Ruggiero's findings.

The Queen, without doubt, had ready for the prophet her entire collection of family birth-charts together with those of the Guise and Navarre families. In Catherine's secret archives, guarded by hidden panels, there probably reposed the most complete collection of court horoscopes to be found in Europe. A large part of Ruggiero's work would have been to keep the more important charts up-to-date in the matter of progressions, eclipses, mutations and significant transits. In this way the Queen could get a *coup d'oeil* of what might be expected. When the Navarre charts were in difficulties she could plan her course, either an attempt to further crush them, or win their gratitude with a helping hand. She could plot the rising curve of the Guises' power and estimate how far it might go, at what time it would show weakness, when she might dare to attack it. However handy Ruggiero may or may not have been with poison and such accessories to Catherine's power as history has credited him with, he was a very fine scholar, and his astrological work must have been well organized and adequate. Catherine was herself an expert in this line and could put up a chart and read it with the best of them. Since this was a branch in which she was qualified and proud of her knowledge she would have wanted Nostradamus' opinion on her charts, as well as in his own chosen field of prophecy.

She would have discussed with him her plan, which she later carried out, of building a private observatory at Blois and requested that he note the intended placing of it, when he went there, and tell her if he thought it good.

How Ruggiero regarded this new-risen star is not known. Like his mistress, he had been well schooled in repression over many years. He may have welcomed some new light on his heavy responsibilities to Catherine. At any rate, one may be sure that this suave, stately Italian scholar greeted his confrère in prophecy with all cordiality and placed the resources of his laboratory at Maître Nostradamus' disposal.

What Nostradamus told the Queen in their first talks cannot even be surmised, except that it is known that Catherine was interested and impressed, but obviously she did not get all that she wanted to know. Whether the prophet hedged or not cannot be said. But Catherine requested him to go to Blois, where her other children were, in order to see them personally and make a closer prediction than he had so far made of their fates.

There must have been some delightful talks between these two keen minds, when prophecy was temporarily in abeyance. Catherine had an objective, intellectual grasp of many things to which emotionally she could not measure up. She could talk and write interestingly and with an impressively high moral tone, strikingly at variance with the cynical remarks made in other moods and with her actions.

Nostradamus' travels in Italy would have interested Catherine, where he went, whom he met, what he thought of Italian alchemy and astrology. As a pope's niece she would have been particularly eager to question him about the two fine verses in which he prophesied that the Church would confirm the doctrine of transubstantiation, which was done seven years later by the Council of Trent in 1563.

The Church had for some time been at work on various reforms with which to combat the theology of Luther and Calvin. Many people today do not realize that it was not until the time of the Council of Trent that the rite of the bread and wine became accepted as miraculous reality. These are the quatrains in which Nostradamus prophesied acceptance of this doctrine:

III—2

The Divine Word shall become flesh,
Through the mystical act (of transubstantiation),
    and the ritual of occult manifestation, celebrated on
    earth, shall give attunement with heaven,
And the ground beneath man's feet shall become as
    the footstool of God.

II—13

No longer will man's body be a soul-less sacrifice,
The day of death will be thought of as a day of birth
When the Divine Spirit shall give the soul felicity,
Perceiving The Word in its eternity.

Nostradamus expressed his wish to visit while in the city the great shrines which were the sacred pride of Paris. The Queen approved this pious desire and assured him that the guardian prelates would be happy to show him their treasures.

The prophet's first night in Paris was destined to be a restless one. From early morning he had been in the thick of audiences and introductions, and he was still not rested from his wearing journey. With more such days ahead, his bed at the Hôtel de Sens looked very good, even to a man who required but little sleep. Late in the night he was disturbed by noise at his front door. Looking out from his window he saw one of the royal pages hammering in a youth-must-be-served fashion on the portal.

"What is it, page?" called out the prophet. "You are making a lot of noise about a lost dog. Go down the Orleans road and you will find your dog being led on a leash."

This page, who came of the aristocratic family of Beauveau, had lost one of his pedigreed hounds. Perhaps he wanted to show off to his friends that he wasn't afraid of the old prophet who, he would bet, wouldn't know where his hound was anyhow. But Nostradamus did know, and the excited boy found his dog being brought home on leash by a servant, just where Nostradamus had said, on the Orleans road. Such minor incidents caught popular fancy and spread the prophet's fame, because they could be understood better than his impressively puzzling stanzas.

Naturally the Seneschal Diane, and the King's sister, Marguerite of Valois, were not kept waiting for their turn with the oracle. Nostradamus was presented to these two ladies next in order after the royal audiences.

Diane de Poictiers was then a miracle of fifty-seven years. "The old hag," her enemies called her, attacking her in street verses of scurrilous ribaldry. But this missed its mark, for she was still beautiful, still the enchantress of the King. Some said that her secret was cold baths, some said it was sorcery—whichever it was, her "pretty and pompous dress," which was always of black and white, encased her northern fairness as the printer's art holds the time-defying lines of a love-sonnet. Perhaps the prophet paid her some such compliment. It was her daily meed, but coming from a fresh source it was always pleasant. She may have inquired if he meant to immortalize her in his prophecies, as Goujon did in his sculpture. If so, he might have told her,

"A prophecy dies when it is fulfilled. But true poetry lives forever. I, Your Grace, am a prophet telling of times and seasons. Your beauty belongs to poetry, which is timeless."

Nostradamus makes few mentions of women in his prophecies, and only in their capacity as heads of state. This seems strange in a country so politically affected by women throughout its history. Perhaps the prophet disapproved of this. Or it may have been his respect for the Salic law of France forbidding women to rule in their own right, except as regent for a child.

Studying the pictured face of Diane, cool and strong like the women of old Germanic Gaul, one does not get the feeling that she would have been much interested in prophecy. She knew her strength. She could hold Henry. But with his passing her destiny would end. She had heard all about the prophecies of the King's duel and death. Did she really want to know if and when this would occur? Probably not.

In the King's sister, Marguerite, the prophet made a genuine and delightful friend. History does not tell a great deal of this princess, but it does say that she was witty and wise and learned. She was charmed with Nostradamus' conversation and ideas. They talked together of books, personalities and public trends. Nostradamus had foreseen, and indicated in a verse not then published, the marriage, eventually, of Marguerite to Emmanuel-Philibert, Duke of Savoy. He would have taken delight in informing the lively princess of the admirable and apparently happy match in store for her, and also in sketching the illustrious future of the house of Savoy destined long after to rule a united Italy.

"My brother, the King, has wanted Piedmont for years," Marguerite said. "I shall tease him about my conquest of Savoy, where his armies have failed."

Nostradamus did not tell her that the event of her betrothal to the Duke would also be the sad occasion of her brother's death in the midst of a gay tournament staged to celebrate the marriages of Marguerite and the King's young daughter, Elizabeth.

"Maître Nostradamus," Marguerite told the prophet seriously, "I shall see you again after you leave Paris. This is not the end of the friendship which you inspire in me. But there are too many people trying to talk to you now. It is bad enough with all those of my own sex appealing to your prophetic gifts, but when I must also compete with my brother and all the gentlemen of the court to get a word with you, what chance have I to talk of the things I long to know? I am going to seek you out some day in Salon!"

Nostradamus smiled indulgently at the charming young woman.

"The royal Pearl of Paris would be a glorious jewel for Provence to honor."

"You turn a compliment," the princess said, "as neatly as any courtier, yet you have spent your years far from the court."

"It is because we Provençals live in the sun, and we know that in France the sun and the monarchy are one."

Throughout the *Centuries* the prophet's favorite and radiant symbol for the French monarchy is *Le Sol*. In astrology the sun is held to rule kings in general, but the prophet applies the meaning only to the sovereign of his own country.

"I shall pick a time to come to Salon," Marguerite continued, "when all the gentlemen have gone to war, and all the ladies are occupied with children. And I shall hope, Maître Nostradamus, that all your patients will be cured. And then we shall talk, and talk!"

It was to be some time before the democratic Marguerite made good her promise, but she meant it, and eventually she did find her way to the prophet's door in Provence.

The Queen was impatient to have Nostradamus go to Blois and see the other children.

"We have not yet asked you, Maître Nostradamus," Catherine said to him, "concerning your two verses which appear to refer to our children. But surely you understand how they disturb us. It may be that when you have seen and studied all of the children, you will be able to give us an encouraging report. The health of the dauphin gives cause for anxiety, but he is young, and our physician, Ambroise Paré, thinks that he may outgrow his delicate constitution. The other children are sturdy and promising. But since, as you know, we have already been saddened by the loss of three children, a mother's heart beats in anxious solicitude for the others."

"Indeed, Madame, I comprehend that," Nostradamus gravely assured her.

Blois is about a hundred miles southwest of Paris, which meant another not inconsiderable trip for the prophet. He probably traveled in a ponderous, much begilded royal coach, but the trip required more than two days on the road. Still, it was August, with fair, warm weather, and the country, delightful all the way, was enchanting the nearer he came to the banks of the Loire. When the plateau of the palace at last loomed before his eyes and he had his first sight of the castle, its fabulous size and the enormous dignity of its towers and broad flat roofs seemed to him, more than any other building in France, to symbolize the might of the monarchy.

The kings of France always loved the banks of the Loire for their country residences, and of all the beautiful castles they built there, Blois is the one which bears the most regal stamp of the magnificence of the Orleans and Valois princes. It was set on a triangle-plateau separated from the town by a stream. Its position was isolated and formerly a strongly defended one. But its military strength was now more apparent than real, and perhaps this, too, was a symbol of the Valois dynasty which had made the latest contributions to its architectural splendor. We would like to know to which room in this vast pile the major-domo directed the steps of the prophet. All that is certain is that it was in the most modern wing, which Francis I had built, and which housed the apartments and guest rooms of the present royal family. The private rooms all faced north to escape the heat. Their balconied, arcaded windows looked out over the country of the Vendômois and the moats of the town. It was in the midst of the carved and frescoed magnificence of one of these rooms that Nostradamus was installed.

As the prophet followed the steward to his apartment, he hardly knew where to look, so bewildered was his vision by the multiplicity and variety of fantastic beauty. The stone staircase which he mounted wound upward through a hexagonal hollow tower, "an arabesque device invented by giants and executed by dwarfs to give the effect of a dream. The delicate, ingenious marvels of workmanship are like super-wrought, deeply cut Chinese ivories." So Balzac describes the staircase which the prophet is now ascending. As he mounts he can see further and further over the Loire, its living color framed in the pale, elaborate artifice of stone.

The apartments of Catherine and Henry occupied the entire first floor. The monarchs spent, however, little time at Blois, for Henry preferred other châteaux. Not until his death would Blois resume its historic role as the setting for the royal drama. When Nostradamus had rested and had something to eat he asked to see the royal children, whose laughter had already reached him from some unseen play-nook.

Blois was well staffed while the children were in residence. Besides the major-domo and his staff, there was a confessor who looked after the spiritual welfare of the young charges and the household. Each of the children had a personal nurse. Over the nurses were Madame de Curton, the governess of the three little girls, a woman whose superior virtues and abilities were eulogized in the writings of the day; and the Abbé Amyot, the instructor of the three boys, who would one day be the source of a bitter quarrel between Charles IX and Catherine, through the young king's love and loyalty toward his childhood teacher.

The confessor and the two instructors welcomed
Nostradamus cordially. They, too, were used to prophets. Their young charges had been horoscoped and
studied by owlish men of purported wisdom ever since
their birth. To them, Nostradamus, whatever his reputation, was just one more of the same. Each was so
devoted to the royal charges and so loved in return,
that to imagine fate as ever cruel to these lovely children was more than their simple faith could compass.
The prophet quickly established friendly relations by
encouraging them to talk about the children. Enthusi-
astically they told him in what this one excelled, how
modest the deportment of that one, and where another
needed curbing. The Princess Elizabeth was so fine a
Latin scholar, Madame de Curton vowed, that soon
she would rival the young Queen of Scotland. Claude,
it seemed, was somewhat stubborn, like her father,
but with her mother's good sense. As for baby Margot,
the whole staff adored her. The Abbé Amyot allowed
Madame de Curton to take the floor, and when she
asked in what arrangement Maître Nostradamus
would like to see the children, Amyot said promptly,
"Ladies first. Display your charges, Madame."

Elizabeth, the eldest of the daughters of Catherine
and Henry, was at this time eleven years old. Nostradamus was charmed with the singular sweetness and
strength of her young face, which still glows through
the stiff conventionality of her portraits. It was this
quality which so captivated Philip II of Spain, three
years later, that he married her, although she was

intended for his son. "He cut the ground under his son's feet," writes Brantôme, "and took her for himself, beginning all charity at home."

Catherine, who had expected, after Elizabeth's marriage, to pump her advantageously about the state affairs of Spain, ran up against a sense of honor rare in the Valois family. Eizabeth refused to betray Spanish confidence. She was only twenty-three when she died, and about her passing has always hung the dark aura of suspicion. Philip may not, as was reported, have poisoned his charming young wife out of jealousy of his mad son, Carlos. But the legend that he did has persisted.

She smiled on the prophet and gave him her carefully coached greeting in faultless Latin, which he praised to Madame de Curton's content. Then he talked to Elizabeth a little of her studies and her interest in flowers.

Mademoiselle Claude, who was nine, came next. She would grow up to marry the Duke of Lorraine, and to try, weeping, to shield her newly married little sister, Margot, from the horror of blood on Saint Bartholomew's night. Her life lacked the spectacular elements of the other two daughters, for which she was doubtless grateful. She, too, made her little Latin speech, but was more reserved than the frank Elizabeth.

Baby Margot was only three years old. Nostradamus had met the two older girls in one of the formal

galleries. Now Madame de Curton guided the prophet
to the nursery in the Queen's apartments, which occupied the first floor. These rooms had formerly been
those of Queen Claude, the wife of Francis I. They
were still adorned with her delicate sculpture of double
C's, with a device in pure white of swans and lilies
signifying her motto *Candidior Candidis*, the whitest
of the white. The entire apartments were gorgeously
furnished, and to the heavier pieces were added a pro-
fusion of little inlaid and silver tables, ivories, enamels
and other *objets d'art*, which were for the most part
of Italian workmanship.

Baby Margot was already a siren and knew it. She
stopped playing with her doll when the governess and
Nostradamus entered, and came running toward them.
She tossed her cloud of blue-black curls, and used
devastatingly her roguish brown eyes at the visitor.
She chattered with adorable fearlessness to the strange,
grave man and promptly claimed another conquest.

"Is she not beautiful! Is she not an angel!" cried
Madame de Curton, while the nurse stood by, beam-
ing with the same adoration.

La Reine Margot! The dry pages of history still
tingle electrically with memories of her beauty, her
grand romantic glamour, her loves, and her tragedies.
Yet something of all the future sadness which he perceived, too, came momentarily into the prophet's eyes,
causing the governess to exclaim anxiously.

"You will see no misfortune for my little ones, Maître Nostradamus? You will foretell only happiness? Surely they are too good and sweet for anything else. Is not each one a little queen of hearts?"

"Alas, Madame," the prophet told her, "hearts are the most uncertain of all thrones. But you may be very sure that your pupils will grow up to reflect every credit upon your admirable teaching, in the exalted positions which all three shall fill."

Madame de Curton and the nurse exchanged pleased looks. They read into the prophet's words their own interpretation, the fulfilled picture of a wish, so different from the realization.

Later Nostradamus walked in the gardens with the Abbé Amyot, and saw the three boys at their play. Charles, Duke of Orleans, and Henry of Anjou, were but six and five years old, and the little Duke of Alençon was a baby of two years. Nostradamus' quick perception noted the nurse in charge of the eldest boy, Charles, a deep-bosomed northern type with a face of endless patience and brooding calm. When she looked at the little boy, the prophet saw a passionate depth of devotion such as one seldom sees except in the expression of the actual mother. He mentioned it to the Abbé.

"Yes," the Abbé replied. "It is so, and she is a superb nurse. It is unfortunate that she is a Huguenot, but she handles the child, who is high-strung, so wonderfully that the Queen will not let her go. The little prince, doctor, is going to make a splendid man," the

Abbé told him, smiling. "Look at his fine, honest blue eyes, the noble set of his head."

A sick feeling swept over the prophet like a spiritual nausea. He turned away from the Abbé lest it should show in his face.

This manly little child was the monarch he had seen in his visions. "The savage king," he had called him. He was to be the one who would mount the throne when Saturn came into water. He it was who would "slaughter the innocents." Dear God, that loving, happy little boy, become the bloodstained man at the palace window holding an arquebus in his hand trained on Frenchmen! The Abbé was talking on, extolling the qualities of his charge, but Nostradamus did not hear him. A tiger-kitten that licked the hand of the man who fed him could one day tear that man to bloody bits. So it would be with this child. And those who fed the tiger his first meat, they were to blame, too.

Henry of Anjou, with two small dogs leaping about him, came shyly up and stood by his teacher's knee and fixed his big violet eyes on Nostradamus.

"Our young lord of Anjou is a fine prince too." Amyot stroked Henry's wind-ruffled hair affectionately, yet his tone told the prophet that Charles was his favorite.

"Who are you?" the child wanted to know of Nostradamus.

And who are you? The prophet's thoughts echoed in suffering, the child's words. A man stood mistily between him and the boy. A man with a weary, cynical, painted face and a dagger in his hand. He could smell the perfume of his silken clothes. This was the man that Henry of Anjou would be. Only the little dogs playing at his feet were unchanged. It was unbearable. Abruptly Nostradamus got up from the stone bench where he and the Abbé were resting and walked toward the infant Duke of Alençon, who was learning his first steps. The faltering efforts stopped at his approach, and eyes that were too solemn above a nose too long for a baby fixed themselves intently upon him.

"He is doing well with his steps," the nurse said proudly. "Soon he will walk alone."

And one day to perdition and an early death, was the prophet's bitter reflection. He recalled the words of Machiavelli: "It is probable that the atmosphere is full of intelligences which announce the future out of commiseration for mortals." What of commiseration was there in foresight such as this? Nearer was he to calling his gift cursed than ever in his life. Suddenly he wished to be away from Blois. A mist of blood seemed to wreathe the castle and tint the pallid stone. He would have ordered the coach and returned to Paris but that it was late afternoon. Not until morning could he leave. The Abbé noticed his abstraction and restless movements. Tactfully he suggested that the prophet might need a little rest and reflection before they supped. Nostradamus was glad to agree, he wanted to be alone.

I—10

When the coffin is lowered behind the iron grille
Where the seven children of the king shall be laid,
The ancient and ancestral dead shall rise from the
    depths of the nether world
With outcry, seeing the death of this their withered
    fruit.

He should have changed that line, he thought.
Their ancestors should rejoice for France, to see the
dropping of such rotted fruit.

That evening the prophet ate little. He summoned
his self-control and talked with brilliance. But he
retired to his room early. He said that he was a night-
owl and asked if it would be disturbing if he should
roam about the castle in the late hours. The others,
having heard that such visions as his usually came by
night, were a little awed by his request. He was
assured that he would be free to ramble, and the guard
should be so instructed. Yes, the castle was all open,
he could go where he liked.

Deep in the night, while all but the guards were
sleeping, the prophet left his room and by the light of
a lonely candle traversed the dim length of empty
corridors to the moon-haunted chapel of the ancient
kings of Blois who had built their temple to God in
an age of surer faith. As he went his way down endless stretches of chilly stone, the ghosts of the past and
the ghosts of the future peopled the shadowed halls.
Out of the blackness gleamed faintly old crowns of

pointed gold above stern faces, or was it a pattern
of yellow moonlight? Surely the presence of Louis XII,
who had so loved this castle, was near, with that of his
friend, the Cardinal d'Amboise. Near, too, was the dagger, not yet forged, which would strike down young
Balafré, the Guise. And here walked Catherine, the
Queen, and the pale young dauphin with reproachful
eyes upon his mother. From farther in the future
peered the fat face of the other Medici, Marie, with
treacherous d'Epernon. Some seemed to follow the
prophet within the chapel, others whose hands were
red, halted outside the door.

The prophet entered and knelt before the Christ and
Virgin, dim in the uncertain candlelight. His fingers
touched the beads of his rosary, his lips moved in
prayer. The candle burned lower, guttered into blackness, unnoticed by the man whose ceaselessly moving
lips pleaded for pity on the seven children of the King.

In the morning Nostradamus said farewell to Blois
and left for Paris. He was beginning to feel the strain
of all he was experiencing. On the way back his mind
was busy with his coming interview with the Queen.
Carefully he composed the answers he would make to
her questions. He knew he could satisfy her ambitions.
But if she asked his guidance and advice that would
be difficult. There was so little to be said that would be
acceptable to her or that she would follow. He sighed
heavily as he thought how futile was, after all, such a
gift as his to change conditions.

Catherine, who had been impatiently awaiting his

return, sent for him at once on hearing that he was back. No one knows what took place at that interview. The Venetian ambassador, Lorenzo, writing in 1560, refers to Nostradamus' forecast to Catherine as very well known in France, and as predicting that her three eldest sons would all occupy the throne. The ambassador speaks of this as a prophecy which menaced the lives of the princes, since their succession could only come about through death. Many commentators have quoted this accepted story of what Catherine heard from the prophet. It would, if true, however, have been but a small part of the amplitude of information which Catherine would have demanded. All that we really know of what Nostradamus predicted are his brilliantly accurate, published verses. That, and one thing more. He satisfied the Queen and retained her confidence and friendship. Had this not been the case she would not have sought him out again, as she did.

The interview over, Nostradamus returned to the Hôtel de Sens a sick man. His foot was paining him with what appeared to be a somewhat serious attack of his enemy the gout. The food in Paris had been very hard on him. It was heavy, with too much meat, spices and sweets. He missed his green vegetables, garlic and simple, wholesome stews that he had at home, and his wife's good housekeeping. He was sick at heart, too, in the midst of all the adulation he was receiving. Paris was filled with greed, ambition and wickedness. She was like Agrippina, the mother of Nero. And Paris would pay for her sins, and then the whole of France would be involved and would suffer. He saw it coming with dreadful clarity of vision.

His foot swelled and grew steadily worse. He had to take to his bed, hating it, and remain in it helpless for ten days. The acid condition induced by change of diet and water combined with the long traveling and emotional strain of Blois were too much for him. He could no longer stand what he used to. Everyone was wonderfully kind to him in his illness. The King and Queen sent constant inquiries for his welfare, and each sent a purse heavy with a hundred gold écus. The Princess Margaret came to see him and sent him more of the indigestible food and heating wines of which he could not partake.

Ronsard sent him a tribute of verses, which pleased him greatly, likening him to an antique oracle and rebuking the scoffers. This more than offset the Latin distych of Jodelle, another famous poet of the day, who attacked Nostradamus with this punning rhyme:

"Nostradamus cum falsa damus, nam fallere nostrum est,
Et cum falsa damus, nil nisi nostra damus."

Which means, though it has a double interpretation with a play on the name,

"We give our own when we give lies, for cheating is our affair,
When we give what is false, we give nothing but what is our own."

His friends countered in this merry, malicious little war with a couplet using almost the same words but changed enough to give an opposite meaning.

The Hôtel de Sens was busy receiving and answering inquiries from the stream of callers that came and went all day. Scholars, physicians, prelates mingled with the courtiers in their puffed and slashed velvet costumes, their jewels and feathers. As soon as Nostradamus felt well enough, he received some of the more important of these visitors in his room.

Of the notables who prayed the exercise of his vision, the great Duke Francis of Guise was not to be denied, nor his crafty brother, the dark Cardinal of Lorraine. Even more than the Bourbons, these two were the most ambitious men in the kingdom. As the uncles of Mary Stuart, they seemed in a fair way to realize the dreams of their house, if and when the King did pass on in a duel, and the dauphin, Mary's betrothed, came to the throne. Duke Francis, the hero of the siege of Metz, was the military idol of France. A very handsome, very haughty man, he claimed descent from Charlemagne, and had pretensions to the throne itself. He had married Anne d'Este, a granddaughter of Louis XII, and daughter of the tolerant, scholarly Renée, Duchess of Ferrara. The Duke brought his wife with him, both eager for a forecast for their son Henry, whom Henry III was one day to murder in the castle of Blois.

"My mother, the Duchess of Ferrara, has rare skill with astrology," the Duchess of Guise told the prophet. "I have known her tell marvelous things. I wish that she might return to France if only for the mutual pleasure which she and the Queen might have in.such discussion."

When Renée did return several years later, one of the few bright spots in her life was the conversations which she and Catherine had on the subject of the stars in the Queen's new observatory at Blois.

Both the Duc de Guise and the Cardinal of Lorraine plied the prophet with questions. Nostradamus predicted a considerable advance in the Guise fortunes. He would scarcely have courted trouble from these fierce, proud, determined men by revealing the ultimate tragedy of their house, but he has set it down in his verses with a full sense of its dramatic significance and its disaster to France.

If he had told them that they would lose to the Bourbons, then very weak, they would probably have scoffed at him. Their star was then too powerful for the concept of defeat to enter into their minds.

The gout wore off slowly, but at last Nostradamus was free of it for the time being, and in spite of all flattery and solicitation, he was anxious to return to Salon. Nor would he be deterred. His room at the Hôtel de Sens looked like a dream of Christmas, so loaded was it with presents of every description. Some of the King's servants packed them for him, while he, himself, packed his valued ink horn and writing materials, his treasured Aristotle and the other simple needs he had brought.

César Nostradamus, writing of these gifts, after his father's death, says of them:

"As to the honors, royal gifts, and presents of jewels which he received from their Majesties, I would rather have their list on the tip of my tongue than to give myself the exquisite pleasure of relating them, fearing lest I should say more than modesty permits."

When all was in readiness for departure, Nostradamus went to the Louvre to say his farewells to royalty.

"Your Majesty," he told the King with genuine feeling, "I never thought that I should envy any man. Yet now I find myself very much envying those who have the gift of ready and golden speech. Lacking this I am but helpless to express my opinion of Your Majesty's grandeur and generosity of nature, and of the kindness which I, your humblest servant, have received from you. The treasures of gifts which your royal goodness has bestowed on me are even surpassed by the treasure of royal memories which I take away with me to brighten all my years."

The King smiled at him with genial regard.

"We have, Maître Nostradamus, one more, and I think well deserved, token of our favor. You are herewith appointed by us to the rank of Physician-in-Ordinary and Councilor to ourself."

The prophet, deeply moved, bowed low. "Your Majesty, I am overcome with this further honor."

"We have enjoyed your visit," the King said, "and

hope to profit by those matters in which you have advised us. Now, the Queen is waiting to see you."

Catherine, like Marguerite, told the prophet, "We shall see you again, Maître Nostradamus, and meanwhile you may hear from us by letter touching some further service which you can render, or some point on which we can better act through your advice."

The last farewell was finally said, the last handshake given. Over the bridge the way led, past the soot-blackened beauty of Notre Dame and the Ile de la Cité, across to the left bank, and the road to Lyons. Nostradamus looked back at the spires and towers of Paris, scene of his proudest triumph. He lifted his hand in salute to the city.

"Vale Lutetia! Ave Salona!"

Last resting place of the older Capetian kings.

CHAPTER TEN

Toward Familiar Country

NEARLY THREE MONTHS had gone by from the time that Nostradamus had left Salon, to his return, laden with gifts and the honor of the King's appointment. It was a great day in the life of the little town when he came back to his people with laurels of this new adventure. Family and friends rejoiced at his success. His triumphs, though pleasing to Nostradamus, made no difference in his way of life. As soon as he had rested up he resumed the busy even tenor of his days as if Paris had never called him.

Yet there was a difference. He was no longer merely the wonderful Doctor Nostradamus of Provence. He was now the celebrated prophet of France, honored by his king, and known throughout Europe. In those days when personalities counted more than policies in the political arena—because personalities then made policies—diplomatic reports on royalty were as gossipy as a tabloid. They were expected to be. In the lives of kings and queens, everything relative to them had political significance.

"Whatever they did was an act of state
From taking a pill to taking a mate."

The least occurrence that an ambassador could find
out was incentive to him to seize his quill and write a
dispatch to his soverign. Ink had flowed like water
during the visit of Nostradamus to Paris, and copious
reports had been sent home by the diplomats describing this amazing man. Some of the diplomats had
made an effort to meet him in order to size up what
sort of influence he might exert on the King. The
Queen's patronage of prophets was well known. But
Henry's interest was something else. It made Nostradamus potentially high politics.

After his return to Salon, foreign rulers began to
send private emissaries there to see him. This was with
the double hope that he might let drop some information of value, and, on the other hand, if he was as
amazing as reported, there was not a ruler in Europe
who did not yearn for a little advance knowledge on
the aims of his competitors. A good prophet was worth
his weight in gold to any king. So the people of Salon
had one more thing to wonder and gossip over in the
important looking men with a foreign air who now
came and went mysteriously at the house of Nostradamus. Naturally these consultations were of the utmost secrecy, and nothing is known of them except
the rumors and observations of the townspeople.

In his leisure time Nostradamus took up the work
on his verses for another volume of prophecies. He also

turned his attention to other kinds of writing. He had published in 1552 a little book, *Traité des Fardements*. In 1557 he brought out in Anvers another, *Des Confitures*. These two were later on combined into one work, perhaps supplemented, and formed the two little volumes to which Bareste refers, one of which contained the recipe for the troches.

It was not strange in that day for a famous doctor to occupy himself with writing about beauty secrets and cooking. In that pre-beautician, pre-dietician age, the doctor was the only safe authority on such matters. The cult of the body, which the pagan revival raised to romantic heights, demanded to be served with formulae which contributed to the effectiveness of feminine charm and preserved its loveliness from age. Every beauty of the day had her private collection of formulae. Some of these were very old family secrets, carefully guarded and passed on from mother to daughter. Valuable additions to this tested knowledge were greatly prized. Perfumes, too, were a part of the doctor's field. The sixteenth century drenched itself in sweet-smelling essences not alone because they were fashionable and much enjoyed, but they were thought to have some prophylactic value too.

There was also the matter of cooking, which was by no means beneath a physician's notice. Culinary recipes, like those for beauty, were especially important in France, and were hoarded and prized in every household. Nothing was known about diet, but it was recognized that in illness special feeding was required, and usually this took the most unfortunate form. Scurvy, which was one of the commonest diseases, was considered, then as now, a deficiency disease. They knew that much about it. But the sufferers were denied the citrus fruits which would have cured them and were "strengthened" with rich meats and heavy wines. The doctors of the day not only recommended the foods which they considered most efficacious for various types of illness, but wrote books of recipes for cooking of every sort. Their wives must have laughed in their capacious sleeves over this, for of course it was *their* recipes these learned doctors brought forward with such *éclat*. They did the cooking, and the doctor took the cash and credit. A little compendium of what every woman should know—perfumes, cookery, beauty hints, household remedies and how to keep the silver clean was a popular, practical book and met a real need. When doctors stopped writing these books, much of this old, generalized information found its way into almanacs. Doctor Nostradamus had many highborn feminine patients. These might not have cared so much for the doctor's ideas on cooking, but they would certainly have demanded that he produce a few miracle-aids for beauty.

Now that he was so famous, the plain people of the countryside, who knew well his kindness, began to claim their need of attention. Their concern was with the land, its crops and harvests. Farmers, laborers, shepherds, estate managers and gardeners swarmed to ask the prophet to tell them when to plant, how their crops would turn out, how to destroy pests, what the weather would be, how to cure livestock, and the thousand and one things a farmer wants to know. They took up so much of his valuable time that something had to be done about it.

So Nostradamus, in order to help them, and, so it is said, for his own diversion too, wrote and published his astrological almanacs. These gave the times and seasons for the farmers' work, and included a number of public forecasts in prose. These almanacs were dedicated to Pope Paul IV, and presumably met with his august approval. King Henry II was overlooked in the matter of dedication which, one would think, by all the laws of hospitality received, would have been made to him. Unless it was that the need for the good will and protection of the Church made the gesture desirable.

Like everything he did, the almanacks caught on at once. They sold like wildfire. Printers all over France, seeing a gold-mine in Nostradamus' name, began to pirate it. Bogus almanacs, imitating his style and using his name, were put out everywhere. The common people, greedy for the prophet's words, were unable to discriminate between the publications, but they knew false prophecy when they saw it, and blamed Nostradamus. His enemies fed the fuel of undeserved criticism, and in consequence of all the ensuing furor Nostradamus' reputation took a fall among the people at large. This was not true of the court, the people of position and culture who knew him realized the situation, and their loyalty never wavered.

There were no copyright laws. The almanacs were at once translated and republished in England. They were the ancestors of *Old Moore's* and other famous English prophetic almanacs which have always been popular there. Nostradamus had no protection or redress. He consulted a Lyons lawyer about the misuse of his name but there was nothing to be done. In Lyons particularly, the city for which he had done so much at the time of the plague, old acquaintances cold-shouldered him and he found that his popularity was gone. He is said to have been deeply wounded by his treatment there.

In 1557 he published at Lyons his *Paraphrase of Galen*, a philosophic discourse which was well received by scholars.

All was quiet in little Salon as the prophet pursued his peaceful studies. But in the great world large events were taking place, fulfilling incredibly his prophecies. While the bourgeois and the common people who bought the paper almanacs were attacking him, kings and their courts who owned and studied the small, finely bound leather volumes of his quatrains were according him new and breathless acclaim.

In January of 1557 Henry II, unable to contain himself longer, sent Guise into Italy to join the Pope in his war against Philip II of Spain.

II—72

The French army in Italy, will be troubled
Throughout the conflict, and sustain great loss,
Flee, citizens of Rome. Oh, France, driven back
Near to the Tessin in your doubtful struggle to reach
    the Rubicon!

Bloody Mary of England was then the wife of
Philip II of Spain. Philip persuaded Mary to help him
by declaring war on France.

Presage—18

The travelling herald of the Lion seeks out the Dog
While the city is consumed by battle, pillage and fresh
    capture,
Princes, defenses opened up, are captured by hard
    blows,
The Herald returns to his country, the French who
    went on an expedition are captured, a great alliance
    is contracted with a royal virgin.

The dog (sometimes the great mastiff) is a symbol
sometimes used by the prophet for the guardian qualities of the kings of France, the watch dogs. The lion
is here the heraldic one of the Tudor family. Mary
declared war by sending a single herald to France to
give in person, in the old mediaeval fashion, her personal defiance to Henry. Henry told him to begone

the kingdom and that had he not come from a woman
he would have told him some worse things. Philip,
with some English help, then landed fifty thousand
men in Picardy and Flanders. The Duke de Guise had
to rush back from the Italian failure to meet this new
threat as best he could. Meanwhile "the alliance with
the royal virgin" goes forward and, while Philip's
army is landing, Mary Stuart is married to the
dauphin of France.

10—55

The unfortunate nuptials will be celebrated
With great joyousness, but the end will be unhappy,
Mary and the mother of the groom will scorn each
    other
When Phoebus, dead, is a more than piteous spouse.

This verse is in the later quatrains, then withheld.
It is interesting that he used "Mary," the English
word, rather than Marie, as she was called in France.
The rivalry of Mary and the Medici queen, after
Henry's death, is history. Piteous Phoebus, the Sun of
the French Monarchy, is Francis II.

Meanwhile the armies of Philip were before Saint-
Quentin, considered one of the bulwarks of France.
The Spaniards were commanded by the Duke of Savoy,
who would later marry the prophet's friend, the Princess Marguerite. King Henry was ill prepared to meet
this siege. His forces were tied up in Italy. The defense army hurriedly mustered was only twenty thou-

sand men. It developed that Saint-Quentin was in a deplorable state, an impressive shell with only dated equipment, as Philip had privately found out.

IV—8

The great city, suddenly and to its repentance, will be
  taken by assault,
Surprised in the night, its defenses will be broken
  down.
The guards and lines of communication at San Quentin
Will be destroyed, and its gates battered in.

VI—96

The fine city will be abandoned to the soldiery,
Never was mortal tumult closer at hand.
O what hideous death is closing in,
Except one crime, nothing will be spared the people.

Soldiers, munitions and food were all lacking. Coligny got there first, sent away the useless mouths and began trying to strengthen the weakest points. Old Constable de Montmorency, *Bossu* of Condé, Francis d'Andelot, men who would soon be murdering each other in deadliest hate, were there with the flower of the nobles of France of whatever creed. They stood together then as Frenchmen and fought as Frenchmen can. But it was one of those never heeded lessons in preparedness. They were unprepared and their defeat was bloody and total, just as the prophecy had said.

Francis of Guise, arriving from Italy after Saint-Quentin had fallen, sought for some brilliant counter-stroke to humble Spain. Calais, like Saint-Quentin, was poorly defended and its equipment was run down. Very secretly Guise moved before Philip could get wind of it, and:

VII—28

The great Duke of Alva will enter the war
In a manner traitorous to his grandsires,
The great Duke of Guise will put an end to the war
With a captivity that shall be his enduring monument.

IX—29

The country which has accomplished nothing will give place,
It will eventually abandon what was captured but not captured,
The Church will be on fire over the bloodshed,
Guines, Calais and Oye will be returned.

The capture of Calais did indeed confer immortality upon the name of Guise and give him an enduring monument. The Pope said it was worth more than the capture of half of England. Mary Tudor, who was dying, cried out: "If they open my heart, they will find Calais graven on it." Guizot lists in his history the vast extent of the "captivity" of the British commander, "cannon and munitions, the gold and silver furniture, merchandise, and horses" which passed to Guise. England had held Calais for over two hundred years. From this capture it remained with France until 1940. Spain had accomplished nothing whatever by the war, for the peace terms gave back to France everything she had lost, all her "captured but not captured towns." The Duke of Alva was general-in-chief for Charles V and Philip II of Spain.

All wars come to an end and this one closed with the Peace of Cateau-Cambresis in the spring of 1559. Nostradamus saw it only as the prelude to worse and internal war.

IX—52

Peace approaches from one side, but war
Will be pursued on a greater scale than ever.
Men and women will weep, innocent blood will flow
   throughout the land
And it will happen throughout all France.

But not while Henry lived would the storm break. Bloody Mary had died while the war was on, which changed the political lineup, as Protestant Elizabeth inherited the English throne, and it was too early yet to foresee the character of her rule. Philip and Henry had decided for a change to be friends; besides, Philip had seen young Elizabeth's picture, the little daughter of Henry II whose sweetness had so charmed the prophet at Blois.

Nostradamus has given a pen picture of Philip.

This cruel king, although Nostradamus doesn't seem
to think so except when Philip is fighting France or
her interests, did, as Nostradamus says, continue the
policy of ridding Spain of Moors, and encouraged the
Inquisition to do its worst. He is to be credited with
the major effort in defeating the Turks (who as Moslems hold Friday sacred) at Lepanto. Perhaps that is
what the prophet means rather than the Inquisition
by "returning the Church to its pre-eminence."

V—74

Sprung from Italian blood, born in the heart of Ger-
    many,
Is the leader who shall become of such high power
That he will drive the foreign Moorish people from
    his realm,
Returning the Church to its original prestige.

10—95

Within Spain there shall arise a very powerful ruler,
He will conquer the Midy by land and sea,
This vigorous man will beat back the Crescent
And lower the wings of the people to whom Friday is
    a sacred day.

Henry II decided that his sister Marguerite had
better marry a late enemy too. So her marriage was
planned with the Duke of Savoy on whose hands the
blood of three thousand Frenchmen slain at Saint-

Quentin had hardly dried. Henry had got Saint-Quentin back in the peace settlement.

VI—8

Under the pretext of a marriage settlement,
Great Henry will, conformably to the situation, act
with generosity.
Quentin and Arras being recovered through a journey,
The Spanish will at this time take a back seat at
slaughter.

Henry acted with generosity by presenting Mary Stuart, now dauphiness, with Saint-Quentin as a wedding present. Kings have to make rather expensive gifts, and this would stay in the family.

VI—74

The great king will acquire new relatives,
Before he shall have rendered up his soul
The people will see him take for kindred
Eagles, Lions and Cross; in doing this he will sell out
the Crown.

The heraldic imperial eagle of the Spanish Empire, the Lion of Scotland and the Cross of Savoy were represented in the three royal marriages with Spain, Scotland and Savoy. But Henry's wedding presents were too much for the French. Others besides Nostradamus said the weddings had cost too much good crown land and felt it was a sell-out for France.

The peace had been signed in April. The marriages took place at the end of June. Henry II celebrated the acquisition of his new relatives with a splendid tourney.

The three-day sports event was attended by the entire royal family—even to Baby Margot. Society turned out in the full magnificence of its jewels, its laces and its stiff brocades. Before this audience of the rank, wealth and beauty of France was played a long-awaited tragic drama. Staged against a background of damascened silks, feathers, tassels and fluttering streamers, with the trumpets of heralds in parti-colored dress calling the final act, on the 29th June 1559 occurred the "duel" in which Henry II lost his life, as prophesied.

Henry II loved to joust, a sport at which he excelled most of his court. He had already run several tilts "like a sturdy and skillful cavalier," and he wanted one more before he stopped. He challenged his young Scottish captain of the guard, the Earl of Montgomery. The Earl, like everyone else, knew the prophecy. He excused himself, but the King wouldn't have it. It was a command. The Seneschal, radiant in her black and white, was looking on from the royal dais, at her colors flying from her lover's lance and shield. The King was mounted on a curvetting Spanish barb, caparisoned with crimson velvet. Henry's armor, as was royalty's privilege, flashed with the goldsmith's art of cunning and intricate gold inlay, which covered the steel like a golden lace. His casque was gilded and crested with plumes.

A fragment of Montgomery's lance struck the King's neck—a piece forced up the visor, and a splinter of wood entered Henry's eye and injured the brain. He lingered for eleven days in horrible agony, then died.

Probably of all the prophetic verses which Nostradamus has written, none is so widely familiar as have always been the quatrains describing this tragic affair.

I—35

The young Lion shall overcome the old
In single combat on a martial field,
His eyes, encased in gold, will be put out,
When two are in the lists, fighting as one, he will
    receive a mortal blow and die a cruel death.

Young Montgomery was a Scot, indicated by the heraldic Lion.

III—55

In the year when a single eye reigns in France
The court will be in grievous trouble.
His friend will kill the Great One of Blois
The Kingdom will be thrown into evil condition and
    double uncertainty.

The Great One of Blois is of course the King, and the young Earl of Montgomery, his friend. Almost

over the King's dead body the struggle began between
the Guise and Bourbon factions, with Catherine as a
helpless factor in the fight for power. Francis II, the
boy-king, doubled the uncertainty of the situation
through his frail health.

VI—63

The Royal Lady shall dwell alone in power
After the passing of her matchless husband, first on
    the field of honor.
For seven years she will lament her sorrow,
Then, gifted with long life, she will rule to an ad-
    vanced age.

Nostradamus must have been looking ahead to the
continued protection of Catherine's favor when he
mentions her seven years' lament. Seven days would
have been stretching it. This line was a courtier's
phrase for a practical purpose. But it is true that seven
years after Henry's death Catherine made a grand
tour of France with Charles IX, and it was the first
time she had indulged in such a public display of
social pomp since King Henry's death. She lived to be
seventy years old. Few royalties in her day lived so
long.

The working out of the prognostications of Maître
Nostradamus had the court gasping with awe. With
Henry dead, everyone set to with a will for a fresh
bout with the quatrains to see if they could wrest an

inkling of where the next blow would fall. The boy-king, Francis II, with lovely Mary Stuart, were now the King and Queen of France. It was the triumphal hour of Francis, Duke of Guise and the Cardinal of Lorraine. It was Catherine's hour to mourn, not for Henry gone, but for herself, alive and beset by enemies on every hand. But who knows what secret prophecies she hugged to her bosom while outwardly dutifully meek, as became a sorrowing widow? Only Nostradamus and Ruggiero could have told.

Bossu, Coligny and their crowd had no intention of letting the Guises rule France without a struggle. They had their own prophecies that some day a Bourbon would unseat a Valois. And prophecy or not, they meant to keep fighting.

IV—62

There will be an ambitious plot against the crown
By a powerful army leader who will think to seize
    the King.
And he will feign a situation, by a planned ruse,
But the plot will be uncovered under the boughs of
    the forest.

Had Condé and Coligny seen that verse when the plot was hatched, and did they only scoff at the Catholic sorcerer? Did no one whisper in their ears, saying, this man has a record for truth, Saint-Quentin, the King's death and all the other things he has foretold should give you pause?

The conspiracy of Amboise was the Protestants' opening gun in the bloody religious wars that would devastate France for more than thirty years. The French historian, Malet, says that Condé, *Bossu*, was the secret head of the plot to kidnap the King and break up the influence of the Guises. The forces of the plotters were stationed in the forest of Amboise. There, under the trees, they were discovered, beheaded or hanged.

Nostradamus heard of all these things in Salon; there was another of his forecasts destined to come true very shortly; one he hadn't published yet, it would be included in the last three Centuries.

X—39

The widow of the unfortunate marriage will survive
    the death of the eldest son,
No children will be born of the marriage. Two Isles
    will be put in discord.
He will die before eighteen, still of incompetent age.
The succession will be harmoniously settled upon the
    next of age.

Mary of Scotland had married the dauphin while he was still "the eldest son" of the seven children the King was to leave behind him. There were no children of this marriage and Mary returned to her native heath, unwanted in France by Catherine, and set two Isles in discord through feud with Elizabeth. The dauphin, King at his death, poor "Phoebus," was only sixteen years old and he was king for but sixteen months.

The story has come down that before the death of Francis II the Venetian ambassador, Lorenzo, wrote to his government that all the court was quoting verse 39 of Century X under the breath. Yet this verse was not published until 1568 and the boy-king died in 1560. So many legends have grown up about Nostradamus, inspired no doubt by the natural desire of the *raconteur* to top the other fellow's story, that one is constantly finding these inconsistencies in old accounts. The court would have been far more likely to discuss the ingress of Saturn into Cancer hinted at as the date for a new king. That verse was in the first edition.

The month before Francis died, the blow, also predicted in the first edition, struck the Bailiff of Orleans, Jerome Groslot.

III—66

The important Bailiff of Orleans will be in peril of his life,
Through one of vindictive nature.
But neither fate nor his deserts shall bring his death,
Because though captive, his hands and feet will be loosely bound.

The court would have been watching for developments on this verse indicating a prominent man.

Perhaps Groslot had studied the verse too, and taken heart from the prophecy that he would escape. He allowed the Calvinists to seize Orleans, for which the Inquisition promptly condemned him to be beheaded. Nostradamus makes it clear that he thought he deserved the sentence as a Calvinist traitor, but foresaw that he would get away. Groslot escaped death in just the way that Nostradamus said it would happen.

During this period, since Nostradamus had paid his visit to the court, while war and turmoil had brought so many of his forecasts to fulfillment, he had published another edition of his prophecies. This had been in 1558.

This edition is spoken of by many commentators as *princeps,* but it was the second edition supplemented by more of the verses. It contained all that the first volume printed, with three hundred and ninety-one additional quatrains, bringing the number up to seven full Centuries of a hundred verses each, and one of forty-four verses, seven hundred and forty-four in all. Between the sixth and seventh Centuries was interpolated an unnumbered Latin verse which he titled:

Invocation of the Law Against Stupid Critics

Let those who read these verses consider them with
   mature mind,
Let not the profane and ignorant mob be drawn to
   study them,

Let all of the Astrologers, the Fools and the Barbarians
keep aloof,
Let him who acts otherwise be cursed according to
ritual.

Nostradamus reveals in this peculiar verse his savage resentment against the people who had insulted
his work. He warns that his book is for the serious
minded only. And to those who have called him sorcerer he will offer a curse, as they have so long accused
him of doing. It is also revealing that though he constantly asserts, for reasons of his own, in his letters
that he is himself an astrologer, he includes astrologers
here among the people who are to keep hands off his
work. He gives away in these lines the fact that he
did not use astrology, and that he even despised the
popular practice of this esoteric art. His mention of
the common mob seems inconsistent with the public
presentation and sale of his book, as if he both wanted
and hated the acclaim it brought him. There is no
doubt that he was very thin-skinned to censure, for
certainly he was not alone in suffering it. Every
scholar who came before the public risked it. Nostradamus was indeed among the fortunate in that he
never endured worse, and that the chorus of his praises
swelled at all times louder than the minority voices
of those who disliked him.

It seems odd that, when Nostradamus had been so
recently and highly honored by the King, he did not
dedicate to him this new edition, or that he did not

bring out the fresh quatrains in a small separate book devoted to the King. Nostradamus knew, none better, when the King would die. If he had ever intended a dedication to Henry II, then was his last opportunity to make it, for Henry died the following year. If, however, the dedication to Henry II which prefaced the third and last book of the *Centuries* was never intended for this king, but was meant for another Henry, fifth of his name, *who is yet to come*, then it was entirely logical that Nostradamus should have arranged matters as he did. The preface to the complete edition, though written ostensibly as a letter to Henry II, was never seen by him. It was not published until he had been dead a decade. Nostradamus himself planned it that way and made his own arrangements for the letter and final volume to be brought out only after he and the King were both gone.

Moreover, the letter begins with a salutation which does not use the word *deux*, as one would expect, but addresses him as Henry, King of France *Second*. The connotation of *second* is a little different from *deux*. It has the implication of "following," and the words seem intended to convey the idea of a king of France which is to follow, *or a second France*.

Had he, during the King's lifetime, dedicated a book to Henry II, no one would ever have considered it as other than it seemed. It was only by holding the letter back until the man for whom it seemed to be written had died without receiving it, that he could get his idea across to some people.

Why, one may ask, all this fuss? Why didn't he just write to Henry V in the first place? Because he foresaw the Duke de Bordeaux who, if he had reigned, would have been Henry V, and did claim the title. People would have mistaken the Duke de Bordeaux for the man for whom the letter was written, then branded Nostradamus as a false prophet because he never reigned. Nostradamus' wording was perfect for his purpose. He knew that the human mind seeks always a conclusion. He knew the world would hang on to the quatrains and preserve them as long as they hadn't solved the mystery. And four hundred years have proved him right.

This would also account for his sensitivity to criticism. One can scarcely imagine his modest, natively retiring personality going after the sensational reputation which his book brought him, unless he had a secret and definite reason for doing it. He could not explain this, he could only suffer through what he felt was its necessity, when people called him a sensation-seeker and attacked him for his pretensions as a prophet.

Everything Nostradamus did, and his personal reactions in regard to the *Centuries*, appear to point to an ulterior purpose in writing them.

With the passing of Francis II, another boy-king assumed the throne. This time there was no lovely, inconvenient wife to menace Catherine de' Medici. Charles IX was only ten years old, and his mother ruled as regent of France in his name. Catherine's power-dream had at last come true.

IV—86

In the year when Saturn shall be in a water sign and
Conjoined with the Sun, the strong and puissant King
Will be crowned at Rheims and received and anointed
   at Aix,
Thereafter he will murder the conquered innocents.

Francis II had died in December of 1560. Catherine, though *de facto* regent at once, did not receive parliamentary confirmation of this until sometime in the following summer, just the time when Saturn was making its ingress into Cancer, a water sign. One must bear always in mind that we are looking at astrology through the eyes of the sixteenth century, remembering too that Nostradamus gave indications of the timing of events by astronomical positions. This verse is of particular interest analyzed with that understanding. One must not forget, either, the wide familiarity which cultivated people then had with famous birthcharts. Even without this verse, people who followed their charts would have said, "Oh, Oh! When Saturn goes into Cancer that will hit the King and the Queenmother. His Sun and her Mars are closely conjoined in that sign, which bodes ill for the country staying at peace. Saturn will touch that off. There will be trouble."

The two, mother and son, were astrologically linked together. That is just what Nostradamus means when he speaks of a strong king. He refers to the mother-son combination which he treats as one force, which it was. He was not speaking alone of the little boy he had seen at Blois, who was still unspoiled and fine. In another passage forecasting the eventual rise of Henry of Navarre he says, "he will shave the beard of Catherine." Indication enough that she was the strong king, it would be only as accessory that the boy would be responsible for "the slaughter of the innocents." Quoting the French historian, Guizot, "From 1561 to 1572 there were about twenty-five massacres, thirty or forty single murders unfortunate enough to be remembered by history. Formal civil war, religious and partisan, broke out in four campaigns signalized by great battles, ending in 1572 with the greatest massacre in French history"—Saint Bartholomew, for slaughtering the innocents. The reign of Charles covered the years 1561–1574, and he was only twenty-four when he died. Not until the Revolution would there be again such "slaughter of the innocents" as filled these blood-drenched years. Trouble began at once with minor slaughters on both the Catholic and Protestant sides. But it was in July, 1562, when the Sun was conjoined with Saturn and both bodies were over the birth Sun of Charles and the birth Mars of Catherine, 14 and 17 degrees of Cancer, that the first religious war was opened.

This quatrain has never been understood by analysts because none has understood the astronomical reference the way Nostradamus used these to date and characterize the thirteen tragic years of this mother-son kingship. We may be sure that there were plenty of people at that time who were quick to grasp the allusions, including Catherine. It may be why the Queen tried so hard in the earlier years of this joint rule to pacify both sides. Catherine didn't want slaughter, she wanted peace, but no woman could have handled and tamed the unbridled, passionate fanaticism which broke all bounds. Later, when it was a question of losing her own power or killing Hugenots, Catherine killed. From her point of view she had no choice.

Some modern students of the *Centuries,* noting this verse, have wondered if it might not relate to the coming king of France, the prophesied Henry V. *In June of 1944 Saturn makes its new ingress into Cancer attended by the Sun, Mercury and Venus in a powerful quadruple conjunction. The present Duke of Guise has his birth Sun and Mars in Cancer.* It could be. Interpretations of Nostradamus are tricky, and dualistic, and this is as much due to history as to the prophet. "Destiny is an eternal chain ... looping upon itself" in repeating patterns, the same and never the same. The author, however, feels that this verse specifically referred to Charles IX and Catherine.

Nostradamus, better than any other in France, understood the terrible threat of the mounting strife. Already it was reaching deeply into Provence and men were dying there for their beliefs. But there were still bright spots to be enjoyed. Chief of this was the promised visit from the Princess Marguerite, who was now the Duchess of Savoy. She came to Salon bringing with her Emmanuel-Philibert. They were on their grand honeymoon swing through the country and probably a little bored with all the public entertainments that were given them everywhere. Nostradamus gave the usual Latin oration on behalf of Salon, as the town always liked him to do for their distinguished visitors. Emmanuel-Philibert seems to have been as charmed by Nostradamus as was his wife. They made quite a stay in the town, longer, that is, than they had planned. They invited Nostradamus to sup with them, and they in turn visited him informally. There were the long and interesting talks that Marguerite had looked forward to. It violated, however, the etiquette of her day, and there was some criticism to mar the pleasure. Nostradamus was a gentleman but not a noble. The sixteenth century made fine distinctions in rank, and Catherine had rigidly tightened all matters of etiquette. She even made such a fuss about the Constable de Montmorency riding his horse into the Louvre courtyard, that he said it was easier for him to win a battle than to get inside the Louvre.

People said that the Savoys were too high in rank to associate with Nostradamus as an equal. It was all right to employ and honor him as a prophet, but not to make a familiar friend of him. The Duchess' new home was now just over the Alps from Provence. The

democratic Duchess and her independent husband no
doubt valued the intellectual interest of the prophet's
friendship above all criticism, and one would like to
know if they continued by letter their agreeable acquaintance. So very little is known of the private contacts and friendships of Nostradamus in these late, important years, that we who cannot see through time
must regretfully forego the reading of this varied and
fascinating chapter of his life. What part he played,
what influence he had upon the great who came or
sent their messengers to him, as in the days of Delphi,
we have no way of knowing.

His friend, the Count de Tende, was increasingly
disturbed over heavy Protestant gains through Provence. In 1560 the Governor had occasion to notify
the Duke de Guise of an election of entirely Protestant
deputies in Languedoc. The Duke de Guise tried ac-
commodatingly to have the deputies killed, but they
escaped him. They had been legally elected, and if not
murdered could serve, as they did. This heavy conversion to the religion which was going on in Provence was naturally a threat to so prominent a personage and so rigid a Catholic as Nostradamus. The
friendship of the Governor was powerful protection,
but there must have been times when he and his family went in fear of their lives.

One of the popular and much embroidered stories
of the prophet is concerning the personal reading he
made for Henry of Navarre, a story of which Tronc

de Condoulet is said to have been the author, and he should certainly have known. But Henry was only three years old when Nostradamus went to court, and seems to have made his own court debut not until two years later when his father, King Antoine, took him to Paris. Nostradamus, now ill, living in retirement, would hardly have risked his life in Protestant Béarn, certainly not without the royal protection of that court. Jeanne, Queen of Navarre, mother of Henry, was the inspired and fanatical leader of the Protestants. It is hard to imagine a more unlikely situation than Jeanne allowing her baby to be prophesied for by an old Catholic sorcerer, for as such she would certainly have regarded him. So it is difficult to see how this story could be true. Nostradamus made many prophecies about Henry of Navarre, for which he did not need to see him and probably never did.

The first prophecy made for the house of Navarre by Nostradamus concerned the father of Henry and appeared in the first edition of the *Centuries*. Since he called by name King Antoine, whom for some reason he seems to have admired, the veiled reference to lead might easily mean the next king of Navarre, Antoine's successor, Henry, whom Nostradamus did not like and never failed to say as much. This verse further gives the lie to the story of the examination of Henry by the prophet. Probably neither of the child's parents would have wanted it. Antoine was a weak man with the turn-coat propensities of his family. He was by turns Protestant and Catholic, but he was Catholic when he died, killed at the siege of Rouen in 1562.

IV—38

The Lice will gnaw great Antoine for his least sordid
  deed
Even unto the last day of his life.
He who shall covet lead shall, after his election, use
  his lead as a plumb for depths to which he shall be
  plunged.

The Lice are of course the Protestants who assailed Antoine and killed him at Rouen. The last lines are a play on words. Lead is the base metal of the alchemists in contrast to gold, the metal of spiritual purity. Henry, the son of Antoine, shall not value gold, but will covet the baser things, and these will be the measure of the man and his ultimate tragedy of assassination.

In view of the many prophecies in circulation that the heir of Navarre would supplant the Valois, these unflattering comments would have been well understood. It gains in aptness from the fact that both Henry and the prophet, having the same birthday, came under the sign and planet ruling lead. But Nostradamus may have considered that in his own case spiritual alchemy had done its work of transmutation.

The prophet's time was growing short now. The town of Salon, holding many of the religion, had greatly changed, and so had, in consequence, its affection and respect for the prophet. In place of that had come gradually a sullen fear of the strange old man and his secret and sorcerous works. The town avoided him, all but a few close, loyal friends like de Condoulet. He lived in great retirement, receiving distinguished visitors from outside, who were still as numerous as ever, and working on the last group of his *Centuries*. His strength has greatly failed but he knows to the day how much time he has left.

In 1564–1566, the Queen-mother thought it might be a good and pacific idea if between wars she and Charles made a publicity tour through the whole realm, and let the people see and know their King. Great pomp and ceremony characterized the trip. It was the seventh year since the death of Henry II. Catherine adopted for the trip richer, more elaborate dress, in keeping with the occasion which might be said to mark the end of her official mourning.

When the royal progress brought the King and the Queen-mother to Salon, the town turned out in full array for them. The Mayor and the town fathers were the spearhead of the welcoming, enthusiastic crowd. Among the magistrates stood Nostradamus. It is said that the young King brusquely ignored the demonstration, cutting the Latin oratory short with,

"I have come to see Nostradamus."

The little boy whom the prophet had seen at Blois was growing up into a tall youth whose fierce blue eyes and restless, curt manner were an indication of the changes taking place in him. Catherine, who was stout when Nostradamus had visited the court, was now frankly fat. She might have posed for one of the famous Seine frogs which the old Merovingian kings took for their device. What secret interview took place at this second meeting with royalty was not recounted. Yet surely there was a private meeting, with questions asked and talk of the fulfilled forecasts of the last eight years. The Venetian ambassador, who seems to have wielded an active, if not always accurate pen, was not there to chronicle the rumors, otherwise we might have had a story.

Charles IX confirmed at this time the appointment of Physician-in-Ordinary and Councilor which his father had bestowed on the prophet. Some writers say that it was not Henry, but Charles who first gave it. Others speak of the prophet holding his appointment under three kings, Henry II, Francis II and Charles IX. In view of the facts this seems the more likely assumption.

On his way back to Paris Charles again summoned Nostradamus. On this occasion he gave him a purse of two hundred gold écus. Whether in the past years Nostradamus had carried out secret missions for the crown is not known. There would hardly have been a record of it if it had been so. However, the King, on the occasion of this second meeting, did send the prophet on some kind of embassy which the prophet mentions, together with the King's gift, in his fare-well quatrain. It must have been an important, delicate matter which Catherine felt no one else could so well undertake. Otherwise she would scarcely have chosen a man who was crippled with his malady and near death. This was the last time, though it may not have been the first, in which he served the Queen in other than his prophetic capacity.

Nostradamus knew exactly how long he had left to live. After his passing, there was found written in his own hand in his copy of the Ephemeris of Jean Stadius, beside the last date in June, *"Hic prope mors est."* "Here my death draws near." It was on that day that he sent for the notary and dictated his will.

"June 30th, in the year 1566, Maître Michel Nostradamus, doctor of medicine, astrophile, Physician-in-Ordinary and councilor to the king, bequeaths to his daughter Magdeleine 600 écus of gold, and to his other daughters, Anne and Diane, 500 écus of gold. To his dear wife, Anne Ponsart, 400 écus of gold, together with certain household furniture. I bequeath, moreover, all my books to that one of my sons who improves himself or profits most from study, together with all letters, notes and manuscripts found in the dwelling of the testator, who has not at all desired that an inventory should be taken, but that his effects should be gathered and closed up in one of the rooms of the house until the one who should have them will be of age to receive them."

There follow a few generous bequests to churchly orders, and six hundred écus in gold to be distributed among the poor. Nostradamus was himself a member of the third order of the *Cordeliers,* a lay rank in which obligations are assumed rather than vows taken.

"The aforesaid testator has furthermore declared that he possesses in currency the sum of 3444 écus in gold and 10 sols, which he declares in the pieces hereinafter specified." Follows a picturesque enumeration of coinage to charm the heart of a numismatist. There were so many of rose nobles, of double ducats and imperials, 1 gold écu of King Louis, 1 gold medal, florins of Germany and pieces called Portuguese.

Nostradamus has without any doubt planted clues to the dates of his undated quatrains. They are all over the place, and if one were versed in the wiles of the *rhétoriqueurs* and the ancient number cycles, they might perhaps be decoded. The "seven men with seven mops" have been trying, with so far no results. This author has a mop too, but it has not as yet done its perfect work. Nor is there space in this book for speculative findings. No one else has noted, however, that there may be a major clue in the numbers of coins mentioned in the will, but this author believes it is there. Nostradamus, in his letter to his son, prefacing the first edition of the prophecies, mentions the year 3797. This is undoubtedly a cryptic, symbolic date rather than an actual one. If the number of verses in the first edition, 353, is subtracted from the year figure, the difference is 3444, the total number of gold écus in the will. If 353 is added to the date of publication of the first edition, 1555, the sum is 1908, *the year of birth of the present Duke de Guise, whose name is Henry, and who, as pretender to the throne of France, may become the Henry V of Nostradamus'* prophecy. These number oddities may be only co-incidental, but there are a great many curious such correspondencies.

Presage 141

On my return from an embassy, with a gift from the King, my affairs are in order,
Nothing more will happen, I shall have gone to God,
Near to my parents. Friends and brothers of my blood
Will find me dead beside my bed and bench.

On the morning of July 2nd, O. S., they found him at his bench bent in the last study that comes to all. The Ephemeris of Jean Stadius, near at hand, showed for that day the Sun, symbol of man's life, just departed from its conjunction with Saturn, the Grim Reaper, and making an aspect with Neptune, the strange planet of timeless things, still undiscovered in that day. Under the mysterious influence of this star the prophet's gift had been developed, under its guidance this titan of two worlds entered his new home in the farther country of Time, whose boundaries between the seen and unseen lands he had so often crossed.

In the church of the Cordeliers at Salon the prophet was "honorably inhumed" in the tomb which he had long ago prepared for himself, upright in the massive church wall where he still reposes. Above the tomb is the bust which César made of his father from memory. "Quietam posteri ne invidete." "Let those who come after disturb not my peace," was the inscription which Nostradamus caused to be cut in the stone. To these words his wife added her further tribute in a Latin epitaph, inscribed on the tomb, which translated reads:

Here rest the bones of the most illustrious

MICHEL NOSTRADAMUS

alone in the judgment of mortals worthy to record the future events of the entire world under the influence of the stars.

He lived 62 years, 6 months, and 17 days.

He died at Salon in the year 1566. Let not posterity disturb his peace. Anne Ponsart Jumelle wishes her husband true felicity.

So ends all that we know of the Seer of the *Centuries*. At the close of the third edition of his prophecies, he wrote the word *Fin*. More fitting words for ending the final chapter of the life story of this timeless traveler and man of tomorrow are

SANS FIN

PART TWO

Tel fut Ronſard, autheur de cét ouurage,
Tel fut ſon œil, ſa bouche & ſon viſage,
Portrait au vif de deux crayons diuers:
Icy le Corps & l'Eſprit en ſes vers.

Ronsard, who celebrated the arrival of Nostradamus at court
with verses in his honor.

CHAPTER ONE

The Cycle of Valois-Navarre

THE SEVEN CHILDREN OF THE KING

Presage 40

A succession of fatalities will decimate the house of
seven,
Hail, tempests, pestilent misfortune and furies.
A ruler of the Orient will put all the Occident in flight
And subdue those who were once his conquerors.

IV—60

Seven children shall he leave behind him in his house,
The Third Estate will eventually murder one,
Two (people) will be pierced by the sword of one of
the children,
Genoa and Florence will contribute to the disorder.

VI—14

The seven branches will be reduced to three,
Death will surprise more than one of the elder born,

293

The two males will be corrupted to the point of fratri-
cide,
Conspirators will die in their sleep.

ONE OF THE CHILDREN, Francis II, was now gone.
The Biblical scourges were unleashing their furies in
the religious wars between the Catholics and Protestants, which had begun in 1561, while Nostradamus
still lived. Solyman the Great was on the throne of
Turkey, his pirates were sweeping the length of the
Mediterranean, harrying Venice, preying on the commerce of all Europe. Hatred and rivalry were between
Charles IX and his brother, the Duke d'Anjou, Catherine's favorite child.

These three quatrains are like the opening bars of
a tragic symphony, giving the *leit-motif* which the
music will interweave with other patterns, amplifying
and developing the theme. Covering the reign of
Charles IX were the four religious wars which spread
death and ruin over the country. The Protestants
numbered more than a quarter of the population of
France, a large number to do away with or even crush,
yet such was the only idea that presented itself to the
Catholics.

VIII—85

Between Bayonne and Saint Jean de Luz
The promontory of Mars will rise,

The effort of the Nymph of the North will remove the
light,
Then it will be snuffed out at the bedside without help.

In 1565 Catherine and Charles IX met the Duke of
Alva at Bayonne to consult about means of quenching
the fire of the Protestant menace. The time was set for
the massacre which was later postponed until Saint
Bartholomew's because the Protestants got wind of it.
The Nymph of the North is Queen Elizabeth, whose
encouragement and active support were invaluable to
the Protestants. The prophet sees the unity of faith
lost to France, snuffed out never to return, largely by
virtue of this support. Elizabeth also removed the light
of the Duke d'Anjou's hope to marry her, which died
aborning.

In 1558, two years after the prophet's death, a new
and final edition of the *Prophecies* was published at
Lyons by Rigaud. The arrangement of the *Centuries*
was in two parts. The first comprised all of the two
previous editions together with the letter to César. The
second half consisted of three new Centuries of a hundred verses each, preceded by a letter of dedication to
Henry, King of France Second. The edition was
brought out under the direction and supervision of
Brother Jean Vallier of the monastery of the Mineurs
Conventuals, and with the permission of his ecclesiastical superiors. It is evident that this must have been
in accordance with a pre-arranged plan made during
the prophet's lifetime. It also shows the support and

approval which the Church accorded to his prophetic powers.· In this time of high excitement, war and death, the publication of fresh prophecies was an event of prime importance in court circles. So many forecasts had already been fulfilled that, as Nostradamus had predicted, he was even more famous in death than he had been in life.

In this same year occurred another event of importance to the court, and saddening to all France. This was the death of the Princess Elizabeth, then Queen of Spain. Of her marriage to Philip, Nostradamus had this to say:

S—49

Venus, Sun, Jupiter and Mercury
Shall augment events of the class coming under their
    influence,
A grand alliance will take place in France,
And the blood-sucker of the Midi himself,
The flame of war being extinguished by this extreme
    remedy,
Will plant the Olive branch in solid ground.

Jupiter and Sun, stars of pomp and royalty, had been in friendly aspect during the splendid, fatal tourney which celebrated the match. Philip, from the time he became King of Sicily, was called by the French the "Blood-Sucker of the Midi." The prophet, remembering the sweet child he had seen at Blois, called the marriage an "extreme remedy," but he saw that the sacrifice was justified for France. The long peace was as foretold. It was only broken after the death of Henry III, when the rise of Navarre, allied with the Nymph of the North, roused Spanish fears.

CRESCENT AND CROSS

While the turmoil of civil war was obsessing France, momentous happenings in the Mediterranean were fulfilling more of the prophet's visions, which were a continuation of what Villiers de L'Isle Adam, the soldier of Rhodes, had told him so many years before.

II—5

When sword and doctrine are shut up within the fish
There shall go forth one who will wreak worse than war,
His fleet will be well rowed across the sea,
Appearing off the coast of Italy.

IX—61

The pillage made along the seacoast
Will be provoked and induced in the new city,
(Geneva)
Certain Christian Knights of Malta, through the act of Messina,
Will be poorly rewarded when they are squeezed in the straits.

In 1565 the Turks boldly attacked Malta, killing
eight thousand of the Knights and possessing themselves of half the island. The island had, you will remember, been given to the Knights of Rhodes, under
Nostradamus' patient, the Knight Commander de
L'Isle Adam, by Spain, as a reward for their valor at
Rhodes. Therefore, says Nostradamus, it is poor guer-
don for Philip II of Spain and King of Sicily (the
deed of Messina, Sicily) to leave them to be squeezed
in the straits without sending any help in their dire
extremity. John Calvin made Geneva his headquarters. The prophet refers to the "New City," as it was
called, in this connection, as contributing to the war.

II—4

From Monaco to Sicily
The whole shore dwells in desolation,
There will not be a town, city or village
Which has not been the prey of Barbarian theft and
    pillage.

IV—39

The Rhodians will demand help
Through the neglect with which their heirs have
    abandoned them,
The Arabian Empire will turn on its course
When the Western Nations have redressed the Chris-
    tian cause.

Lepanto IX—30

From the port of Erzeroum and the country of Saint
Nicholas (Turkey)
There is Peril to Frenchmen in the Gulf of Fanati-
cism,
From the streets of Constantinople will go up cries and
appeals to the house of Capet.
Help will go out from Cadiz and the forces of great
Philip.

IX—43

The neighboring descendants of the Crusaders
Will be ambushed by the Mussulmans,
But these will be beaten on all sides by the forces of
the barque of the Papacy,
They will be promptly assailed by the galleys filled
with the picked men of ten nations.

The Holy Father shall heed the cry of Sicily,
All preparations will go forward from the Gulf of
Trieste
Extending down to Sicily,
Comprising many galleys. Flee, flee from the horrible
scourge.

III—31

From the lands of Media, Arabia, and Armenia
Two great leaders shall thrice assemble expeditions.
Near the shores of Asia Minor the house
Of Sulyman the Great will meet defeat.

III—64

The Shah of Persia will replenish his great commercial
navy
When the trireme galleys go against the Mohamme-
dans,
Because of Parthia and Media and the pillage of the
Cyclades,
And bring a long peace to the port of Smyrna.

In 1571 the Battle of Lepanto turned back and
seriously crippled Turkish sea power. In that year the
island of Cyprus, "The neighboring descendants of
the Crusaders will be ambushed," was seized by Turkey
with a massacre so complete and dreadful that at last
Christian Europe was galvanized into action. Indi-
vidual soldiers went from France to take part in the
expedition, as did soldiers from all over Europe and
England. But France as a nation remained aloof. Philip
of Spain and the Pope were the organizers of the
naval expedition which did include ten governments,
counting the states of Italy. "The picked men" were
the flower of Europe's chivalry. Great princes in person led the boarding parties that took the Moslem
ships. Cervantes was among the heroes at the battle.
The colorful Don John of Austria was the military
commander of the allied fleet.

The losses on both sides were very heavy, but the
Christians administered a smashing defeat from which
Turkey never recovered. Lepanto is one of the most

important naval engagements in history. Its spirit was that of the ancient Crusaders. Its "trireme galleys," little changed from the days when Rome defeated Carthage, saw their last use in a major engagement at Lepanto. These romantic ships of war were shortly discarded for boats of different build adapted to hold the new artillery, and to a complete change in the methods of sea war.

It was some years later, but in direct consequence of Lepanto, that the Shah of Persia seized important Turkish provinces, and also one of the great ports on the Persian Gulf, which enabled him to enrich himself by expansion of his maritime commerce.

THE MASSACRE OF SAINT BARTHOLOMEW

Meanwhile the civil wars of religion went on interminably in France. Leaders on both sides were killed. The ability and faith of Admiral Coligny, after the Prince of Condé died, made him the greatest leader and military commander whom the Protestants had.

VI—75

The master pilot commissioned by the king
Will leave the fleet to assume a higher post,
Seven years later he will be in opposition to his king
At a time when Venice is dreading the coming of
    Barbarian armies.

V—83

Those whose enterprise is the ruin of France
Of the matchless, powerful and invincible realm of
   France
Will carry on with deceit. Three nights a watch will
   be kept
On their leader as he sits at his table reading the Bible.

Presage III

The great bronze bell that rings in the succession of
   the hours
Will sound full volley at the Tyrant's death,
Tears, groans and cries, but no bread from revolution's
   icy waters,
Carolus Victor Sanctus abandons *peace* for the sword.

VIII—85

A hot wind, deliberations going on, tears, hesitations,
Assault by night on one unarmed in bed,
A grand disaster of oppression,
The wedding-song converted into tears and lamen-
   tations.

III—30

He who by sword and prowess on the field of battle
Had carried the prize from one of greater rank than he,

In his bed at night will be stabbed to death, by six,
Stripped, without his armor, taken by surprise.

IV—47

When the savage King shall have tried his hand
Bloody with the work of fire, sword and arquebus
The people will be completely terrified
To see the greatest in the land strung up by neck and
heels.

Sixain 52

The great City which has but half enough bread to eat
(Paris)
Will have the further blow of Saint Bartholomew
Engraved upon the depths of its soul.
Nîmes, Rochelle, Geneva, and Montpellier,
Castres and Lyons, when Mars enters Aries
These cities will have civil war, and all because of a
government.

Admiral Coligny resigned his commission as commander-in-chief of the French navy seven years after he had received it, in order to head the Protestant party. He came within an ace of carrying off "the prize" of power by his ascendancy over Charles IX. For a time, he and his party, as well as his enemies, thought that he had. His domination was so great that Catherine dared delay no longer in putting into execution the plans made seven years previously with the

Duke of Alva, at Bayonne. And the first death must be Coligny's. An assassin was sent, Maurevert, to kill the Admiral. Guizot says he watched Coligny's house for three days before the Admiral went out, and the killer got his chance. Nostradamus' vivid picture of the old man reading his Bible under the eye of the murderer is a perfect bit. Coligny was only wounded, so that the general mass murder was ordered at once. This occurred on the twenty-fourth of August, 1572. Six days earlier, Marguerite of Valois had married Henry of Navarre, and the court was still celebrating the wedding. The feverish deliberations and last minute conferences which preceded the ringing of the tocsin happened precisely as Nostradamus describes. Coligny was murdered at night, unarmed, by the Duke de Guise, his servant, Besme, and three or four of the Swiss mercenaries. The towns mentioned were those in which Protestants were strong, particularly New La Rochelle.

The prophet had no sympathy for Coligny, the spearhead of the faction he believed undermining France. The anointed King acted within his rights to kill the "Traitor." But he deplored that the savagery of that same King should massacre his people, "the slaughtered innocents" of the quatrain quoted earlier. Charles IX was said to have stood at the palace window, arquebus in hand, and shot down Protestants until exhausted.

Events of importance followed two years later, in 1574.

VII—35

The Important Fish will weep and wail
Because he has been elected. They will be deceived in
the times,
Their political guide will not be desirous of making
his home with them.
He will be killed by the people of his own language.

The Fish was the Duke d'Anjou. The Pope, in the
Centuries, is often called the Fisherman. France, politically and religiously, was always the best-loved fish
of the papacy. Henry of Anjou was heir presumptive
to the throne. The quarrel between himself and
Charles had become so acute that neither was safe
from the other. Henry was offered the crown of Poland, which he accepted to get out of France. After
sophisticated Paris, he loathed living in Poland. The
Poles quite misjudged the character of the times in
France when they invited Henry. He was only there
three months. Charles IX, racked with remorse and
illness, died, soothed at the last only by the old Protestant nurse whom the prophet had seen with the little
boy in the gardens of Blois. Henry left Poland at once
to become Henry III of France, until such time as one
of his own people would murder him.

DUEL A OUTRANCE

Henry III was weak, vicious, perverted; but like
all the Valois he had charm. The psychopathic jeal-

ousy and hatred which he had felt for his brother, Charles IX, now that Charles was dead, he projected upon the strong, brilliant Henry, Duke de Guise, son of the warrior who took Calais. Courtly, eloquent, magnetic, Guise was the idol of Paris. He was twice wounded in action, once in the arm, and again in the leg and head. A bullet clipped his ear and scarred his cheek which gave him his nickname, Le Balafré, in spite of which he was considered very handsome. One of the cardinals at court remarked of the Guises, father and son, that they made other people seem common by comparison.

Guise as the descendant of Charlemagne, and having also the royal blood of the Capet line, was one of the two royal brothers whom Nostradamus describes in the following accurate picture of their deadly duel, which was half personal hatred, half desire for power. Guise, like the Bourbons, wanted the throne. As the leader of the Catholic faction, he was in consequence close to the palace, and had in a fashion the inside track. He was at this time far more powerful than the coming King, Henry of Navarre. Guise had every confidence that he would win the crown. The weak King, Catherine supporting her son with her craft, and the Duke de Guise are the actors in this tragedy.

IV—38

While the Duke, the King and the Queen are in occupation of power

Captives will be taken in Byzantium and Samothrace,
Before the showdown (between the Duke and King)
  one shall consume the other,
Then the sword will turn against the survivor and its
  track will be made in blood.

IV—62

Two royal brothers will wage war so powerfully
Against each other that it will be a mortal combat,
Each in turn will occupy the seats of power,
The great quarrel will involve both power and life.

II—54

The insensate ire of furious combat
Will place a gleaming sword between two brothers
  who were once companions at the same table,
He who is the quarry will be struck to his death,
In the fierce duel that will injure all France.

VIII—45

His hand in a sling and his leg bandaged,
Junior of Calais and a long line of ancestors (Guise),
He will avert his death through a warning of ambush,
His blood will be shed in a palace after Communion.

X—56

King against King and Duke against Prince,
Hatred between them and horrible dissension,

Rage and fury will sweep the whole country,
In France there will be great war and terrible changes.

III—51

Paris conspires to commit a great murder,
Blois will carry it into full effect,
The citizens of Orleans will wish to depose him (the
   King),
Angers, Troyes, and Langres will commit an offense.

II—57

Before the final conflict and the fall of the wall
A Great Personage (Guise) will be done to death, his
   end will be sudden and lamented,
The policy of the Church will be imperfect. The
   greater part of the nation shall welter,
Hard by the river blood will stain the earth.

VII—2

Many will come and will talk about peace
Between the Monarques and their very puissant Lords,
But it will not come about in the near future
Because none of them will swear fealty to any of the
   others.

VIII—3

Alas what fury! Alas what pity
For what will happen between so many of the nation,

Never will one have seen such good will
Except among diligently coursing wolves.

VIII—4

Much of the nation will wish for negotiation
Between the great Lords who will be responsible for
   the war,
But no one will be willing to listen to anything,
Alas! If only God would send peace to the earth.

The religious wars were more than a fight between
Catholic and Protestant. They were a three-cornered
fight for power between Catherine de' Mcdici, backing
successively her sons, and the great competing houses
of Guise-Lorraine and Bourbon-Navarre. None of the
three would yield to the others; it had to be, as it was,
a duel to the death.

Note how the Oriental motif is sustained. Lepanto
had defeated Turkey, but not crushed her, and France
had not fulfilled her obligation then. No Turkish
armies threaten, but the Turk still takes his captives
as pirates' prey, while Christian France quarrels internally. The Duke de Guise organized the Catholic
League to wrest the power from the King. Spain supported this effort, the King was losing. Assassination
was the answer. The King had gone to Blois. The
Duke, as Lieutenant-General of France and High
Steward of the Royal Household, was also there, both
being present for the meeting of the States-General.

So one has the strange picture of these two deadly
enemies and rivals under the same roof and dining at
the same table. The King summoned the Duke for a
private conference. As the Duke raised the tapestry to
enter the room, known as the old closet, he was stabbed
five times by the King's men. The King and the Duke
had taken communion together shortly before the
murder.

When the Duke was dead the King exclaimed,
"Now I am sole King. The King of Paris is dead!"
Catherine said, "You have done the cutting, now we
must sew it well." But there was little time for her
sewing. Her own death, in bed, occurred thirteen days
after the murder of the Duke de Guise. France was
outraged at the murder. Orleans turned against the
King. The other towns mentioned by the prophet
promptly went over to the Protestants, for which Nostradamus blames them. Sixtus V, whom, as we have
seen, the prophet did not admire, was subservient to
Spain, and in many ways vacillating or afraid to adopt
a strong policy. The Cardinal de Guise, brother ("Two
shall be killed by one of the children") of Le Balafré,
was murdered by Henry a few days after the Duke.
The third Guise brother, the Duke de Mayenne, then
took over the leadership of the Catholic League.

I—85

The King shall be troubled by the response of the
    nation,

Ambassadors will scorn their lives in fulfilling their missions,
The Great Personage will act for both his brothers
Slain by hatred and malice.

The Great Personage is the Duke de Mayenne.

V—72

For the satisfaction of passing an edict that caters to self-indulgence
Poison will be mingled with holy faith,
Venus in her course will show such power
As will shadow the unalloyed gold of the Sun.

The edict of Poictiers, passed by Henry III in 1577, among other things permitted Protestant ministers to marry. Nostradamus saw this as a threat to Catholicism. It was a temptation away from the ascetic standards of the priesthood, into the freer customs of the Protestant ministry. Venus, here a metaphor for self-indulgence, clouds the Sun of the monarchy.

HENRY OF NAVARRE

V—1

Before the onset of the ruin of France
Two shall negotiate within a palace,
A death stroke to the heart, someone mounts a courser,
The Great Personage will be buried without publicity.

II—15

A short while before the King is killed
We shall see Castor and Pollux in the same ship, there
will be a comet visible near that time,
The public taxes will have been emptied over land and
sea,
Throughout the cities of Italy the land (of France)
will be interdict.

The two royal brothers, Henry III and Henry of Navarre, sinking their religious differences and agreeing
on a common plan, climb into the same ship of state
which is also the barque of religion in a country having a state religion. The condition of the treasury, and
the reaction of Italy to the combination of the two
rulers were as the prophet indicates.

IV—95

Scant space the two shall hold the reign,
But the war will last three years and seven months.
The two vestals will be in rebellion against France,
but from opposite sides.
The victor, from the cadet branch, will plant his foot
on Armoric soil (Brittany).

The great King will be taken by a Young Man
Not far from Easter, when there will be confusion and
knife thrust,

The perpetration of the deed is at the time when there
are captives, and powder in the tower,
This murder follows the death of three brothers who
injured themselves.

V—67

While the leader of Perouse (Sixtus V) is afraid to
take off his shirt
For fear of being totally despoiled and left bare
The last of the seven will be taken, a shock to court
circles,
Father and son both struck in the neck.

Presage 58

When the King—King is no more, destroyed by the
Gentle One,
The year will be feverish, stirred with sedition,
Let him who holds hold fast. Not for the nobles (Guise
faction) is Lutetia,
He will pass (outlast) the period of his cavillers.

After the furor over the murder of the two Guises,
Henry III, twice King, once of Poland, once of France,
desperately in need of backing, with the Duke de
Mayenne, the third and sole surviving Guise brother,
in virtual control of Paris, sought out Henry of Navarre and made an alliance with him. But, "scant

space"—only a few months later the King was assassinated by Jacques Clément, believed to be the agent of the Third Estate. "The Third Estate shall murder one." Clément, the name meaning clement or gentle, is exactly indicated by the prophet as the murderer. The alliance with Navarre was at Easter, the murder —"not long after."

Paris, in the hands of the Duke de Mayenne, preparing its defenses and arresting Protestants and royalists, there were "captives and powder." Pope Sixtus, "the leader of Perouse," after the papacy having been despoiled of England by Henry VIII, was terrified lest it happen now with France. Henry II had been struck on his armored neck-piece by Montgomery's lance. Henry III was stabbed in "the little gut," or neck of the colon. "Father and son both struck in the neck." Henry of Navarre, surviving member of the alliance, is advised to hang on, for not to the nobles under the Duke de Mayenne shall fall Lutetia, Paris. Henry will survive his opponents.

The Seven Children of the King are now dead, all but Marguerite, the wife of Henry of Navarre, who had no children. Under the Salic law she cannot rule, and in time Navarre will divorce her.

S—26

There will be two brothers, each the leader of an
    ecclesiastical faction,
One of them will take France at sword's point.

There will be another *coup* in six hundred and six
If he is not then afflicted with grave illness.
His armes and power will flourish to six hundred and
ten,
His life expectation will hardly go beyond that time.

II—95

Places long peopled will become uninhabitable,
Throughout the country there will be a great division,
Factions of government will be in the hands of men
incapable of wisdom,
Between the brothers there will be dissension and death.

X—26

The successor to the kingdom shall avenge his brother-
in-law,
He will occupy the realm under the pretense of ven-
geance,
After the obstacle to his power is cut down, he will
show great anger over the death of his own blood,
And Brittany will long be held by France.

VII—24

The buried shall go out from the tomb
To bind with his chains the power of the bridge (of
Seine).
Poisoned with the eggs of the great Barbel
The Leader of Lorraine will be defeated by the Lord
Warden of the Marches.

IX—50

Vendôme the deceitful shall soon come into his high
power
Putting those of Lorraine somewhat in the background.
The pale Cardinal will be the male of the interregnum,
The young man will be apprehensive, dreading for-
eign influence.

IX—41

The great Henry will seize Avignon,
From Rome the letters will be bitter-sweet,
A letter will be dispatched to an accredited agent to go
to Chavigny at Chinon,
Carpentras will be taken by the dark Duke, who wears
the Cardinal's panache.

Presage 22

Cut off by sea, trenches are dug around the occupied
city,
The Great Personage and the newly chosen King are
weakened,
Follow the Fleur de Lis, enter the camp of broken faith.
The white plume will have to put forth a strong effort.

V—18

The unfortunate contender in the duel (the Cardinal)
will die,

His victor will celebrate with a hecatomb.
He will draw up an Edict of freedom based on early
law,
The wall will fall to the Prince on the seventh day.

I—18

The house of Lorraine will give place to Vendôme,
The high will be put low, and the low exalted to high
places,
The son of Amon will be chosen at Rome
And the two great personages will be defeated.

Cryptic as these verses read, they tell a perfectly
straight story. Two brothers in royalty, Navarre and
Mayenne, lead the Protestant and Catholic factions.
The winner of the war, Navarre, will not live beyond
1610. He was assassinated then. A *coup* or an illness
will mark his year in 1606. He nearly died of illness
in 1608, but Guizot speaks of it as if it were of long
standing, and it may have begun when the prophet
said.

Henry of Navarre did claim the crown to avenge
Henry III, his brother-in-law. He seized Brittany,
previously tributary, but autonomous under France.
It had belonged to Queen Claude, grandmother of
Henry III. Nostradamus said in a verse, previously
given, "the cadet branch," the Bourbon, "will plant
its foot on Armoric soil." Armorica was the old name
of Brittany. Thereafter Brittany remained as a province of the crown.

"The buried" is Coligny who, through his Protestant successor, Henry of Navarre, will enchain the power of Paris. The Barbel is a fish equipped with prongs to spear its prey. The fish, in the *Centuries*, is always a religious symbol. Here, the Barbel, the vicious fish of the false religion, Protestantism, will poison with the eggs it lays, hopes of the house of the Catholic faction under Guise-Lorraine, so that it is defeated by Navarre. The latter is Lord Warden of the Marches because he comes from the border kingdom of Navarre, a bulwark against Spanish aggression.

But when Henry claimed the throne, the Duke de Mayenne put up a counter-claimant who was none other than Navarre's uncle, the old Cardinal de Bourbon, who had come over to his side. It was in this Cardinal's house that the prophet had lodged while in Paris. But nothing can stop Vendôme (one of the family names of Navarre) although he is worried and doesn't know what Spain is going to do about all this. His first concern was to see that his uncle, whom he had under guard, didn't escape and get himself crowned. The Cardinal was at Chinon in the care of Sieur Chavigny, who was also old, like the Cardinal, and nearly blind. Henry sent a courier with a letter to the governor of Saumur "bidding him at any price" to get the Cardinal away from Chinon and under proper guard, which was done. But the poor old man, "the contender in the duel," died, as the prophet said, not long after.

The battle of Arques, 1589, the first of Navarre's

two great victories, was as the prophet indicates it. Mayenne was between Henry and the sea, blocking help. Henry had a complete line of trenches dug surrounding the castle and town of Arques. Nor does Nostradamus forget to mention the white plume of Navarre, so famous in song and story. Victory, he tells us, will crown Navarre in the battle, that is what he means by "follow the *Fleur de Lis.*" It is the beginning of the taking over by the house of Bourbon—to the prophet a faithless line—the royal lily emblem of Capet.

Meanwhile the letters from Sixtus were very bittersweet. He admired Navarre, but he didn't want a Protestant ruling France. Henry of Navarre at once began to put into practice his ideas of toleration which later were shaped into the Edict of Nantes. "The son of Amon," the religious turncoat and heretic, Navarre, of course, was chosen at Rome, after his purely political conversion to Catholicism. Thus were the two great personages, Mayenne and the Cardinal, defeated.

The Cardinal is dead, but we are not yet finished with the Duke de Mayenne. (And, reader, if the history of France seems unduly involved, don't shoot the prophet and the author. Like the pianist, we are doing our best.)

IX—57

A King will replace the line of Dreux (the northern branch)

And will seek a law that will change the situation
from Anathema,
While the heaven is thundering with preparations for
war
The new brood will destroy themselves and the King
too.

X—45

The unfulfillment of the promise made at Cambray,
The shadow over the reign of the faithless Navarre
Will make life very precarious (until)
Accepted as King by Orleans he will find a wall to
lean on.

Presage—76

Before the legate of the earth and sea
The head of the Capetian line will accommodate him-
self to all that is required,
Mayenne will listen in silence
And will, of his own advice, grant as little as he can.

IX—39

In Arbrisselle, Vezame and Crevari,
He shall set out at night in the hope of capturing
Savona,
The lively Gascon, with de Givry and La Charry,
Will penetrate the old wall and grab the new palace.

VII—32

Hatred will produce uncommon stratagems,
Rebellion will sow death throughout the country,
When the foreigner returns from his trip
The people will exalt the entry of the Protestant.

Navarre and his rule were under the ban of the Church, they were anathema until his conversion. The prophet in this verse looks forward to Henry's end when fanatical hatred destroys him, and with his passing the new brood, the Protestants, gradually lose their political power, shorn of royal protection. It was, however, hardly true that they were responsible for their own destruction.

Henry had early renounced Protestantism at Chambray, but he hesitated to take the final steps against the feeling of his own party. Only after he was bulwarked by the support of Orleans, which came over to him, did he feel strong enough to take this step, which he did in 1593. He then accommodated himself to the requirements of the Pope, "the legate of the earth and sea."

After his conversion, Henry took Paris the following year. On the 14th of March the civic powers of Paris, having decided to admit him, forbade meetings of the Mayenne faction. Seven days later, as stated by the prophet in a quatrain given earlier, Navarre entered Paris. The reference to the new palace, when Navarre entered the old walls of Paris, is to the Tuileries, which Catherine de' Medici had begun but which was still not entirely finished. De Givry and La Charry are names of two of Navarre's enthusiastic supporters. The three towns mentioned in the same verse were in the Sardinian states with which Henry had a certain amount of fighting and difficulty.

The war continued for a time longer but eventually Mayenne yielded and made the best terms for himself that he could, and became a friend and loyal subject of the King. The Duke of Parma, who led the Spanish forces assisting Mayenne, returned to Spain, and, Spanish influence removed, the people of France, the majority of them, rejoiced in the entry of the Protestant into the monarchy.

VI—70

A world leader shall be Henry the Great,
Respected and feared, he will be more loved long after
    his passing,
The heavens shall ring with his reputation and praise,
With the sole title of Victorious he will be well content.

IX—45

Never will be be without something more to ask for,
The great personage of Vendôme will obtain his em-
    pire (but),

He will spend his time away from court, he will nullify the plans of Piedmont and Picardy, and Paris will
Become like ancient Tyre.

III—88

From Barcelona by sea shall come a great fleet,
All Marseilles will tremble with terror,
Islands will be seized, help blocked by sea,
The traitors will swarm on land.

Philip's plot to seize Marseilles for Spain was in the early years of Henry's rule while he was still fighting for power and had declared war on Spain. When the design was foiled, the traitor killed and dragged in the mud of the streets, Henry exclaimed: "Now I am really King!" Such was the importance, says Guizot, of Marseilles as the queen of the Mediterranean.

The fighting in Picardy was with the Spaniards, mainly, and like that of Piedmont before he came into his full sovereignty.

I—86

The free City (Geneva) which is the slave of liberty
Will give asylum to the defeated and the dreamers.
When France changes her king the application of the
law will not be so hard on them
And (in France) for every hundred (formerly) there
will now be a thousand.

As true of modern Geneva as in the times of Henry IV. The passing of the Edict of Nantes, the great law of religious toleration, of which the prophet disapproved, permitted the return to France of "the defeated and the dreamers," who had received asylum in Geneva during the religious wars.

Sixain 6

When Biron's traitorous undertaking
Shall put a great Prince and his Lords in a difficult situation.
Lafin will know all about it, his chief will be beheaded.
Plume to the wind and letters sent, for he has a friend in Spain,
The postman will be trapped when he enters France,
The writer throws himself into the water.

Two pieces of treachery marked the reign of Henry IV. One was that of the great soldier, Marshal Biron, whom the King said that he loved like a brother. Biron sold out to Spain. He wanted, he said, to see his head on a coin before he died. If he had lived today it might have gone on a stamp; as it was, it went on the block. His agent was Lafin, who confessed to the King. The other traitor, who also wanted Spanish gold, was an obscure clerk in the diplomatic service. He was trapped through a watch set on the post-office, and when pursued by night, near the Marne, fell in the water and was drowned.

Sixain I

A new cycle begins with a new alliance,
A Lord Warden of the Marches establishes accord with
the papal barque,
A galley, uniting a king and a duke, will put out from
Florence,
Making port at Marseilles and landing a royal daugh-
ter in France
To marry the strong leader who shaved the beard of
Catherine.

V—3

The inheritor of the duchy will command advantages
Far beyond the Tuscan sea.
Florence will have a branch in France
And the Frog will be held in the bosom of papal accord.

X—54

Born into this world of a furtive concubine,
Twice raised on high through sad news,
She shall be captured by her enemies
And brought to Malines and Brussels.

Henry IV's second marriage was to Marie de' Medici,
who came by galley to Marseilles as Catherine had
done so long ago. Her father, the prophet lets us know,
did very well for himself when he married his daugh-

ter to the King of France. Marie's mother was said to be what Nostradamus called her, but not particularly furtive about it. Marie was twice regent after Henry's death. Richelieu exiled her to the country. She escaped to Brussels and died in Belgium.

III—21

The noise of armes shall long be raised to heaven,
The tree in the midst of the city falls,
There is a vermin-ridden man with a knife opposite Tyson,
Then falls the monarch Henry.

Henry IV was preparing for war when he was stabbed by Ravaillac, while on his way to the Cathedral for his second coronation. Halted by the congestion in the narrow Rue Ferroniere, he was standing, strangely enough, beneath a sign, The Crown Pierced By An Arrow. In this street of the iron-workers there was one little alley which was occupied by the makers of pokers, les tisoniers. The King was standing opposite the entrance to this, "face Tyson," when he was struck down. It is said that before he left the palace to go to the Cathedral, a tree in the courtyard, decorated in gala style according to old custom for such occasions, fell over.

The accession of Henry of Navarre (he had already been ruling for more than a decade) had established the Bourbon dynasty upon "the golden throne." It had brought to fulfillment the long struggle of the Bourbons for the rulership of France which the Constable de Bourbon had begun sixty years before. The prophet could never bring himself to admire the splendid qualities of Henry, though he admits his greatness. To him Navarre was always the faithless scion of a faithless house, whose leader in the days of his youth, the Constable, had brought treachery, plague and slaughter to Rome and to France. He knew, too, that France was not through with the changeable loyalties of the house of Bourbon. Louis de Condé, called The Great, namesake of *Bossu*, would go against his King, Louis XIII. Philippe Egalité would vote for the beheading of his own brother, Louis XVI. And Louis Philippe would abandon the flag of the *Fleur de Lis* for the Tricolor. The prophet had spoken bitterly of that; it hurt him. However, with the coming of Henry, the Bourbons were henceforward France, and to those who ruled after Henry, Nostradamus gave spiritual allegiance as he followed them in his prophetic visions.

The author regrets that space forbids the presentation of the great periods intervening between Henry IV and the contemporary scene. It is in our own time, as prophesied by Nostradamus, that the last of the Bourbons is to rule France, the man who is to be her greatest King, who is to arise and guide the nation back to glory. This King will close the cycle of both the Bourbons and the monarchy of France.

It was, however, the reign of Henry of Navarre which closed the cycle of the people Nostradamus knew, born in his lifetime. The world had greatly changed since he came into it. Still, there was always something of its familiar character left while there remained some of those born in his lifetime and acquainted with the old ways. Now that is over. The world which he describes from this time on is a world different from his experience, and known only to his prophet's vision.

It was sometime during the reign of Henry of Navarre that César Nostradamus, nephew of the prophet, and governor of Provence under Henry IV, presented to the King the fifty-eight *Sixains* and one hundred and forty-one *Presages* which were among the prophet's effects. In view of Nostradamus' devastating attacks on Henry in so many of his verses, which the King must have seen, it does not seem a too tactful present. One wonders how the King really felt about it, in spite of the records which say that he was interested and pleased. But Henry was a gay, generous, tolerant nature. He probably shrugged it off and, like the *vert galant* the Gascons still call him, sought out the prettiest woman in the room and told her about it as a jest.

CHAPTER TWO

Claude de Savoie

MORE MARS THAN NARBONNE

CLAUDE DE SAVOIE, Duke de Villars, Marshal-General of France, and the man who was "more like Mars than Narbonne," was the hero of France in the War of the Spanish Succession. That tragic struggle, which involved all Europe from 1701 to 1713, is now chiefly notable for the victories of the Duke of Marlborough, whose reputation has overshadowed that of the scarcely less brilliant Villars.

The story of the war, told by Nostradamus virtually in headlines, is extraordinary for its coverage and detail. His prophecy was superb, if his reporting was somewhat prejudiced in favor of his King.

In these verses, as in a number of others about Louis XIV, the prophet calls Louis the "Æmathion," which means a Macedonian Greek. The term is a good illustration of Nostradamus' power of condensed, laconic expression in which art he could have given lessons to Lacon of Sparta. In this one word, Æmathion, he has made an historical commentary on *Le Grand Monarque*. The Capetian kings had a real, if shadowy,

329

claim to the blood of Alexander the Great since the days when a Russian princess, descended from Philip of Macedon, Alexander's father, had married an early king of France. Alexander the Great repudiated the paternity of Philip, and called himself the son of the Sun, claiming Apollo for his father. History has repudiated the paternity of the Sun-king, Louis XIV, and his true father is unknown. Both Alexander and Louis were warriors. The conquests of the former were dissipated after he died, while Louis outlived his winnings, which went in this war.

III—92

The world will be approaching its last cycle,
Saturn will be nearing its slow re-entry (into Aries),
The empire (of Spain) will pass to a Germanic nation,
The eye of the man of Narbonne will be torn out by
    those around him.

IV—2

Because of a death, France will undertake a foreign
    expedition,
The fleet will put to sea, the army will cross the Pyre-
    nees,
Spain, in a difficult situation, will set her army in
    motion
Because royal ladies were conducted into France.

I—99

The great Monarch will associate himself with
Two rulers united to him in bonds of friendship,
Oh, how the royal household shall sigh,
What piteous conditions are around the son of Narbonne!

IX—38

The great Æmathion will hold the harbor-mouth at Blaye
Now cleared of English and Rochellese resistance,
The Gauls who wait for help near Agen
Will be fooled in their enterprise, the help will be for the man of Narbonne.

X—69

Savoy approaches, his military array stretches from Lake Geneva,
The great leaders draw up their lines of strength,
Far from the heirs, there will be great fighting around Geneva,
All the people will be involved in flight.

II—34

Livestock savage with hunger will cross rivers,
The greater part of the field will be encamped over against the Danube,
The great general will be taken prisoner (Villefroy),
While German youth are keeping watch on the Rhine.

VIII—73

The Foreign Soldier will smite the great Monarch
Unjustly, when he is already near his end,
The avaricious mother will be the cause of his activity
And plotter and realm will greatly repent of it.

VI—53

The great Celtic prelate suspected by his king
Will lay a course by night and leave the kingdom,
Arranged by the ingenious Duke acting for his British
    king,
He (the Cardinal) will pass through the towns of Bel-
    gium undiscovered.

IV—64

The armies of the Æmathion will cross the Pyrenees,
Mars of Narbonne will not be able to withstand the
    enemy,
On land and sea so great will be the enemy's advance
That the house of Capet can occupy no terrain in safety.

IV—5

At Arras, Bourges and in Germany the standards of
    the mighty will be raised,
A large number of Gascons will fight in the infantry,

Soldiers from up and down the Rhone will shed Spanish blood
Close to the mountain where Sagunto sits.

IV—14

The two royal brothers of Spain will be driven out,
The elder will be vanquished beneath the Pyrenees mountains,
The Rhone, Lake Constance and Germany will be red with blood,
Narbonne, eastern Berry and Ath will be regions soiled by the invasions.

VI—56

Fear of the army of Narbonne's enemy
Will terrify the Spaniards very greatly,
Perpignon will be emptied through the blindness of Narbonne,
Barcelona will be taken by naval attack at the point of the pike.

II—59

The French fleet, supporting the country's defense,
Will be in conflict with great Neptune and his trident soldiers,
Provence will be gnawed to the bone to sustain the horde of troops,
The general who is more like Mars than Narbonne will be attacked by the javelins and darts of the enemy.

Presage I

The Ocean and the Tyrrhenian Sea will be under the
anchor-watch
Of mighty Neptune and his trident soldiers,
But Provence will be held in safety by the army of the
great Tende,
The heroic Villars whose nature will be more like
Mars than Narbonne.

The mutation of Saturn and Jupiter in the warlike
sign Aries introduced the conflict. Spain was already
declining, and Austria was the continental rival of
France. Two Spanish princesses married two French
Kings, Louis XIII and XIV. The Spanish King, dying
without heir, willed his realm to the part-Spanish
grandson of Louis XIV. Spain was divided over this
arrangement, and the rest of Europe strenuously objected to it. So Louis marched, the others counter-
marched with a counter claimant, and the fight was
on with everybody in it, including England.

Louvet, Louis' war minister, was so jealous of Villars
that he would not give him command until a series
of disasters had made the French situation desperate.
Marshal Villefroy, commanding for the French against
Prince Eugene of Savoy and the Duke of Marlborough,
was beaten and taken prisoner. Louis started out with
two weak allies, and only a German Elector stayed
with him. Villars was given command after the dam-

age had been done; he couldn't then stand up against
Marlborough, and failed in one battle to foresee his
moves. He had his eyes snatched out metaphorically in
several ways. The fighting raged from the Danube to
the west coast of Spain, and from the lowlands to the
Midi. This war saw the first use of the technique so
familiar today, the large-scale devastation of areas affecting civilian population, and it was France that used
it. Louis was criticized by the rest of the civilized world
for doing it. "Livestock maddened by hunger"—but
the prophet wouldn't say that it was Louis' fault. Capet
could do no wrong.

"The Foreign Soldier" is the Duke of Marlborough.
Nostradamus sees him attacking Louis, then an old
man, unjustly. The avaricious mother who put him up
to it was Queen Anne's England. Marlborough was
recalled, and English feeling later turned against him.
He was criticized on the home front for the enormous
slaughter of Englishmen which marked his victories.
Villars said to Louis after Malplaquet, "If our enemies
win one more such victory they are ruined."

The Celtic prelate was the Cardinal de Bouillon, who
left France and traveled secretly across Belgium under
an escort from Marlborough.

Both candidates for the Spanish throne were in turn
driven out, but eventually Louis' grandson carried the
day, with the rival, descendant of an elder branch, out
of the picture, and the era of the Spanish Bourbons
began.

England's trident soldiers won her Gibraltar in this

war and gave her "the anchor-watch" of the Mediterranean.

In the early part of the war, the Camisards, French Protestants, revolted and expected help would come from the coalition; they awaited it near Agen, but Villars broke their revolt, and the help did not come.

Villars was more than a match for Prince Eugene, and after Marlborough had gone home, won the spectacular victory over him at Denain, which ended the war. Voltaire called Villars "*fanfaron plein d'honneur*," which is very close to "more Mars than Narbonne." Nostradamus often uses the part to denote the whole. He does this in his mention of "Provence will be safely held—" He means France, but he wanted to imply a tribute too in the recollection which Provence evokes of the earlier Claude de Savoie, his friend, whose valor was more exclusively associated with that part of France.

CHAPTER THREE

In the Twentieth Century

As THIS LAST CHAPTER IS BEING assembled with the horrid word "deadline"—Oh, anathema to writers!—ringing in the author's ears, one portion of her attention is on the radio, one on the newspaper, and the rest on the ancient quatrains, written so long ago, and yet so full of meaning for those who live in the present day. Today's news is in the prophecies of the *Centuries*. Russia and England are now fighting on the same side, while war rages in the Orient, just as Nostradamus predicted. Before this book is off the presses, more striking predictions may have seen fulfillment. And perhaps there will be verses, omitted here because their meaning was not yet clear, which will have become clear through the rapid onrush of events. It is difficult to indicate chronological sequence in events of the future, and any interpreter's confusion on this point in unavoidable. Nostradamus may have juggled order to further mask identification and meaning. Also many of the quatrains had to be omitted for lack of space. Those most pertinent to our time, and to the de-

velopment of the future, are given first consideration
here.

The final chapter of the historic cycle of the Nostradamus predictions is naturally the most exciting to
us who live in the midst of its predicted alarms and
tragic drama and can foresee, in part, some of the fear-
some days of the future. Nostradamus has given in
the course of the *Centuries* many dates, both actual
years and astronomically stated times. He has not
given, directly, the date for the emergence of France
from her yoke of bondage. But in the opinion of this
author he has given it in the number of his verses, one
of the cryptic methods which he enjoyed using for his
half-concealments. The final edition of his work contained ten Centuries which by right should have to-
taled a thousand quatrains. There were but nine hundred and forty-four. If one takes these two facts as
giving the elements of a historic date, and adds them,
the date is 1944.

This is not to be taken, however, as the date for the
crowning of a new king of France, but rather perhaps
of his coming to the fore, or raising the royal standard, together with a new attitude in France. In other
words, it is the turning point. Several verses indicate
that the stabilization of Europe, and the fullness of a
new king's power will not come until 1952–3.

The present Pretender to the French throne is
Henri, Duc de Guise. He corresponds in the facts of
his life to the description given by the prophet of the
coming king. The last king of his line, he would be the

first to bear the name Henry since the founder of the Bourbon dynasty, Henry of Navarre, and would complete the cycle of the house of Bourbon-Orleans, whose first ruler was born within the lifetime of Nostradamus.

1914 AND ITS CONSEQUENCES

A horrible war in the Occident draws near.
The year following its outbreak there will be a scourge
So powerful and terrible that young, old and livestock
    will be affected.
There will be blood and battle when Mercury, Mars
    and Jupiter are in France.

In March, 1915, the second year of World War I, these three planets were in conjunction in Pisces; the Sun, in the chart of the Third Republic, is in the ninth degree of Virgo, the opposing sign to that of the conjunction. The full Moon of that month, occurring March 1st, on the day of the second battle of Ypres, fell on nine of Virgo, exactly on the Sun of the Republic.

The new Moon of the 15th of March fell in Pisces, thus giving emphasis to the other planets in that sign which, since it is opposite Virgo, is the house of enemies of the government, and of war. It is in the precision of such details as this that the vision of Nostradamus seems the most fabulous. For vision it was. No astrologer on earth, lacking the chart of the Republic (and it was then of course unborn), could have made a forecast based upon it.

VI—81

A bridge made of small boats will be quickly built (pontoons)
To attack the great Prince of the Belgians.
There will be fighting in trenches not far from Brussels,
They (the enemy) will outstrip him, putting seven at a time to the sword.

III—18

After a considerable period of plenty (forty-four years)
The sky will touch the country around Rheims.
Oh, what bloody conflict raging around the people of this locality, draws near.
Nor fathers, nor sons, nor rulers will dare go near it.

Around Rheims, center of the two battles of the Marne, the artillery duel developed such clouds of smoke that the sky seemed to touch the land, and the horror of so many dead deterred even relatives and officials from the agony of the place. The prophet's picture is as accurate as it is harrowing.

VIII—61

Never shall the day dawn to attain the flag of rulership
Until the seats of government are returned to their
   proper places
And it will be the armed Cock (France)
Who shall bear the gift of *Der Tag.*

III—7

Fugitives, aerial warfare above the bayonets,
Sportive ravens neighboring the conflict,
The cry goes up from earth for heavenly aid and rescue
When the fighting comes close to the walls (of Paris).

III—6

A cannon shot shall enter within a closed church.
The citizens within shall be killed in their refuge.
Horses, cattle, and men shall suffer. The swelling wave
   will touch them,
Hunger and thirst will deplete them, even the weakest
   will be under armes.

In 1917 a shot from a Big Bertha killed people in a
church in Paris. The Seine was very high that year,
at times touching the walls.

VIII—48

Saturn in Cancer, Jupiter with Mars,
A university professor, wise as a Chaldean seer, under

the aegis of a vigorous young nation, with the full-
est round measure will save the country in February.
There will be the fall of Château-fort, and assault on
three fronts.
The conflict will take place near Serbia. It is a mortal
war.

Saturn was in Cancer throughout the first six months
of 1917, leaving the sign at the end of June. On the
3rd of February Woodrow Wilson broke off diplomatic relations with Germany. In June Mars and
Jupiter came to conjunction when the first American
contingent of troops sailed for France. Nothing could
be more precise than this astronomical timing of the
period from the first cheering announcement to France
of the break which meant this country was coming in,
to the sailing of the first troops of the A.E.F. to "save
the land."

Nostradamus made use of a triple anagram to characterize President Wilson, which is a triumph of in-
genuity and condensation.

III—71

The inhabitants of the isles (Britain) will be blockaded for a long time.
They will summon their vigor and might against the
enemies.
Those outside shall die, defeated by hunger.
They will experience a greater hunger than they have
ever known.

IX—100

A naval battle will be won in darkness.
The fight will be disastrous to the Occidental navies.
A new ruse will be employed, that of coloring the ships,
There will be wrath toward the vanquished, and the
victory won in a drizzle of rain.

X—2

The galleys will screen the ships of the line.
The grand fleet will draw forth the lesser one.
The ships will maneuver to encircle the opponent.
The great navy, which is vanquished, will draw off
and reassemble its scattered units.

The battle of Jutland is very well indicated in these
two verses and the device of camouflage is duly observed by the prophet.

IV—12

The larger of the countries will be routed and put to
flight.
It will hardly be pursued beyond the frontiers (of
France).
The country will be reconstructed and a region re-
gained,
Then all of the invaders will have been driven outside
of France.

Alsace-Lorraine was regained by this war.

II—82

Through hunger the wolf (Germany) will become the captive of its prey.
The assailant will be driven to great distress.
A man of high birth (the Kaiser) will arrive at his end.
The great leader will not avoid the central pressure.

X—I

The enemy, which is always the same enemy, faithless to its word,
Will not stand fast, nor keep its captives. Its people will be captives.
Taken, overwhelmed, its people dead or stripped to their shirts,
They will give all they have left to be helped.

VII—25

The whole army will be exhausted by long war.
There shall not be found money enough to pay off the troops.
Money will be devalued to the worthlessness of stamped leather.
The ancient Gaulish coinage will shrink (from full moon size) to a crescent.

An illustration in the *Jour*, for the 26th of February, 1937, showed coins of 1914 as a full moon, those for 1918 as half moon, those for 1936, a quarter crescent, and those for 1937 as a thin crescent. (*Extrait du "Jour,"* Georges Lachapelle, Les Finances de la III° République.)

VI—72

By frenzy feigning divine emotion
The wife of a great and powerful man will suffer
transgression.
The judges desiring to condemn such teachings
Will sacrifice her as a victim to an ignorant populace.

The Czarina of Russia and the influence of Rasputin.

I—14

The Slavic nation will sing songs and chants, they
will present their petitions.
Their Princes will be captured and their Lords imprisoned
At the coming into power of brainless idiots
Who will be accepted as if they were divinely inspired.

This is a clear picture of the Russian Revolution.

X—22

For being unwilling to agree to separation,
He will be recognized thereafter as unfitted and
The King of the Isles will definitely be driven out

And another will occupy the throne when he will no
longer sign himself King.

VIII—58

When the kingdom is divided and quarreling over the
brothers,
One of them will take the arms and name of Britain.
The English title (of the other) will be tardily con-
sidered.
Night overtaking him, he will leave for France.

These are the events around the abdication of Edward VIII.

*

V—49

Not from Spain but from ancient France
Shall be he who is elected to guide the tossing barque
of the Church.
He will have trust in the enemy,
Who during his reign shall become a great scourge.

In the papal elections of 1922 many thought that
the papacy would go to the Spanish cardinal, Merry
del Val. It was given instead to Monsignor Ratti, Pius
XI, who though Italian, came from what was an-
ciently Cisalpine Gaul.

V—92

After the elevation to the papacy, which will last for
seventeen years,
Five will change in the revolution of this term,
Then one will be elected from the same time
Who will not be very conformable to the Romans.

Pope Pius XI reigned seventeen years. The five gov-
ernments which underwent changes in his time were
Italy, Germany, Austria, Czechoslovakia and Spain.
Pius XII is not too "conformable" to Mussolini's ideas.

*

THE LEAGUE OF NATIONS

V—13

Near Lake Leman there will be a house of prostitution
Presided over by a foreign woman, who will seek to
betray the city.
Before she is murdered by the Germans, there will be
a great flight.
Then those from the Rhineland will begin their invasion.

The house is the League of Nations, run by foreign
policies. Nostradamus, as we have seen, in earlier
quatrains here included, did not trust the League.

X—49

The garden of the world where is the New City
(Geneva),
Situated in the corridor between two mountains,
Will be seized and plunged into the vat
And forced to drink the envenomed, sulphurous waters.

I—47

At Lake Leman the preachments will cause irritation.
Days will drag into weeks,
Then months, then years. Then they will fade away
completely
And the Judges will condemn their empty laws.

IX—92

The King will desire to enter into the New City
But his enemies will eventually drive him out.
A captive, he will be free. False things will be spoken
and perpetrated.
The King, living outside, will keep himself aloof from
his enemies.

The captive king is Haile Selassie.

II—64

The gentry of Geneva will be parched with hunger
and thirst.

Their closest hope will eventually fade away.
The imposition of the law will have the Genevese
trembling on the point of war,
But the fleet will not be able to protect itself in the
great port (Toulon).

Yes, that was the time they imposed the Italian
sanctions and the British fleet backed down.

I—100

For a long time in the sky a gray bird will be seen
Near Dole and the land of Tuscany
Holding in its beak a green branch.
Soon the great man will die and he will conclude the
war.

The reference to the dove and the olive branch of
the League of Nations seems to close with a reference
to the death of Woodrow Wilson. Perhaps the exigen-
cies of rhyme induced the prophet to mention his concluding war, after the man "will die". The meaning
is clear enough, but cart-before-horse.

II—23

The palace birds will be driven off by another bird
(German eagle)
Soon after the prince (Hitler) comes into power.
How many times that enemy (Germany) has been
driven back across the river (Rhine).

Caught outside its own country the tether of the bird
has been seized and held.

I—87

The central fire of the earth which causes temblors
Will make a trembling around the new city.
Two great boulders will for a long time make war
 (England and Germany),
Then Arethusa's fountain will be red with a new flood.

II—39

A year before Italy is in the conflict
The Germans, French and Spanish will be struggling
 for power.
The schoolhouse of the republic will fall (League of
 Nations)
It and its people stifled to death.

IV—59

Two will be besieged with burning anger.
They will quench their thirst in two level cups,
To the strong man who has had the edges of his power
 filed off, and to the old dreamer.
And to the Genevese, will be exhibited the track of the
 Aryan country.

The two besieged, or limited, by the League, are
Hitler and Mussolini quenching their thirst for power

with Czechoslovakia and Ethiopia. The strong man is
Daladier; the dreamer, Chamberlain.

*

1940

II—40

A little later, but no great interval,
By land and sea will come the great tumult.
Naval warfare on a scale greater than ever
With explosions and guns will increase the onslaught.

V—85

The Germans and their neighbors
Will be in a war for the control of the regions of the
    clouds.
The country will suffer from marine locusts and from
    gnats (hydroplanes and airplanes),
The faults of Geneva will be laid bare.

III—12

Through the tumult that reigns along the Ebro, the
    Tagus, the Tiber, and at Rome
As well as at Geneva and around the man who is like
    Aretino,
The two great headwaters and the cities of the Ga-
    ronne will be affected,

Captives, dead and injured, the human booty will be divided up.

One can only say that the comparison of Mussolini to Aretino is unflattering to the early journalist and satirist.

*

THE SPANISH REVOLUTION

The Greek dame of despicable beauty
With her lucky achievement of innumerable civil
  processes,
Will be imported into Spain,
Where she will be captured and perish miserably.

Because of the Greek ideas which characterized the French Revolution and Directorate, foreseen by Nostradamus, he usually calls a government *la dame*, and uses throughout the *Centuries* the Greek Woman, or Castula to signify it. Here he sees the importation of democratic principles into Spain, crystallized in the Spanish Republic.

I—19

When they shall complete the area of the Coffin
The Spaniards will make trouble for their aristocratic
  blood.
Their population will be greatly decimated,

Their leader will be in flight, hidden by the troughs of blood.

The author has seen a newspaper reference to the flight of the late ex-King, Alfonso, in a boat carrying a cargo of fresh-killed meat, but cannot cite the reference.

The reference to the Coffin area is fascinating. Bertina Harding, in *The Phantom Crown*, tells how young Maximilian visited the tombs of his ancestors while in Spain in 1856. "The mystery of Philip II's oracle confronted him. In the octagon-shaped chamber, at the center of the mausoleum, the eccentric monarch had fitted out a permanent abode for his embalmed ancestors. That was not all. After providing accommodation for ten defunct forebears, he had added with dreadful insight, space for as many crowned successors to himself as he deemed probable. Tier on tier the marble coffins stood, thirty in all. And only three were empty . . . but the Queen, Isabella II, was fitting up a nursery in her palace at Madrid for this expected heir, Alfonso XII. Would there then be but one more Alfonso? A thirteenth? The Archduke fell into uncomfortable reflections while a phlegmatic guide rattled a bunch of keys.

" 'When they are quite full', the man said, pointing at the coffins, 'we will get the Republic.' "

The construction of the tombs (the Coffin) was probably begun by Philip II during the lifetime of Nostradamus.

X—48

In the southernmost part of Spain the standard will be
raised
And will go out to the end and the confines of Europe.
The revolution will touch closely the bridgehead of
the Aisne.
It will be defeated by the great expedition of a coalition.

It is generally recognized that Franco's revolt was
the real beginning of the present world war.

VI—64

No one will keep any treaties of peace.
All who accept them will agitate through deceit.
While peace and truce are protested by land and sea
At Barcelona the fleet will be caught in its activity.

III—75

Pau, Verona, Vicence, Saragossa (throughout Spain
and Italy)
There will be the long swords, the lands humid with
blood.
The corruption of the great granary will be so great
That though help will be near, the remedies will be
very far off.

VI—10

For a time the Church will follow its colors,
Black and white, the two will be intermingled.
The reds and yellows will seem to be like their own.
The land will suffer blood, scourge, hunger, battle and
will be maddened by revolution.

The robes of nuns and of the priesthood are black and
white. Red and yellow are the Spanish colors. Franco's party will have the confidence of the Church for
a while, because ostensibly the Franco revolt is on behalf of royal restoration.

X—14

The Republic of Valencia, without guidance, and by
reason of its nature
Will be hardy and timid by turns. Seized by fear, it
will be conquered.
Accompanied by its pale prostitutes
It will be convicted in the prisons of Barcelona.

In place of the wife, the daughters will be killed.
Murdered by a criminal fault which will not be allowed to endure.
Little clad, within trenches they will be overwhelmed.
The wife will quench her thirst in the Italian Sea.

The wife is the royal government whose principles
will survive, though her children are murdered.

VI—19

The true flame will engulf the government
Which wished to put to death the innocents.
Near the time of assault the army will become inflamed,
And one will see a prodigious thing in the Bull of
    Seville.

III—62

Near the Douro, the sea of Cap Cires not having been
    cut off,
The great mountains of the Pyrenees will be pierced.
The man with the short hand and the pierced tongue
    (a criminal; meaning the survivors of the Republic)
Will carry his plots into the south of France near
    Carcassonne.

IV—70

Contiguous to the Pyrenees
A leader will raise a great force against the eagle
    (Italy),
Exposed and futile forces will be exterminated.
The leader will be pursued as far as Navarre.

III—19

In the south of Spain both blood and prosperity will be spent.
A little before they change their proconsul
There will be great scourge and war; famine and thirst will be seen.
Their prince, their great warden, will die away from his own land.

The recent death of Alfonso XIII confirms his prophecy for Spain's "great warden."

*

THE SECOND GREAT WAR

II—56

When corruption and massacre have not put a stop to the situation
And there is death in the bomb-craters struck from high heaven,
The head of the Church will die when he sees the ruin
And those who are shipwrecked clinging to the rock.

The death of Pius XI in 1939 six months before the outbreak of war.

I—91

The myths acting in human guise
Will be the authors of this great conflict.

Before serene heaven, sword and lance
Will be a less mighty affliction than will be the trend
toward the left hand.

The meaning of this is that the old gods and myths
revived will dominate human action. Such a revival
has been seen in Germany, and Hitler's belief in his
relationship to the figures in Wagnerian drama is well
known to all readers of magazines and newspapers today. The left hand meant in the prophet's day, not
Communism but peace or pacificism. This verse, from
a man of peace, is a powerful indictment of the pre-
war policy of his country.

Interesting is the phraseology of a *New York Times*
editorial (June 22, 1941) on the subject of myths,
commenting on a speech by President Conant, of
Harvard: "President Conant's new nihilists are the
people who believe in the Myth as the great motive
force in history. To stir the masses you don't need to
tell them the truth. Just tell them anything that gets
them excited."

III—26

The kings and the princes will raise up chimeras.
There will be empty prophecies and divination will be
exalted.
The golden horn of plenty will be a victim, and from
the heaven of the cruel
Will come the interpretations of the oracles.

Everyone has heard that Hitler uses astrology and other occult methods to guide his life and activities as well as the destiny of Germany.

VII—14

Natural topography will come to be falsely abandoned.
The monuments created for posterity will stand as open as pitchers.
Factions will multiply, philosophy will be proclaimed.
Black will be put for white, and green wine drunk for ancient vintage.

Presage 27

Aerial warfare will be over the shores of the Occident,
And of the Midi, rushing even to the Levant.
About half the people will die without being able to take root.
This third age shall belong to Mars the Warrior.
The Firebrands will make their appearance to light the fires,
It is the age of the Firebrand, and its end is famine.

X—99

The end of the wolf, the lion, the bull, the ass
And the timid deer will be with the dogs.
No more will sweet manna fall to them.
The watch-dogs will give more vigilance and guardianship.

*

ITALY AND SPAIN

VII—32

Born in a hovel and elevated to a regal height
Is he who, empty and vain, will come to tyrannize
  over the land.
He will raise a force for the march from Milan,
He will exhaust Fayence and Florence of men and
  money.

This is Mussolini, even to the "march," by train,
from Milan.

VI—36

It is not by earthly battle that good or evil
Will rule the confines of the Perusian plain (Italy).
Pisa and Florence, through revolution, will see the
  birth of misfortune.
The King wounded by night will be lifted up on his
  mule and set upon a black saddle-cloth.

The wounding of Victor Emmanuel is metaphor-
ical, as is the black saddle-cloth of Fascism.

II—65

The calamity of a declining economy will afflict
Spain and there will be disaster for Italy.

The Church will be inflamed, there will be corruption
and captivity
When Mercury is in the sign of the Archer and Saturn
becomes a usurer.

Saturn in Aries is associated with acquisitiveness.
The prophet appears here to indicate the period of
January 1938, when Saturn entered the sign and
Mercury became direct in Sagittarius, to January of
1939 when Saturn turned direct preparatory to leaving the sign, and again Mercury was in the Archer's
sign. Nostradamus pays close attention to the times
when the planets change from retrograde to direct motion, as did all of the older astrologers who would have
noted these details in the prophet's mention of astronomical timing. This time was a period of new and
grave economic problems for both Italy, which had
not then entered the war, and for the United States
whose economic policy, born of the war, was not then
fully formulated. The death of a pope during this
period would have been felt by Nostradamus as a further deep affliction to Italy.

VII—20

Agents speaking the Italian language
During April and May will cross the Alps and travel
overseas.
He of the Calf will explain in a harangue
That he is not coming with the purpose of wiping out
the life of France.

This verse seems to describe 1940 in the spring, when Mussolini's agents were active on all fronts before his entrance into the war. He of the Calf is Hitler born under Taurus, sign of the Bull, Ox or Calf. The prophet here implies that he is not only Taurus, but the Golden Calf as well. He, Hitler, was, as one recalls, busily explaining that he had nothing against the French—only their government.

IV—35

When the virgins are faithless to their trust the homefires will become extinct.
The largest number will join the new league (Hitler's new order).
Rulers alone will have in their keeping the means to make war,
Etruria and Corsica will become a fiery gorge by night.

VI—33

The last army raised by bloody Saul
Will not have power to guarantee the sea.
Between two rivers he shall dread a military power.
The black one of wrath will repent his actions.

Obviously a reference to Mussolini, the dark man with his black-shirt legions. The land between the two rivers, referring to the Po and the Tiber, is Italy. The defeat of the Italians, so recently, is clearly given.

IV—20

The proclaimed union (Axis) will not last a great
while.
The greater of the two will make changes and reforms.
When the nation is paralyzed in its ships,
Then Rome will have a new Leopard.

It was the Mediterranean defeats of the Italian navy
which paralyzed the power of Italy and threw her at
the mercy of Britain, causing Hitler to move in and
take control.

Leopards were the famous device of the Plan-
tagenets, and Richard I, the Crusader, carried them to
the Orient. This provides one analogy to the present
crusade of England, and the fact that the Mediterranean battles were fought for control of the Eastern
bases.

III—68

The leaderless people of Spain and Italy
Will see death and defeat within Italy.
Their leader (Mussolini) will be betrayed by his ir-
responsible folly.
Blood will flow everywhere across the latitude (of
Spain and Italy).

VII—30

The sack approaches with battle and a fire and a great
shedding of blood.

Along the Po and the other great rivers, the initiative
will be held by ox-tenders.
After expecting it for a long time, Genoa, Nice,
Fossano, Turin, all the way to Savillano will be captured.

Ox-tenders is a play on words referring to Hitler's
birth under Taurus, and also is a reference to the low,
or ordinary, parentage of Hitler and Mussolini.

IX—76

The Rapacious leader, dark and bloody,
Issued from the hide of inhuman Nero,
Will have his left wing defeated between two waters
 (Po and Tiber).
He will be destroyed by a young man who will re-
organize everything.

Dictatorship organized by Mussolini eventually defeated by the coming Henry V.

VI—98

Ruin to the Italians in terrible plight through the
power of fear.
Their great city will be captured, a corrupt deed.
Monarchy, populace and temples will be violated.
The Po and the Tiber will flow reddened with blood.

II—54

By a foreign nation quite different from the Romans
Their great city (Rome) will be affected after they
    have already gone through a powerful revolution.
The government (Fascist) without forces, because of
    a different country,
Will see their chief captured for lack of a burnished
    sword.

It has all been reported in the newspapers. First the
Fascist revolution, then the coming of Hitler. Italy
helpless, her sword in a beautiful scabbard, but dull
and rusty when drawn.

X—20

All the friends who held together the party (Fascism)
Will be pillaged and put to death for their harsh un-
    civilized propaganda.
Their effects will be declared confiscated,
For never will the people of Rome have been so out-
    raged.

V—21

The death of a Latin monarch
Will involve those whom his rule has assisted.
The fires will be lighted, the booty divided,
There will be public death for his hardy associates
    (Fascists).

V—14

When Saturn and Mars are (conjoined) in Leo, Spain
will be captured,
The African leader will be trapped in the conflict.
Near Malta there will be an engagement. Herod will
be taken alive,
The scepter of Rome will be struck down by the Cock.

This warlike conjunction will occur on November
12, 1947. It would seem to indicate General Franco,
whose prestige has always been bound up with his
African influence; it was from the coast of Africa that
he planned and led his invasion of Spain. It also speci-
fies the final overthrow of dictatorial power in Italy.
Exit the Fascists and Falangists.

IV—34

The great leader will be led captive in a foreign land.
In chains of gold he will be offered to King Henry.
He who in Italy at Milan will lose the war
With all his host will be put to fire and sword.

Since there was nothing in the rule of Henry of
Navarre corresponding with this verse, it must apply
to the coming Henry V and the downfall of the Italian dictatorship. Fascism is particularly associated
with Milan.

III—54

A man of very high rank will flee into Spain
After the blood-letting of the long wound.
Armed forces will cross the high mountains
Devastating everything, after that he will reign in
peace.

The heir to the Spanish throne, Don Juan, or another?

III—21

In Italy, on the Adriatic coast,
There shall appear a horrible fish.
It will have a human face and an aquatic fin,
It will be taken outside on the hook.

Just what this means is uncertain, except that the
fish in Nostradamus' writings indicates an heretical
religion or ideology.

VII—49

Saturn in Taurus sporting with revolution, Mars in
Sagittarius,
The sixth of February will be a day of mortality,
Those of the north of Italy will make a great breach
in the walls of Brussels
While at Ponteroso the Barbarian leader dies.

This prediction refers to February 6th, 1971—for
readers of another day to check!

THE COMING OF HITLER

III—76

Germany will give birth to divers creeds
Strongly resembling a happy paganism.
But the heart will be prisoner and there will be little
   profit.
The people will return to their payment of the true
   tithe.

II—45

Even the heavens will lament when the Androgyne is
   born.
Near to those same heavens human blood shall be shed.
Through death too late will a great people be renewed
   (the French).
Late though early the expected succor will come.

The bi-sexual interests of Hitler have been frequently commented on in the press. Late and early refers to the long interval elapsing between the fall of
the monarchy and this modern restoration, which will
begin early in the great struggle (1944).

IX—68

From the Aryan height there shall arise one who is
   both elevated and obscure.
His evil will affect the country at the junction of the
   Saone and the Rhone (Lyons).

On the Day of Saint Lucia (December 13) his soldiers will be hidden in the woods
Of him who has the most horrible throne ever known.

X—46

In life, destiny and death he will be a base, unworthy
man of gold,
But he will not be the new elector of Saxony.
From Brunswick will come the token of affection,
The hypocritical seducer will pose as the restorer of
the peoples' rights.

Hitler will not be a second Martin Luther, nor the
patron of Luther, the Elector of Saxony. His "reform"
movement will not be lasting.

V—5

Under the holy pretense of giving freedom from servitude
He will himself usurp the power of the people and the
city.
He will be able to do his worst because of the falsity of
the young prostitute (French Republic).
The treacherous, pre-eminent one will read his book
to the country.

Probably no one will heed to have it pointed out
that the *dramatis personae* of this verse are Hitler,
France and *Mein Kampf*.

X—10

Stained with murder and enormous adulteries,
The great enemy of the entire human race,
Who will be worse than his forefathers, his uncles and
his fathers
Will be, in fire, battle and revolution, bloody and in-
human.

This sounds like what a large part of the world
thinks of Adolf Hitler today, and recalls to the frivolous, "his sisters and his cousins and his aunts etc."

IV—66

Under the protective coloration of seven revolution-
aries
Divers experimenters will sow their seed.
Pits and fountains will run with poison,
These human devourers will be inspired by the power
of Italy.

It has been noted that Hitler, who was inspired by
Mussolini's success, has consistently surrounded himself with seven leaders who carry out his orders and
develop his ideas. Whether this is happenstance or related to some of his ideas on occultism is not known,
but the number seven has some association with the occult in the minds of many and its legends are very
ancient.

II—9

Nine years the vegetarian will hold his power in peace
Then he will meet downfall in a thirst so bloody
That on account of him a great people without faith
  or legality
Will be destroyed by one who is more easy-going.

1933 + 9 = 1942 unless the time should be
counted from Hitler's rise in 1932.

V—18

The besieged peoples will strain at their agreements
A week after they are faced with the cruel issue.
Blood will flow in their repulse. Seven will get the axe
When the government which wove the fabric of the
  peace is itself a captive.

This very well describes conditions after the fall of
France. The author does not know the exact number
of members of the former government now dead or
imprisoned at Rion; but it is close on seven. France,
through Clemenceau, was responsible for the peace of
Versailles.

VIII—13

The crossed brother maddened by lust
Will kill Bellerophon because of Praytus.

The enraged woman whose fleet has sailed for a thou-
sound years
Will drink bitter brew, thereafter both shall perish.

This verse is as puzzling as it is intriguing. The
Bellerophon was the ship that took Napoleon to Saint
Helena. Here it is a symbol of England. Classically,
Bellerophon was a hero who retired after involuntarily
causing the death of Praytus, his friend and hunting
companion, while both were guests in the house of
Praytus' father-in-law. The meaning could be that
England allied with a government of France, the Republic (which is not the true son of France but an in-
law), while both are guests of France, will meet
tragedy; that England (at Dunquerque) will be responsible for the death of (Praytus) the French government.

Then the symbolism changes, and seems to indicate
Britannia, "for a thousand years" a sea-going power
from the days of William the Conqueror, will taste
defeat, and thereafter both Britain and her antagonist,
Germany, the crossed brother, will perish.

VI—99

The efficient enemy will turn about in confusion.
The great country, sick, will be defeated by ambushes.
Spain and Western Africa will refuse to play along
    (with Hitler).

There will be defeat near the river where are the remains of antiquity (Tiber).

This appears to be a forecast of the eventual defeat of Italy and Germany, "the efficient enemy."

VIII—90

When among the crossed ones there shall be found a
man with a troubled mind,
Then in the Holy Land shall be seen the horned bull.
The home of the Virgin will be filled with swine,
No ruler will be able any more to sustain order there.

Rudolf Hess is said to have fled because his mind was troubled at the thought of occupation and war in the Holy Land which shocked his Catholicism. The horned bull is Hitler, the Taurean, who has brought the war to the Holy Land.

When the *Robin Moor* was sunk the New York *World-Telegram* carried a story from the survivors which stated that the submarine hoisted no flag, but was painted with the large device of a red bull. So that it would seem that not only the forces of Hitler, but also his actual astrological insignia are in evidence in the far places.

VI—77

By reason of the fraudulent victory of the leader who
shall be cut down,

The two sides will be in battle, when the cycle is clos-
ing in Germany.
The leader and his governmental offspring will be de-
stroyed in home territory,
The monarchy and the papacy will be pursued in
Rome.

This seems to mean Hitler's destruction by his own
people.

VI—18

In the course of events the Great Ruler will be forsaken, and
The Inebriate, drunk not with art but with power, will
be no more of this life,
He and his class having been pushed into such high
power,
Pardon will be given to the race who hated Christ.

*

ENGLAND AND HER ALLIES

IV—50

Libra will see the rise to domination of the Western
hemisphere,
From heaven to earth the Monarchy (of France) will
hold its power.
The forces of Asia will not have perished.
Only seven more will hold the Hierarchic rank.

Many people interpret the old prophecies concerning the popes to mean that the present pope is the prophesied Pastor Angelicus. Libra is England, so called because of her policy of the balance of power.

II—89

One day the two great masters will become friends,
    (Hitler and Stalin).
When their grand power will be greatly augmented.
The new world will be at the height of its development,
The bloody one will make an accounting of its resources.

IV—56

The rise of him who will spread fear on a great scale
    will be sudden
And the principles in the affair will be well concealed;
The red government will no longer be in the public
    eye,
Little by little the important leaders will become displeased with it.

Joseph Stalin is an ally of England as this goes to press, but here and elsewhere his passing, along with Communism, is predicted.

X—81

The treasures kept within a building by the citizens
    of the West (Hesperus)
Shall be withdrawn into a secret place.

The building shall open its fastenings to the starving.
Closed up again, it will be ravished, a horrible prey to
the populace.

This may refer to the gold hoard of the United
States; or it may have reference to Spain, known to
the ancients as Hesperus, and often so designated by
Nostradamus.

III—3

Mars, Mercury and the Moon in conjunction
Will produce extreme scarcity throughout the south
of Europe.
In southernmost Asia the earth will quake (or there
will be revolt).
Corinth and Ephesus will then be in a quandary.

This triple conjunction last occurred September
2nd, 1940, just before the invasion of Greece.

Nostradamus lived too near the time of Jeanne
d'Arc, and he was too passionately French, to feel
other than jealousy and distrust of England, a power
which he saw steadily expanding through centuries to
greater possessions than his own nation. From early
times a prophecy of the downfall of England had been
handed down from the Welsh prophet, Merlin. Eustache Deschamps, the French bard of the early fif-
teenth century, used the Merlin prophecy in one of
his satiric poems. Nostradamus has come very near to

copying it. Both of these troubadours hoped Merlin was right, and, because of that, one may perhaps discount something of the gloom that hangs about Nostradamus' forecasts for England. The lines of Deschamps are these.

According to the prophet of the Isle of Giants,
Which has since been called Albion,
The people were tardily converted to a belief in God.
The Isle will be completely desolated.
Through their pride will come their day of hardship
Concerning which their prophet Merlin
Predicted their dolorous end
When he wrote: "you will lose life and land."
When that has happened, men will point out to foreigners and those from neighboring countries
Where in former times there was England.

Nostradamus elaborates on the theme in the following verses. No specific dates are indicated in these prophecies for England, some of which may be quite distant.

X—100

England will be a great empire,
The all-powerful land surrounded by water will endure for more than three hundred years.
Her commerce will traverse sea and land,
The Portuguese will not be satisfied with that.

Portugal was the great maritime rival of Britain at the time Nostradamus wrote this. There is something deeply symbolic in the fact that this verse is the closing one of the *Centuries*. It is as if there were an implication that the end of England would be the end of the world as we know it. It is like the old saying about Rome: "While stands the Colosseum, Rome shall stand, when falls the Colosseum, Rome shall fall, and when Rome, falls the world." The civilized world today has a similar feeling about England and her relationship to all that is held free and precious.

III—70

Great Britain taken together with England
Will become indeed overwhelming on the seas.
The new Ausonian (Italy) league will be active in
    war
And the two powers will be aligned against each other.

III—57

Seven times you will see the British nation change its
    dynasty,
Bloodstained, in a period of two hundred and ninety
    years.
France, by no means because of German backing,
Will mistrust being harnessed to this Arietic ox-pole.

VI—81

Tears, shrieks, wailings, groans and terrors because of
The inhuman heart of a cruel and icy Ruler.
Lake Leman, the British Isles and Italy will be major
   targets,
There will be bloodshed, famine, and no mercy shown.

The League of Nations and Britain, differently approached, have been Hitler's main objectives.

VI—90

Ignominy stinking and abominable
Will after the event be hailed as felicity.
There will be great excuse for (France) being unfavorable
When Neptune (England) would not be pushed to
   make peace.

These curious lines, which seem only applicable to
1940, admit that France has played a not quite heroic
part—a great admission for the prophet. Yet he manages to blame England for not following in the footsteps of France.

X—32

Everyone will desire to head the great empire,
One shall obtain the power over the others.
But there is little time for his power or life,
Two years his navy will sustain him.

II—100

Within the Isles there will be such a horrible tumult
That nothing will be heard but bellicose factions.
The insults of the brigands (Axis) will become so
    great
That they will go so far as to range themselves in a
    strong league.

III—71

Where there is expectation of creating famine
There will be surfeit.
The patrol of the seas, like a dog in the manger,
Will ration oil and wheat to the various nations.

It was all right with Nostradamus when England
blockaded the seas in 1914 to the advantage of France.
The same situation is all wrong in 1941, and England
is then "dog in the manger."

VI—21

When those of the Arctic Pole are united together,
In the Orient there will be a great terror and fear.
The newly elected pope shall sustain the great Church,
Rhodes and Byzantium will be stained with foreign
    blood.

As this book goes to press, Russia is invaded, and
Winston Churchill announces that England will assist

her, the two northernmost empires, "those of the Arctic Pole." The fighting and terror in the Orient are at peak.

IV—63

At a time very close to an elongation of Venus
The two great leaders of Asia and Africa will be active.
The arrival of the forces from the Rhine and Danube
   will be reported.
There will be cries and tears at Malta and the Italian
   coast.

II—95

The law of More will be seen to decay.
It will be followed by another and much more se-
   ductive doctrine.
The premier of Moscow will eventually fall
Defeated by offerings and propaganda of a leader with
   greater drawing power.

Sir Thomas More, contemporary of the prophet and author of *Utopia*, was the ancestor of Communism. The prophet seems to blame his ideas beyond those of Rousseau, though he mentions the latter for the trag-edies produced by the Communistic ideology. How closely this verse follows the headlines and reports on the Russian-German conflict, as this book goes to press (June, 1941)!

VIII—64

Within the Isles the children will be transported,
Two out of every seven will be in despair.
Those of the soil will be supported by it,
But the name and the skin will be captured by the
league, and hope flees.

S—50

A little later after England
Has laid the wolf (Germany) as low as earth,
War will be seen resisting revolution,
Rekindling in such violence
Of human bloodshed that little but the bodily envelope
of skin will be left.
Bread will be scarce, but swords abundant.

IX—51

The earthquake occurring at Mortara
Will half engulf the navy of Saint George berthed in
near-by waters.
Peace will be asleep, war will awake.
In the Church at Easter the chasms will open.

V—59

The English leader will tarry too long at Nîmes
On the way to Spain to help Ænobarbus.
Many will die through open war that day
When the comet shall fail to strike Artois.

VIII—7

The fortress beside the Thames
Will fall, the government blockaded within.
Thereafter along the coast it will be stripped bare,
Their adversary will behold the corpse, then he will
stand inside the barrier.

III—32

The great sepulchre of the people of Aquitaine (England)
Will be off the shores of Tuscany.
Then war will be near the German frontier
And bringing terror to the people of Mantua.

II—78

Great Neptune will lie at the bottom of the sea
In the mingled blood of Arabs and French.
The Isles will go down in blood because they took up
their oars too late,
And more, because they concealed their plans so badly.

VIII—97

In the confines of the War the destiny of Britain will
change,
Near to the shore where three fine young nations will
be born.

Ruin to the people competent through their seniority,
The government of the country will change and never
grow again.

IX—6

Across Guienne an enormous number of English
Will come to settle under the name Anglaquitaine
(English Aquitanis).
In Toulouse of Languedoc and le Bordelais
They will live and call their settlement Barboxitaine.

*

FRANCE AND THE PAPACY

VI—74

The government which was driven out shall return to
power,
Its enemies will be named as conspirators.
More than ever its times will triumph
For three and seventy years until death well assured.

This is a peculiarly interesting verse. In his letter
to King Henry the prophet speaks of "the great trembling of the earth together with the increase of the
new Babylon, wretched daughter (of the Revolution),
augmented by the abomination of the first holocaust

(1792). It will hold its power for just seventy-three years and seven months. Then there shall issue from the long barren tree (of the monarchy), born at the 50th Parallel (latitude of the Franco-Belgian border), one who will revitalize the entire Christian Church. And there shall be created a peace, union and concord between the children of opposed and separate races."

If 1944, as previously analyzed from the number of verses and Centuries (this author may possibly be alone in seeing such a connection; certainly the first to say so), it consitutes Nostradamus' date for the beginning of "France Second," over which the new and great Henry V is to rule.

If to the date of the Battle of Sedan, September 1st, 1870, the seventy-three years and seven months of the prophet are added, it brings us to March, 1944. If the seventy-three years are subtracted from the date of the downfall of Napoleon III at Sedan one gets 1797, dating the rise of Napoleon I. Napoleon III died in 1873, which is a kind of echo of the number. Nostradamus mentions, not in a prophetic connection, the Hebrew prophet Joel. This is in the letter to the King. It seemed odd to single out for no reason this one short Biblical book and not to refer to other prophets. But on looking into Joel, one discovers that the book has just three chapters and seventy-three verses. The French Republic has had three chapters too, the First, Second and Third Republics. This number 73 is a peculiar one.

Nostradamus gives the precise date of the French Revolution, also in the letter to the King. "Then will be seen the beginning of events of long duration, and in the first year there will be a great persecution of the Christian Church. This will break out in the year one thousand seven hundred and ninety-two. The people will think that it is a renewing of the age."

If 1792 is taken as a starting point, and two additions of the number of Joel, 73, are made, one has the date of 1938.

Returning to the quatrain, the verse of course refers to the government of Napoleon I, which returned to power under Louis Napoleon. Yet as has been shown, the verse has a much more subtle application, and the seventy-three years does not refer to the tenure of power of either man, but to cycles which included their years. The rise of one and the downfall of the other give points of reference for use of the number.

X—28

The Second and Third Republics will make prime music
And be lifted by a king to the summit of prestige.
But the grass will grow thin to emaciation
And the exposé of false self-indulgence will deprive
them of power.

Nostradamus severely blamed Louis Philippe, whose reign was the beginning of the Second Republic, in other verses, for his catering to democratic ideas, and

abandoning the flag of the lilies for the tri-color. He
is the King referred to here.

IV—30

More than eleven times the populace has refused the
monarchy,
All influences have been alternately augmented and
lowered,
And so low will they sink that little gold can be sewed
up for keeping,
Later there will be famine, corruption and exposés of
hidden matters.

There have been twelve elected presidents of France,
in addition to the first two who were royalist in sympathy.

VIII—96

The synagogue, sterile and bearing no fruit
Will be received, accepted among the infidels
Of Babylon where its sad, miserable leader will
Have his wings clipped by the daughter of persecution
(Paris).

Léon Blum's tenure of office.

IV—32

The times and localities will compel meat to be re-
placed by fish.

The law of the Commune will work in an opposite
fashion.
An old man will hold the power, then he will be
removed from office.
The friend of all things pertaining to the mob will be
relegated to the background.

The boomerang in both defense and economics
which marked the Blum régime is predicted.

VI—50

Within the pits the old bones will be found,
The remains of incest committed by the step-mother.
The state will change, the skeleton will rattle,
And Mars will be ascendant on its star.

Nostradamus never fails to ascribe the faults of
democracy in France to its hideous beginnings in the
French Revolution, the step-mother of the Third Republic. He hears the rattle of its bones in the revival
of Communist ideas in the Blum régime.

I—3

When the blown litter of the whirlwind drives against
them,
They will hide their faces with their cloaks,
A new class of people will trouble the Republic
And the Revolutionaries and the Royalists will judge
all matters from opposing points of view.

The Cagoulards, or hooded ones, who hid their faces, arose to fight the leftist tendencies of the French Republic, and by so doing played into Hitler's hands.

IX—51

The people will band themselves together against the red factions.
There will be flame, battle and revolution while the heart is avid for peace.
Those who weave their plots will do so at the point of death,
Save one (Hitler), who will bring ruin upon the entire world.

VIII—91

In the country watered by the Rhone,
Where the crossed ones will be almost united
When the two which constrain (Mars and Saturn) are met in Pisces,
A great number will be punished by the deluge.

This probably referred to the conjunction of 1938, when the harmony between the Axis members was at its height. Mention was made in the press of their conspiracies, notably those of burning French ships. They had their headquarters in the valley and mouth of the Rhone. The deluge here is the figurative one of the onset of tragedy.

VIII—1

A number (in the government) will be confused in
their expectation.
This will not be forgiven by the population,
Who will be of the opinion that they should persevere
in their hope,
But the great leisure to do this will not be given to
them.

Sixain 36

Those without power, wishing to acquire power
Will spread a great rumor all through France.
The honeyed tongue, the veritable chameleons,
The incendiaries, the firebrands, the agitators,
The Toms, Dicks and Harrys, the purveyors of news,
Their bite will be like that of the Scorpion.

VII—33

Through fraudulent government the country will be
despoiled of its forces,
The fleet attacked, channels open to espionage.
Two pretended friends will form an alliance
Awakening hatred long lulled to sleep.

The ancient enmity of France and England.

VI—34

The mechanics of flying fire
Will cause the people who are besieged to revolt against
their leader.

Within the nation there will be such sedition
That they will be defeated in their despair.

II—77

With projectiles, fire and chemicals they will attack,
and be repulsed with fire.
Cries and groans will be heard on the midnight air,
People will be placed within hidden ramparts,
The traitors will escape by an underground route.

VI—43

For a long time the country will be abandoned
Where the Seine and the Marne flow together.
The soldiers from the Thames will be despised,
They will be driven back from those whom they were
supposed to guard.

I—41

The City (Paris) will be assailed by night.
Few will escape in the conflict near to the sea (Dunquerque),
The prostitute (Republic), when her son returns to
her defeated,
Will perish of poison hidden in the folds of propaganda.

II—87

Afterwards there shall come from the neighboring
lands

A German prince who shall sit upon the golden throne
(France).
In captivity and through experiences with the tides of
revolution
The Republic will be reduced to servitude and shall no
longer endure.

The golden throne in Nostradamus' writings is always the throne of France, whose ancient emblem was
the lilies of gold on the white flag. Nostradamus often
uses prince or king when speaking of a foreigner of
great power. Here Hitler.

II—5

Near the frontiers, within two cities
There will be two scourges worse than was ever known.
Famine linked with corruption, the people driven at
the point of the sword,
They will cry for help to the Great God immortal.

Paris and Vichy. Nostradamus uses such terms as
scourge in the Biblical sense of general affliction.

X—85

The tribune so old that he is almost at the point of
trembling,
Will be under pressure to deliver up his captive.

The old man, who is not really old, speaking a cautious evil,
Will attempt by legal means to betray his friends.

Pétain, Laval, and the prisoners at Rion.

IV—21

The change will be very difficult,
But the City and province will gain by it.
A prudent man of high courage put in office will be driven out by the clever man,
Land, sea, and population, the status of all will be greatly changed.

This sounds as if it were a reference to Marshal Pétain and Laval or Darlan.

I—61

The Republic, wretched ingrate,
Will be depopulated under its new Magistrate.
There will be a great mass of exiles and witch-doctors,
Who will rob the Germans of their great agreement.

VI—97

At the five and fortieth parallel the heavens will flame.
The battle will approach the great new city (Geneva).

On the instant a great scattering blaze will leap up,
Then it will be desirable that the Normans should
  prove their capacity.

The degree is that of the city of Lyons, which is indicated elsewhere as the route of conquest, up from
the south and the path which the coming Henry V
will follow. The Normans are the old monarchy of
which he is the descendant.

IV—40

The forts of the besieged will be attacked
With fiery explosives that will reduce them to craters.
The bandits will be ground up alive,
At which time there will be never so piteous a schism
  in the Holy Church.

VIII—6

A lightning splendor appearing at Lyons
Will give illumination; after Malta has been taken
  will be suddenly smothered.
Don Raz will deceitfully deliver up the Moors
While from Geneva to London the treason of the Cock
  is proclaimed.

Don Raz is Franco, so called because of his Moorish connections.

III—82

Fréjus, Antibes and the cities around Nice
Will be devastated by land and sea power.
The locusts (airplanes) will be over land and sea when
the wind is favorable,
People will be captured, killed, bound and pillaged
without regard to the rules of warfare.

S—4

In a round cycle of the lily there shall be born a very
great Prince
Come late indeed yet early into his Province.
Saturn will be in Libra, sign of its exaltation.
The standards of self-indulgence will be in decreasing
strength.
The Republic after her effort to be masculine will be
under her own corpse,
That the happy blood of Bourbon shall be upheld.

Saturn will be in Libra in 1951, when the new King
may be expected to reach the fullness of his power.

II—88

When the cycle of the great ruinous activity is accomplished,
There shall arise he who will be the fifth (Henry V) '
and seventh (of the name of Guise).

At that time Aix will not be able to guarantee Lutetia
Against the foreign Aries warrior and his nation, a
third larger than France.

This verse clearly prophesies that the coming King
of France will arise at this time when France is under
the heel of Germany. Germany, like England, has long
been considered by many astrologers to be under the
general rulership of the sign Aries. The astrologer
Cheiro once told Edward VII 'that the salvation of
both countries lay in peace and agreement because
they were both ruled by Aries.

V—53

The law of the monarchy contending against that of
    self-indulgence
Will confirm the spirit of my prophecy.
Neither the one nor the other of the rival parties
    (Communism and Fascism) will be successful,
Through the Monarchy the law of the Great Messiah
    will be upheld.

III—5

Near the long default of two great luminaries
Which will come to pass in April and March,
Oh, what a dearth! But two great and kindly gentlemen
By land and sea will succor all parts.

Nostradamus indicates in verses, not given here, that the coming King of Spain will be a friend and companion-at-arms of Henry V.

I—51

In the watery triplicity there will be born
One who will have Thursday for his gala day.
His reputation, praise, and power will spread
By land and sea, he will be a tempeste to the people of
the Orient.

The present Pretender was born July 5, 1908, with the Sun in the watery sign Cancer.

X—71

By the forces of earth and air the very great revolu-
tion will be frozen
When in time Thursday shall be venerated.
Never was there one so fair as he shall be,
The four quarters of the earth shall honor him.

Thursday, the day of Jupiter, planet of ecclesiastical hierarchy, is here used in contradistinction to Friday, sacred to the Mohammedans. The meaning is that of the Christian King, Henry V, whose reign will be closely harmonized with the Church.

VI—12

He (Henry V) will assemble forces to carry him to
    Empire
And in the Vatican the Pope will be of the blood royal
    (of France).
The Flemish, the English, Spain and Paris
Will fight against Italy and the rest of France.

By Paris, here, one assumes that he must refer to
the Free French movement representative of the former government seated in Paris. But the verse is
puzzling in advance of the event.

S—15

The newly elected father of the great ship (papacy)
Will for a long time give illumination like a clear flame
Serving as a lamp to this great land,
And at that time the coat-of-arms belonging to his
    name
Will be linked with that of the happy one of Bourbon.
From the Levant to the Western Ocean and the land
    of the Setting Sun his memory will be honored.

X—42

The human rule of Angelic birth
Will base its power on peace and union,
War will be captive and half cloistered,
For a long time peace will be maintained among men.

The Pastor Angelicus, of the prophecy of Malachi, is the pope yet to come, and is the one indicated by the prophet in this verse. Apparently he is to be of royal French blood and hold his office while Henry V is King of France. This prediction does not check with the papal succession given by Malachi.

S—53

Many will die before the Phoenix dies to renew itself.
Until six hundred seventy shall he dwell,
Having passed fifteen years, twenty-one and thirty-nine.
The first is subject to illness,
The second to battle and danger to life,
And to fire and revolution is subject thirty-nine.

If these numbers are added and the sum added to 1870 the resultant date for the rebirth of the Phoenix is 1945.

X—44

When there shall be a ruler who will go contrary to the will of his own people
A scion of Blois (the blood royal of France) will subjugate the Italians,
Memel, Cordova, and the peoples of Dalmatia.
Thereafter the spirit of the seven will be with the King and he will make offerings to the souls of his ancestors.

VI—24

When Mars and the Scepter shall be conjoined
Under Cancer there will be calamitous war.
Not long thereafter a new king will be anointed
Who for a long period will bring peace to the land.

June, 1951. Both Sun and Mars were in Cancer in
1940 but not close enough for conjunction. This
checks the previous verse giving the same year, and
indicates that fighting will go on until the turn of the
decade.

VIII—52

The king of Blois shall reign in Avignon,
From Amboise he will dispose his forces the length of
    the Indre.
In the angle of Poictiers he will break the wings of
    the Holy Empire
In the neighborhood of the *Boni.*

The angle of Poictiers is what military men still
call the strategic position in this terrain which domi-
nates the approach to Paris. The Holy Empire is that
of Germany. *Boni* is thought by Fontbrune to mean
the Bohemians—Czechs. This author doubts it, but
does not know what the interpretation is. The original
line consists of only two words, and there is probably a

trick reading. Such verses were an art in the prophet's day.

VIII—1

PAU, NAY, LORON will be a man who is more of fire than of blood.
He will swim in praise. The great man will put down the insurrectionists.
He will refuse entrance to the despoilers.
He will enclose the Name of the Pope in the country where the Durance flows.

In this verse which begins the three Centuries dedicated to Henry, King of France Second, Nostradamus indicates the Bourbon ancestry by addressing the coming King by the name of the birthplace of the Bourbon line, Pau, and two other towns in Béarn. Avignon, the papal city, is near the confluence of the Rhone and Durance.

V—6

The Pope will lay his hand on the King's head
And implore him to establish peace in Italy.
The King will change his scepter to his left hand (token of peace)
And from being a king he will become the pacific Emperor.

VIII—18

The offspring of the Fleur de Lis will cause its death.
A little after its rebirth the old confusion will arise,
The three lilies will come to an end because of it.
The rescued fruit will change and become as crude
  flesh.

S—34

Princes and Lords, all who are accustomed to make war,
Cousin German, brother with brother,
Ended is The Tree of the happy line of Bourbon.
The very lovable Princes of Jerusalem,
Ended by the commission of an enormous and exe-
  crable deed.
The people will feel the effect when the bottom drops
  out of their economy.

X—75

He who had been so long awaited will never come again
Within Europe. In Asia there will arise
A man of the league, sprung from the Greek tradition
  (democratic or Communistic)
Who will spread his power over all of the Kings of the
  Orient.

In the last three verses the tragic end of the house
of Bourbon is indicated, and reaction against the
monarchy.

VIII—99

By the power of three temporal kings it shall happen.
The Holy See will be changed to another place.
There the bodily substance of the spirit
Will be restored and the new locality will be accepted
as the true seat.

V—46

By reason of quarrels and new schisms among the
cardinals
When the Pope shall be elected
Great amounts of false doctrine will be produced
against him
And Rome will be injured by the Mohammedans.

VIII—98

The blood of the clergy will be shed
Like water in great abundance
And for a long time it will not be stanched.
Woe, woe to the clergy, ruin and sorrow.

There are no dates for these verses.

*

DISCOVERY OF THE TOMB OF A SAINT

The fascinating prophecy given below concerns the
finding of a tomb of some early Christian saint, which
is to happen in April of whatever year. The prophet
does not indicate a closer date except that the "new
party" will be founded upon the bones of the saint,

whom he calls the Great Roman. This presumably means the Christian royalist party of the coming King. The saint may possibly be one of the early Christians of the time of Trajan, who journeyed into Gaul and died there. Under Trajan the Roman Empire reached its greatest expansion of territory. It also achieved a very high and wide-spread culture. The persecution of Christians was, however, very severe. The verses seem to point to an analogy between Trajan and the imperialist ambitions of Mussolini, who is perhaps typified in the mention of Prince Ulpian. Trajan's name was Marcus Ulpius Trajan. Nostradamus' reference to the golden lamp of Trajan would seem to mean the spiritual lamp of Christianity which, though buried under persecution, still glows in its secret place in the old Roman province, now Provence. The parallel is made by the prophet between the persecuted Christians of Trajan's day, of whom the old saint may have been one, and the modern Christians, whose lamp must also burn in secret, persecuted by dictators.

VI—66

At the foundation of the new party
Will be found the bones of the Great Roman,
A fissure will reveal the marble of the sepulchre,
Ill covered, after an earthquake in April.

IX—31

Exposure of the government will put an end to the
hecatomb.

When the source of the stream is traced
A freshet will lay bare the marble and lead of the
tomb
Which will be that of the Great Roman whose motto
was *Deus In Me.*

VIII—59

The weak faction will occupy this locality,
Those in high places will make horrible outcry,
From their vantage point the strong group will stir up
trouble,
The tomb will be found near Embrun, where the in-
scriptions will be uncovered.

VI—15

Beneath the tomb will be found a prince
Worthier than he of Nuremberg.
The Spanish government, its power lessened, will,
when the Sun is in Capricorn (January)
Be denounced and betrayed by the Great Leader of
Wittemberg.

Nuremberg and Wittemberg refer to Hitler.

V—66

Under the ancient buildings sacred to hearth and home,
Not far from the ruined aqueduct (Pont du Garde at
Nîmes)

Are the luminous metals of the Sun and Moon,
There the chased, golden lamp of Trajan is still burning.

VII—66

When the inscription D. M. (*Deus In Me*) is found
And the ancient tomb with its lamp is discovered,
The law, the King and Prince Ulpian will be put to
proof,
The royal standard and the Duke will go into hiding.

III—65

Discovery of the tomb of the Great Roman
Will be followed next day by the election of a new
pontiff.
The College of Cardinals, engrossed in quarrels, will
not ratify the election.
The sacred chalice (the Church itself) will inhibit the
authority of the heir of Saint Peter.

I—25

Lost, refound after concealment for so long a cycle,
an age
The shepherd will be venerated as a demigod,
Until the Moon has completed her grand cycle,
When the ancient saint will be dishonored by those of
another faith.

*

THE RISE OF THE ORIENT

The author, sometime ago, cited some of the predictions in the following verses to a well-known military commentator. He said that they were not news. That men in his particular work who were always scanning future horizons for long-range prophecies of their own had long accepted the rise of the Orient as a *fait accompli* of the future, and that for this reason the political forecasters gave triple attention to every item that came out of Asia and Africa. Nostradamus in his own day saw the might of the Orient and its menace to Christian Europe, and he knew that cycles return.

VIII—59

Twice lifted to power, twice overthrown,
The Orient like the Occident will weaken.
His adversary after numerous struggles,
Routed by the sea, in a pinch will fall.

IX—60

In the conflict with the Barbarian with the black
  Head-dress
Bloodshed will make Dalmatia tremble,
The might of Araby will rear its headland,
The frogs will shake with fear, Portugal will give help.

The frogs are the French; that is the ancient name from Merovingian times.

VI—85

The great city of Constaninople will be destroyed by
  the French;
The forces of the Turban will be taken captive.
Help will come by sea from a great leader of Portugal.
This will happen on the twenty-fifth of May, the day
  of Saint Urban.

Probably the prophet looks back from this advanced time to what is Portugal today, as this is a small country and may be incorporated in a large one. A modern French commentator, realizing its size, says, naïvely enough, that Portugal will send for the U. S. fleet!

VIII—77

Anti-Christ will be three times annihilated,
Seven and twenty years blood will be shed in war.
Dead heretics, captives and exiles there shall be,
Blood, human corpses, crimson waters and hail upon
  the earth.

I—18

Through the negligence and discord of France
An opening will be given to the followers of Moham-
  med.

The earth and sea of the north of Italy will be blood-
soaked,
The harbor of Marseilles will be filled with ships and
sails.

III—44

The ancient monarch driven out of power
Will go to fetch his help among those of the Orient.
For fear of the cross he will fold his standard.
In Greece he will go by land and sea.

V—112

The sea will not be safe for the monarchy,
Those of self-indulgent life will hold all Africa,
No longer will the hypocrites be in occupation,
And a portion of Asia will change.

Life will be frankly hedonistic in Africa without
the mask of moral hypocrisy.

V—55

In the country of Arabia Felix
There shall be born a puissant leader of the Moham-
medans.
He will trouble Spain and conquer Granada,
And from beyond the sea he shall invade the people
of the Italian west coast.

VI—80

From Fez the rule shall attain to the countries of
Europe.
Their cities will be fired and their people pierced with
a blade,
The chief leader of Asia will bring a great troop by
land and sea.
He will pursue the royalists, the priests and the cross
to their death.

III—20

Through the lands watered by the great river Bethis
Far within Spain in the kingdom of Granada,
The cross will be driven back by a Mohammedan
nation,
A man of Cordova will betray his country.

I—73

France, through her neglect, will be assailed on five
fronts,
Tunis and Algiers will be stirred up by the peoples of
Asia,
León, Seville and Barcelona will fall
And they will not have the fleet of Venice to protect
them.

In the coming invasions of Europe, through the rising of the Orient, the prophet makes sarcastic reference to the long years in his own day when the Venetian fleet, unaided, protected Europe against the East

while the nations of Europe quarreled amongst themselves. That situation, he says, will come again, and this time there won't be the Venetian fleet.

II—96

A burning torch shall appear in the heaven
Above the Rhone from source to mouth.
Famine, sword will afflict, succor will be tardily brought.
The Persian will turn to the invasion of Macedonia.

IX—73

The Monarch of the blue Turban when he has entered into Foix
Will rule less than an evolution of Saturn (29 years).
The King of the white Turban and the high courage of Byzantium
Will be manifest near the time of holding when Sun, Mars and Mercury are conjoined in Aquarius.

This conjunction takes place February 18, 1981.

Presage 35

France shall be greatly saddened by a death,
The mother and tutrice shall be bereft of the royal blood.
Government and Lords will be made orphans by the Crocodiles,

Strong cities, castles and towns will be taken by surprise,
May Almighty God guard them from these evils.

The Crocodiles are the people of Africa and tropical Asia who will overwhelm France, the mother and tutrice, after the final fall of the Bourbon dynasty.

V—75

The Church of God will be persecuted,
The sacred temples will be despoiled,
The child shall strip the mother of everything,
The Arabs will join the Jews.

V—25

The rule of the Church will succumb by sea
To the Prince of Arabia when Mars, Sun and Venus
    are conjoined in Leo,
Across Persia will come full near a million troops,
The true serpent will invade Byzantium and Egypt.

The date of this conjunction is August 21, 1987.

*

THE END OF THE AGE

Not only ever since the Christian era, but long before in the songs and lamentations of the Hebrew prophets, the end of the great precessional era of the

Fishes, Pisces, has been foretold in a wealth of tragic and saddening detail. It is not the end of the world, as many people of old times thought, but the end of a grand period, and the birth of a new age with a different type of thought and civilization. Nostradamus prophesied that it would be marked by the downfall of old Europe, and be ushered in with earthquakes and eclipses such as the Bible describes in the scene of the Crucifixion.

Science recognizes that from time to time the earth changes the inclination of its axis. They know this from fossil remains (which, for example, show that Alaska had once a warm climate, and other localities show that similar changes have taken place). But science has no knowledge of what causes this change, nor in what cycle of years its return may be expected. Nor does Nostradamus specify the date for this occurrence, but by implication he links it with the phenomenon of the double eclipse which will take place in 1999.

The two eclipses will occur in the sign Leo, a partial one on July 28th, and a total one on August 11. The event is a very rare astronomical phenomenon. Camille Flammarion wrote of it in detail. All astronomers then living will prepare to observe it with every advanced resource of scientific equipment. Nostradamus, in both his letter to the King and in his verses, has given his picture of what he predicts will affect the entire world. Science is just beginning to have an understanding of terrestrial phenomena, such as floods and earthquakes, coming as the result of celestial phenomena, the doctrine held by astrologers for thousands of years. Science has arrived at some limited conclusions forced by the necessity for better long-range weather forecasting. But the study of earthquakes, floods and volcanoes, made in the light of the gravitational and magnetic strains and stresses of the Sun, Moon and planets, is still in its infancy and as yet almost nothing is known about it. The wise men of old knew these things, and Nostradamus knew them. He needed no telescope for the double eclipse, and he not only saw it, but he saw the train of events that came with it, something no giant telescope can show.

In his letter to the King the prophet has this to say of the last years of the twentieth century:

"Then shall begin the great empire of Antichrist in the invasions of Xerxes and Attila ('one who will revive the King of the Angoumois,' and the Oriental invasion) who will come with a countless throng, so that the advent of the Holy Spirit, from the 48th parallel, will make a great change and chase away the abomination of Antichrist that made war on the sovereign Vicar of Christ (the Pope) and against his Church for a time and to the end of time. This will be preceded by an eclipse of the Sun, of denser darkness than has ever been seen since the Creation and up to the passion and crucifixion of Jesus Christ, and from that time until the coming one. There will take place in the month of October a great translation made so that the earth will seem to lose the weight of its natural motion in an abyss of endless darkness. There will be premonitory signs in the spring, and there will be extreme changes, overthrows of kingdoms, and earthquakes."

* * * *

"In the last period all the Christian kingdoms, and those of the infidels, will be shaken for twenty-five years. The wars and battles will be more injurious. Towns, cities, castles, and other buildings will be burned, laid waste, and destroyed, with great bloodshed of vestals, violation of wives and widows, and children at the breast dashed and broken against the walls of the towns. Satan, the prince infernal, will commit so many evils that nearly the whole world will be afflicted and desolated.

"After this has endured for a certain length of time, Saturn will almost renew his cycle (twenty-nine years), but God the Creator will bring an age of gold. He will heed the affliction of His people, and He will bind Satan and throw him into the abyss. Then shall begin between God and man a universal peace, and Satan will be bound for a thousand years. Then the cycle will return in grand power, Satan will be once more unbound against the Church."

IV—67

The year that Saturn and Mars are conjunct and combust
The air will be very dry and there will be a long trajection (comet),

Through incendiarism a great locality will be consumed by fire,
There will be little rain, with wind, heat, wars and incursions.

This configuration occurs in April, 1998. It is in that year that Nostradamus predicts the great invasion of France. The path of the solar eclipse, which will be total, passes through northern France and Belgium.

V—54

From the Euxine Sea and great Tartary
There will arise a King who will eventually behold Gaul.
He will traverse Turkey and Germany
And in Byzantium will leave his bloody track.

II—29

The Oriental will go out from his home
To cross the Apennines and look on France.
He will traverse the clouds and the snows of heaven,
And everyone will be struck down with his club.

X—72

In the year 1999 and seven months
From the sky will come a great and terrible King
Who will revive the great King of the Angoumois,
Before and after his coming war will rule at full blast.

The Angoumois were an early Gallic people conquered by the invading Goths. The situation will be similar.

III—84

The Great City will be desolate,
Of her inhabitants not one shall remain to dwell there,
Wall, sex, building and virgin will be violated.
By battle, fire, corruption and cannon the people will
die.

II—28

The last but one to be called Pope
Will take Diana for his day and his repose,
He will wander afar on account of his distracted head,
Seeking to deliver a great people from economic
oppression.

Diana is the Moon, so that Monday will be the Pope's day of rest. The Moon rules changes, travels and voyagings, and it is involved in mental frenzies and distracted mentalities. In the famous prophecy of Malachi, in his descriptions of the popes yet to come he names third before Petrus Romanus (the last one named) De Medietate Lunae. *De Medietate Lunae* means "relating to the half-Moon, which is the crescent of Diana." Malachi's further description of this pope is: "From the half-moon proceeds this pope sent to Rome by the Divine Doctor, Hail, our well-beloved Pius XII, most holy Mediator, future victim." The present incumbent of the holy See is Pius XII, and more than any previous pope he has "wandered afar." But otherwise the description does not fit, nor does he come in the order given by Malachi. According to the Monk of Padua there will be two popes after the Lunar, and three more before him. Nostradamus names him as the "penultimate" pope. In the times of the Avignon popes and the Great Schism Cardinal Pietro di Luna was one of the false popes. Eustache Deschamps, a famous satiric poet of that time, whose writings were not only familiar to Nostradamus but imitated and quoted by him, wrote a satire called, "Of the Schism in the Church Which is Much Troubled by the Moon" (Luna). Some of Nostradamus' lines are very close to lines in this satire.

III—17

Mount Aventine will be seen flaming in the night.
The sky will be suddenly obscured in Flanders.
When the Monarch drives out his nephew,
The people of the Church will commit scandals.

VIII—15

Toward the north great efforts will be made by mankind,
Almost all of Europe and the whole world will be tormented.
The two eclipses will put men to such pursuit

And will augment life and death among the Hungarians.

These two eclipses, one of the Sun and the other of the Moon, both occur in August of 1999, in the sign Leo, traditionally associated.

VIII—16

In the place where the Almighty has built His ship (Rome)
The deluge will be so great and so sudden
That there will be no spot of earth for a firm foothold.
The wave will cover the Olympus of Fiesole (Apennines).

I—69

The great round mountain of the seven hills (Rome),
After it has gone through peace, war, famine and inundation,
Will tumble far, sending the great country into the abyss,
Even its antiquities will be lost and its great foundation.

I—56

You will see, early and late, great changes take place,
Extremes of horror and prosecutions

As if the Moon were guided by its spirit,
The heavens approach the time of their tilting.

I—84

The Moon obscured in profound darkness,
Her brother (the Sun) will become the color of rust,
The great one hidden for a long time in darkness
Will turn the sword in the bloody wound.

I—47

For forty years the rainbow shall not appear.
For forty years all the days shall behold
A barren earth and increasing scarcity,
And great deluges will be perceived.

X—74

At the revolution of the grand number seven
There will appear the hazards of the hecatomb,
Not far from the great Millennial age
The dead shall go out from their tomb.

X—73

Past and present times together
Will be judged by the great Jehovah,

The world in its late stage will be abandoned by Him
And sentence will be passed on the disloyal clergy.

VII—41

Those whose bones of hands and feet were shut up
In a dwelling long uninhabited by noise
Will be disinherited while they are in the depths of
their dream
And translated to a house that is salutary and calm.